HEIDEGGER'S MORAL ONTOLOGY

Heidegger's Moral Ontology offers the first comprehensive account of the ethical issues that underwrite Heidegger's early efforts to develop a novel account of human existence. Drawing from a wide array of source materials from the period leading up to the publication of *Being and Time* (1919–27), and in conversation with ancient, modern, and contemporary contributions to moral philosophy, James D. Reid brings Heidegger's early philosophy into fruitful dialogue with the history of ethics, and sheds fresh light on such familiar topics as Heidegger's critique of Husserl, his engagement with Aristotle, his account of mortality, the role played by Kant in the genesis of *Being and Time*, and his early reflections on philosophical language and concepts. This lively book will appeal to all who are interested in Heidegger's early phenomenology and in his thought more generally, and to those interested in the nature, scope, and foundations of ethical life.

JAMES D. REID is Associate Professor of Philosophy at the Metropolitan State University of Denver. He has co-edited *Thoreau's Importance for Philosophy* (2012) and is the author of *Being Here Is Glorious: On Rilke, Poetry, and Philosophy* (2015).

HEIDEGGER'S MORAL ONTOLOGY

JAMES D. REID

Metropolitan State University of Denver

CAMBRIDGE
UNIVERSITY PRESS

CAMBRIDGE
UNIVERSITY PRESS

University Printing House, Cambridge CB2 8BS, United Kingdom

One Liberty Plaza, 20th Floor, New York, NY 10006, USA

477 Williamstown Road, Port Melbourne, VIC 3207, Australia

314–321, 3rd Floor, Plot 3, Splendor Forum, Jasola District Centre, New Delhi – 110025, India

79 Anson Road, #06–04/06, Singapore 079906

Cambridge University Press is part of the University of Cambridge.

It furthers the University's mission by disseminating knowledge in the pursuit of
education, learning, and research at the highest international levels of excellence.

www.cambridge.org
Information on this title: www.cambridge.org/9781108422185
DOI: 10.1017/9781108381055

First published 2019

Printed and bound in Great Britain by Clays Ltd, Elcograf S.p.A.

A catalogue record for this publication is available from the British Library.

ISBN 978-1-108-42218-5 Hardback

Contents

v

Acknowledgments

An early version of the present volume would not have been possible without the intense intellectual atmosphere of the University of Chicago. I single out, above all, Rick Anthony Furtak, a constant friend and interlocutor whose voice and concerns are present in almost everything I think and do, and whose faith that the book would appear never wavered. The late Matthew Geiger (1972–2016) was a friend in every one of Aristotle's three senses. Much of what I have to say about the ethical import of early Heidegger is indebted to conversations in Hyde Park on Levinas's critique of fundamental ontology and his insistence that ethics is, or ought to be, first philosophy.

Several mentors among Chicago's faculty were instrumental in making the present work possible. I'd especially like to thank my dissertation advisors, Michael Forster, Charles Larmore, and Jean-Luc Marion.

I spent the academic year 2005–6 teaching as a visiting instructor at Colorado College, when a first draft of what became *Heidegger's Moral Ontology* was being drafted. I'd like to thank Jonathan Lee, John Riker, and Rory Sadler for their unflagging support, along with my friend Reiko Hillyer, who was visiting in the same year. Among my former students at Colorado College, conversations with Leath Tonino, Rosalie Nell Bouck, and Reid Prebenda were especially productive.

Since coming to the Metropolitan State University of Denver in 2006, several of my colleagues have been helpful in making ongoing work on Heidegger possible. I'd like to thank David Sullivan, Timothy Gould, Adam Graves, and Carol Quinn. My dean, Joan Foster, and provost, Vicki Golich, both provided material support, in the form of course release, without which I would not have been able to make certain last-minute abbreviations to a longer version of the present study in a timely fashion.

Several students at Metro State, some of whom have gone on to pursue graduate study in philosophy, provided occasions for conversation that improved certain chapters. Among them, I'd like to thank especially Sarah

Adair, Nick Barnes, Ali Barrena-Phipps, Alexa Brown, Haley Burke, Nate Galvin, Paul Jacobs, Sam Munroe, Cliff Naylor, Corey Polster, Luke Straka, and Shawn Vigil.

I've presented versions of various chapters in too many places to count. Among those present on such occasions I include Bill Blattner, James Carey, Benjamin Crowe, Steven Crowell, Helen Daly, Carl Ficarrotta, Judy Genova, Alberto Hernandez-Lemus, Marion Hourdequin, Leonard Kahn, Mike Kim, Bruce Krajewski, Samantha Matherne, Dennis McEnnerny, Tucker McKinney, Karin Nisenbaum, J. P. Rosensweig, Matthew Shockey, Robert Stolorow, Iain Thomson, Clinton Tolley, Mark Wrathall, Katherine Withy, and Nate Zuckerman.

I owe special thanks to the two anonymous reviewers who read carefully a penultimate draft of the manuscript in its entirety for several helpful suggestions that made for a better one than I submitted in December of 2016. I should also thank Wayne Martin who said several positive things about a much longer version of the book in progress that encouraged me, a few years later, to take his words to be an invitation to revise and resubmit, without which *Heidegger's Moral Ontology* might have remained homeless. For making the publication of the present volume more immediately possible with Cambridge University Press, I'd like to thank Hilary Gaskin. It is hard to imagine a better, more careful, and patient and receptive editor.

For meticulous, painstaking, and unremunerated work on the index, without which the volume's publication would have been delayed, as well as for discovering several last-minute typographical errors, I would like to thank Corey Polster.

A longer version of the first chapter was first published in *The Review of Metaphysics* 59 (1): 33–71 (2005) and is reprinted with permission. I stole a few pages from the Introduction for inclusion in a chapter of my *Being Here Is Glorious: On Rilke, Poetry, and Philosophy* (Evanston, IL: Northwestern University Press, 2015 pp. 35–7) that I return to their original location and reprint here with permission.

As so much of this work was written or revised during extended stays in Crested Butte, Colorado, I thank the generous Oliphant family – Scott, Allen, Holly, and Sarah – for making available a house situated among the mountain gloom and glory, without which I might not have been able to complete the manuscript.

There are three people (or four) whose influence goes beyond anything that can be reasonably captured in these acknowledgments. To Candace R. Craig I owe more than I can say. It's difficult to avoid cliché facing someone so central to everything that matters. She is at once the source of several enabling background conditions that make intellectual life and work possible and a conversation partner with whom I find myself moved to talk about anything I consider important to discuss. I also owe thanks to Candace for considerable editorial work, for long hours spent compiling the bibliography, and for proofreading and formatting the manuscript at the very last minute. After too many years to count I can still say that the world remains fresh thanks partly to her. A recent addition to the family (Obi, King Oberon) has helped keep me sane by way of his exuberance and *joie de vivre* and by drawing me out of the solitude of intellectual work when he needs to engage with the larger world, regardless of what I think I need. And I'd like, finally, to thank my parents, Mary and David Babuder, to whom I dedicate this volume.

Introduction
Ethics and Ontology

"You don't intend to sing the praises of this book-making epidemic, do you?" So runs one of several questions raised by a fictional critic of eighteenth-century culture in a playful set of dialogues written in 1798 by the German philosophical poet Georg Philipp Friedrich von Hardenberg. Hardenberg's question, situated in a conversation that includes a defense of what was already becoming a publishing industry, anticipates a now commonplace, conservative uneasiness facing the proliferation of books, and books about books: the shadow of the past is too long, the catalog of worthwhile tomes already too large, and time too short to waste on the day's literary produce. Even the defender in the *Dialogues* of the unintended fruit of the revolution initiated by Gutenberg admits that important choices need to be made regarding what to read and what, just as importantly, to write about.

Why, then, devote time and energy to the work of Martin Heidegger, a thinker whose philosophical significance remains debatable, and whose political views during the period of National Socialism are detestable? If time is always *running out*, as Heidegger himself insists against the spurious sense we sometimes have of having all the time in the world, we would, perhaps, do better to come to grips with intellectual labor of less contestable philosophical value, and without any of the disturbing political affiliations that mar Heidegger's life and thought, and (for some) cast doubt upon his work as a whole, beyond the egregious political engagements and disturbing contaminations of the 1930s.

More troubling still: Why bother to take up a book on early Heidegger's contribution to *ethics*?[1] It is one thing to derive anti-Cartesian arguments

---

[1] There are still only a few book-length studies of Heidegger's contribution to ethics available in English, including Joanna Hodge's *Heidegger and Ethics*, Lawrence Vogel's *The Fragile We: Ethical Implications of Heidegger's "Being and Time,"* and Frederick Olafson's *Heidegger and the Ground of Ethics: A Study of Mitsein*. Although not directly concerned with ethics, mention should also be made of Scott M. Campbell's volume on *The Early Heidegger's Philosophy of Life: Facticity, Being, and*

from *Sein und Zeit*, and to argue that what Heidegger means by "being" is just the background intelligibility of our everyday social practices,[2] or to take seriously early Heidegger's contribution to theories of judgment and truth,[3] or to see in Heidegger a Teutonic pragmatist.[4] It is something else to stress Heidegger's importance as a serious moral philosopher and to construe the path that leads to *Sein und Zeit* as the development of a compelling moral ontology and ethical anthropology. And surely we can dismiss without lengthy argument the ethical vision of a philosopher who defended his commitment to National Socialism by appealing to the charm of Hitler's hands,[5] scorned enlightenment and liberal democratic practices and institutions, and officially broke with the philosophical tradition, in the name of the elusive mystery of *Seyn*.

In what follows, I hope to show, against the grain, that the path leading to the existential analytic of *Sein und Zeit* is pervaded by concerns that can plausibly be addressed in ethical terms, broadly construed. And I hope to show that Heidegger's contribution in ontological categories to what goes by the name of "ethics" deserves to be taken seriously by anyone interested today in normative questions and questions about the status of normativity as such.[6]

Ethics, Care, Authenticity

There are several good reasons to think that Heidegger is not interested in the issues that underwrite the discipline of moral philosophy or ethics. Heidegger never places at the center of his thought the question posed by Socrates in the *Gorgias* and the *Republic*: How should one live?[7] Even when his work leans noticeably toward an ethic of spiritual renewal and self-transformation in lecture courses delivered in Freiburg between 1919 and 1923, or displays an interest in what we might call practical problems, as in the Aristotle courses held in Marburg, the question

---

Language and Irene McMullin's exemplary *Time and the Shared World: Heidegger on Social Relations*. Sonia Sikka's *Heidegger, Morality and Politics* appeared in December 2017, too late for me to have benefited from it at any step in the development of the current project.

[2] This is the thesis of Dreyfus' commentary on the first division of *Sein und Zeit*, *Being-in-the-World: A Commentary on Heidegger's "Being and Time," Division I*.

[3] See Wayne Martin's *Theories of Judgment* and Daniel Dahlstrom's *Heidegger's Concept of Truth*.

[4] See Okrent's *Heidegger's Pragmatism*.

[5] Mark Lilla, *The Reckless Mind: Intellectuals in Politics*, 24.

[6] Heidegger's potential contribution to discussions about the normativity of human life, or Dasein, is central to the ongoing work of Steven Crowell and, more recently, of Sacha Golob's informative *Heidegger on Concepts, Freedom, and Normativity*.

[7] See, for instance, *Gorgias*, 500b–c.

concerning the good life seems to stand on the margins of Heidegger's expanding list of fundamental questions. Nowhere does Heidegger defend a moral imperative or justify a list of duties and obligations or rework the principle of utility as the criterion of moral deliberation. (When Mill comes up in the winter semester of 1925–6, it is his logic that matters.) Hegel's defense of *Sittlichkeit* in the third part of the *Philosophy of Right*, a fruitful source of more recent communitarian views on the complex social weave of moral and political life, appears to have made no deep and lasting impression on Heidegger during the phenomenological decade (1919–29). The early works are silent on questions of social justice and the nature, sources, and limits of human rights. With the important exception of Aristotle's *Nicomachean Ethics* and Kant's conceptions of respect and the dignity of the person in the *Groundwork* and second *Critique*, Heidegger rarely engages with the classic texts of our moral tradition with a clearly defined ethical agenda. When he does address the Stagirite's account of the good life, he appears to give the *Nicomachean Ethics* an ontological make-over.[8] When he takes up Kant's conception of the human being as an end in itself, in an important course of lectures on logic or truth (Winter Semester [hereafter, WS] 1925–6), he interprets it as a distorted version of his own apparently morally neutral thesis that Dasein's being is to be defined as care: the moral implications of Kant's ontological distinction between persons and things remain largely unexplored.

If one sets up any of these projects as defining preoccupations of moral philosophy or ethics, it can be difficult to see anything ethically salient in *Sein und Zeit* and the surrounding lecture courses.

There is, to be sure, widespread agreement that the ideal of *Eigentlichkeit* in *Sein und Zeit* is fraught with normative weight, even if Heidegger is eager to frame basic questions of moral philosophy in more neutral, ontological terms.[9] Mark Wrathall, to take one recent example, speaks of Heidegger's "authenticity thesis" as "a normative claim about an ideal form of action," as a claim about how we *ought* to be or to behave and to understand ourselves in practical life.[10] And it has become increasingly common to read Heidegger's philosophy of authenticity as a normative

---

[8] See, for instance, Taminiaux's essays on Heidegger and Aristotle in *The Thracian Maid*. The texts in question include a course of lectures on the basic concepts of Aristotelian philosophy (SS 1924) and the material devoted to Book Six of the *Nicomachean Ethics* in a course on Plato's *Sophist* (WS 1924/5).

[9] See, for instance, Iain Thomson's helpful "Heidegger's Perfectionist Philosophy of Education in *Being and Time*" in *Continental Philosophy Review*.

[10] "Autonomy, Authenticity, and the Self" in *Heidegger, Authenticity and the Self*, 193.

account of human responsibility, moral or otherwise.[11] Not as a bare fact
about us (in Wrathall's reading, that falls to Heidegger's account of
autonomy, which we cannot entirely avoid), but as something we are
called upon to assume, presumably because it would be *better* to act in
certain ways. The source of the claim the "ideal form of action" ostensibly
makes upon us is obscure, but its force in Heidegger's work is hard
to deny.

Heidegger's early ontology appears to have been grafted onto a vision of
what the philosopher of being takes to be a life lived *well*. Decisiveness,
courage in the face of death, and the readiness to be moved by the voice of
conscience seem like moral phenomena, even if the philosophical advantage of becoming authentic is just to be in a better position to discern
ontological differences and to make ontological pronouncements about
space, time, history, the wholeness of Dasein, and the like.[12] It is hard to
read the descriptions of *das Man* in the first division of *Sein und Zeit* –
curious to a fault, chattering idly, indifferent to what truly matters and
insensitive to important distinctions, concerned about social status,
absorbed in the petty details of a dislocated present, and ready to conform
to unquestioned norms and public standards – without hearing ethical
undertones beneath what appear to be neutral structural claims about the
nature of the public sphere and the social structure of normativity.

How to formulate the ethical requirement, what exactly becoming
authentic demands of a social agent, what sort of realignment in social
space it requires, and what the consequences of failure are, are matters of
controversy. But Heidegger is clearly not cataloguing the furniture of the
world and explaining what there is, from a neutral point of view, lacking
normative presuppositions and demands of an ethical sort.[13] If this turns
out to be what it means to do ontology, then it would be closer to the truth
to say that Heidegger's work offers no interesting contributions to the
discipline of ontology. If we think of ontology as an adequate theory of
being and its modes, then the author of *Being and Time* seems to be
suggesting, in an unexpected inversion, that the sort of ontology you do, or
how you think about the modal inflection of being, depends upon the sort

---

[11] See also Denis McManus's chapter in *Heidegger, Authenticity and the Self* on "Anxiety, Choice and
Responsibility in Heidegger's Account of Authenticity."
[12] For a useful account of the methodological role played by authenticity in *Being and Time*, see
Charles Guignon's "Authenticity and the Question of Being" in *Heidegger, Authenticity and the Self*.
[13] Robert Brandom associates the task of cataloguing what there is in the world with Heidegger's
conception of "vulgar ontology" in "Heidegger's Categories in *Sein und Zeit*" in *Tales of the Mighty
Dead: Historical Essays in the Metaphysics of Intentionality*, 299.

of person you aspire to be; and, further, that some varieties of ontology will be deficient because the *lives* that underwrite the theories are spurious or somehow lacking. *Jemeinigkeit* (the fact that life is always owned), a crucial category in *Sein und Zeit* and the early lecture courses, is not merely a neutral structure of Dasein's being, but a polemical concept, directed against more impersonal ways of living. The problem with Descartes's conception of the *ego cogito* as the first philosophical truth, and Husserl's more recent variation on the theme of absolute subjectivity and its certainty, is not merely theoretical, but is grounded in what Heidegger considers an impoverished vision of what human life and its world should be allowed to be. As Heidegger insists throughout the period this study covers (1919–27), the Cartesian quest for certainty in its many guises is best understood as a motivated flight from being in uncertainties and mysteries. Our prevailing ideas of what exists and how to interpret what exists are in contention in early Heidegger because certain ways of life and the ends they embody are in question. Heidegger's various attacks on extant ontology are in some measure *ad hominem*, and rooted in a normative ideal that underwrites the abstract ontological pronouncements.

This is, I hope, a promising start in the defense of the ethical significance of the project that came to public expression in 1927 in *Being and Time*. We shall develop this point in some detail in the opening chapter below. But doubts about the *moral* worth of Heidegger's account of authenticity are likely to persist. If, for instance, morality involves certain duties to behave in certain ways, then Heidegger's account of authentic human existence does not seem to have much in common with moral experience, unless, as Golob notes, we can be said to have a duty to become authentic.[14] I don't believe that Heidegger thinks we have a duty or an obligation to own up. Authenticity places certain demands upon the agent, but there seems to be nothing like a categorical imperative (anchored, as Kant argues, in the very structure of finite rational agency as such) to live more transparently. And as we shall see below in the discussion of things and persons, the very capacity to be moved by moral requirements is not entirely up to us, at least not for Heidegger. One can say, at best, that owning up to the human condition is somehow more satisfying than failing to do so; but that still leaves the individual free to ignore the demand. There may be culpability in this, but it does not appear to resemble the sort of *moral* culpability at stake in, e.g., Kantian ethics. That may not prove fatal to the very idea of moral ontology (which,

[14] *Heidegger on Concepts, Freedom and Normativity*, 213.

as we shall soon see, embraces and elucidates a wide array of ethical phenomena, grounded in care), but it does place certain limits on what can be said on its behalf.

But there are other problems as well, at least on the surface. In some ears, Heidegger's various descriptions of the normative (or "ontic") ideal that makes his own fundamental ontology possible will strike a note of selfishness and self-absorption or, if it demands total detachment from what *we* think and do, impossible in principle (call this the Hegelian objection). To someone sympathetic to Russell's *The Conquest of Happiness*, the call might seem to subvert the proper order of the happy human life, where the task is precisely to forget yourself and "to center [your] attention increasingly on external objects: the state of the world, various branches of knowledge, individuals for whom [one feels] affection."[15] In the minds of still others, the jargon of authenticity is the sophisticated philosophical expression of a rebellious commonplace, with more distant (and richer) historical roots in the individualism we associate with the early modern era.[16] From this point of view, Heidegger might appear to have more in common with Descartes than is usually thought, despite his own self-proclaimed anti-Cartesian aspirations.[17]

We have, therefore, several questions to ask: What are we prepared to embrace under the umbrella of ethical or moral reflection and its objects? What does it mean to aspire after *Eigentlichkeit*? And can we locate points of contact between what we acknowledge as a moral or ethical concern and the aspirations of *Eigentlichkeit*? We may find points of convergence in the idea of what it would be good to be, not as a displacement of what it would be good or right to do, but as another register of the moral life.

We should probably be as suspicious as Heidegger was when it comes to saying something about *the* essence of ethical concern. Iris Murdoch voices a difficulty we ought to take seriously: "It is a peculiarity of ethics that the initial segregation of the items to be studied is less easy than in other branches of philosophy."[18] An important feature of our intellectual landscape is our lack of clarity about what ethics and ethical concern are

[15] *The Conquest of Happiness*, 18.
[16] Benjamin Crowe situates Heidegger's conception of authenticity within the context of romantic individualism in the fifth chapter of his *Heidegger's Religious Origins*.
[17] See, inter alia, Marion's *Reduction and Givenness* and several essays in *The Cambridge Companion to Heidegger*. Jacques Taminiaux argues at some length along these lines in *Heidegger and the Project of Fundamental Ontology*. Matthew Shockey offers perhaps the most compelling case for a Cartesian line of thought in early Heidegger in "Heidegger's Descartes and Heidegger's Cartesianism" (*European Journal of Philosophy*).
[18] "Vision and Choice in Morality" in *Existentialists and Mystics*, 76.

about in the first place, and how far philosophy is able to ground an ethical vision of the world.

Our burden might seem lightened by important work on the difference between moral concerns and ethical matters, where the latter is said to consider not, or not exclusively, what we ought to do (what actions we have certain duties to perform) but what sort of life is best.[19] But taking seriously the broader claims and questions of ethical life has its own difficulties. If Kant and the Kantians limit themselves to the domain of moral obligation, the ethicist has to consider a wide range of values and concerns, including (perhaps in a different key) what the moralist analyzes; and she has to take more seriously the potential conflicts between areas of concern and the difficulty of assigning relative weight to what is discovered to be important in our various pursuits of human flourishing. Here it is not only a matter of what choices are morally required or permitted; we are equally interested in what form of life best satisfies whatever human strivings we take to be important, and these ambitions and their relative worth are difficult to pin down. Something like this broadening of concern is needed to appreciate what Heidegger is up to in *Sein und Zeit* and the early lecture courses and essays.

In several essays, Harry Frankfurt paints a compelling picture of *care* as the basic concern of a certain style of ethical reflection; and I would like to take this as my point of departure here, partly because Frankfurt, like Murdoch and Williams and others, situates moral concerns in a larger space of human interest (where the moral is often awarded second-place), in part because he offers a convenient summary of an important strand in the fabric of recent moral philosophy. But Frankfurt is also attuned to the *reflective* reach of our concerns and, most importantly, *Sorgen* stands at the center of Heidegger's view of being human and having world. Because Heidegger's ontology includes an account of what it is properly to care and what sorts of matters ought to matter, it is possible to read *Sein und Zeit* and related documents from the early period as contributions to ethics.[20] So why place concepts of caring, concern, importance, and mattering at the heart of ethics?

We ought to begin with care because "the fact that we do actually care about various things is of fundamental significance to the character of

---

[19] See Bernard Williams' *Ethics and the Limits of Philosophy* and Martha Nussbaum's *The Fragility of Goodness*.

[20] For Frankfurt on the importance of moral considerations and contexts in which they are less authoritative, see *The Reasons of Love*, 6ff. "Morality," Frankfurt writes, "can provide at most only a severely limited and insufficient answer to the question how a person should live."

human life."[21] It is a fundamental fact about us that we are creatures for whom things matter. We do not first encounter mere objects to be observed, classified, and explained, but things to be used and things of pressing concern (*pragmata*). It calls for no sophisticated piece of reasoning to conclude that things of use serve because they play a role in what we take to be worthwhile. Whatever enters into the context of our engagement plays whatever role it does in light of the point of what we take ourselves to be about. And care can be said to be fundamental in the sense that it cannot be derived from something more basic. Here we reach something like what the ancients called an *archê*, at once a first principle and a chronological beginning. The interest we take in reason, the desire to understand the cosmos, the affection between parents and children and among siblings, the aspirations of a novelist – these things, however diverse, are unthinkable in the absence of care. Their very quality, or being, is shaped and determined by the fact that we care about them. If we are incapable of caring, if we remain truly apathetic, we will be unmoved by the claim of reason, indifferent to the cosmos of ideas, unconcerned about what others call "loved ones," and unreachable by moral or ethical considerations: "What is *not* possible is for a person who does not already care about *something* to discover reasons for caring about anything."[22] For Frankfurt and, I suggest, for Heidegger as well, caring is the original source of reasons.[23] As Kant argues in his work on conscience and the "fact of reason" (*Faktum der Vernunft*) in the second *Critique*, you cannot be reasoned into a moral view of the world from the ground up. Moral philosophy has only to make explicit and to clarify what lies in the untutored understanding and moral preoccupation of every human being. Immorality is not ignorance of what we ought to do but an inclined refusal to do it. Someone who, *per impossibile*, truly doesn't care about the claim of moral reason cannot be reasoned into taking an interest in a genuinely moral life. She could only feign an interest in appearing moral.

On Heidegger's view (and here we depart from Frankfurt), care grounds even our most trivial activities: an interest in distraction and mere entertainment is conditioned by care as much as our commitments to more serious pursuits in philosophy, science, politics, religion, and the arts. The care-structure of human existence can be ignored (Heidegger seems to think that the philosophical tradition as a whole has failed to acknowledge

[21] *The Reasons of Love*, 16.   [22] Ibid., 26.
[23] Steven Crowell develops the connection between care and reason in "Responsibility, Autonomy, Affectivity: A Heideggerian Approach" in *Heidegger, Authenticity and the Self*.

the phenomenon), but it cannot be circumvented. Some of the things we care about may turn out to be unworthy of our concern; but any attempt to argue us out of an ethical stance will have to begin with what we do in fact care about and why. The fact that we care is nothing the ethical thinker, interested in the interest we take in our ethical existence, can afford to ignore; and Heidegger has a rich and compelling account of this fundamental, grounding condition of our engagement with the world, in theoretical and practical life alike.

We should also note that the importance of what we care about and the caring itself constitute whatever identity, moral or otherwise, we can be said to have or to win. "Caring is indispensably foundational as an activity that connects and binds us to ourselves."[24] Or, in one of Heidegger's earliest ways of speaking about the formation of identity, the *Selbstwelt*, the world that forms around an entity able to say "I," is a *Sorgenwelt* (a world of care).[25] The differences between one person and the next, and what makes a difference in our own lives and identities as moral agents, are partly constituted by the different objects of our concern, the intensity and constancy our commitments display, and the *way* we care for those persons and things we find important. Care is at work from the ground up in the formation of human agency and intelligence.

The standpoint of care is, further, large enough to allow us to puzzle over the diverse range of things we might be led to care about, without shuttling ethical inquiry too quickly down one highway at the expense of other, equally important paths. From this vantage point we can weigh, say, the values of the Kantian conception of the moral life against the claims of Aristotelian ethics, ponder the significance of utilitarian principles, reflect upon the worth of certain external goods, like friendship, wealth, and material possessions, and take more seriously the difficulty of living and choosing well. And we will take these questions seriously if Frankfurt is right that "what it is in particular that we care about has a considerable bearing upon the character and the quality of our lives. It makes a great difference that certain things, and not others, are important to us."[26] Getting clear about what ought to be important is hardly a simple affair. And developing the ontological and ethical implications of the point of departure in *Sorgen* would by itself be a significant philosophical achievement.

If Heidegger's ontology belongs to ethics or if ethics becomes an ontological affair, it is because the path to *Sein und Zeit* (and *Sein und*

---

[24] Ibid., 17.   [25] *Phenomenological Interpretations of Aristotle*, 70–1.   [26] Ibid., 17.

Zeit itself) is pervaded by an interest in *authentic* care. Throughout the lecture courses and manuscripts I draw from in what follows, we discover various ways of marking the distinction between caring well or poorly, owning up to life and struggling to avoid what life demands. At times *Eigentlichkeit* appears to be the virtue of a solitary hero, detached from the crowd, indifferent to the vagaries of public opinion, disdainful of what we share with others, and unwilling to get situated in relation to a larger space of social concern. But more importantly (and, I think, more plausibly), *Eigentlichkeit* is often portrayed as the proper way to care about our own lives in relation to others and, just as importantly, about the *world* in which it is our shared lot to live. Far from being an isolating experience, authentic care could be said to consolidate an ethical interest in what lies beyond the *solus ipse*. In this light, *Eigentlichkeit* means something like coming to grips with the human condition, being true *not* (or not only) to our solitary selves, but to the sort of being we all have and are (owning up to life, owning up to the human); and this on the grounds that it is possible to evade or avoid something about ourselves, or to close ourselves off to the things of this world and to other persons.[27] Again, this may not add up to a definitive ethical vision of what we ought always to pursue and avoid in the concrete life of our uncertain affairs (and there is good reason to think that Heidegger never intended to offer anything of the sort); but it is, I hope to show, part of an effort to weave ethical concerns into what we think there is in the world of what we care about.

The Shadow of the Object: Responding to Moral Skepticism

In "Metaphysics and Ethics," Iris Murdoch suggests that the more ancient question "What is goodness?" has been replaced by the question "What is the activity of valuing or commending?"[28] "The philosopher is now to speak no longer of the Good, as something real or transcendent, but to analyse the familiar human activity of endowing things with value."[29] We have a handy and familiar vocabulary of more or less interchangeable terms to name what we do when we experience something important or valuable: we *endow* the world with significance; we *project* meaning onto the world;

---

[27] I argue for this position, shared by Golob, at some length in Chapter 5: in Golob's words, one of the defining characteristics of authenticity "is that Dasein accurately understands its own nature . . . in a way that reflects facts about Dasein" (*Heidegger on Concepts, Freedom and Normativity*, 214).

[28] This section repeats, with slight modification, a passage of argument in my *Being Here Is Glorious: On Rilke, Poetry, and Philosophy*, pp. 35–7.

[29] *Existentialists and Mystics*, 60.

we *bestow* value on what would be worthless without the impact of a valuing mind on indifferent matter. Endowing or projecting or bestowing is the work of a mind straining to find value in a world that remains indifferent to our projections, and making up for what the world lacks through its own, perhaps hollow activity.

This view finds, perhaps, its most extreme expression in J. L. Mackie's *Ethics: Inventing Right and Wrong*. As Mackie informs us, values "are not part of the fabric of the world."[30] And if values form no part of the fabric or furniture of the (objective) world, then certainly they can only be in us. Where else are we to discover their sources if we cannot find them out there, in the physical world? When we cannot discover a value in the realm of fact, it seems natural to look for it in the searching subject: "No doubt if moral values are not objective they are in some very broad sense subjective."[31]

Although it remains a controversial thesis concerning the nature of value, this view is pervasive enough, especially beyond the academy, that something must speak in favor of it. Mackie offers several now familiar sorts of arguments for the subjective thesis concerning the ultimate source of value: arguments from the relativity of what matters across cultures, within a culture over time, and within a culture at any give time; arguments from the strangeness or "queerness" of objective values (the fact that we don't encounter values in the same way that we experience stones, plants, animals, and the like); and several arguments targeting specific claims made by objectivists. The arguments from the relativity of what we consider important and worth becoming or doing are perhaps the oldest and, from the standpoint of what often passes today for common sense, the weightiest. For it does seem obvious that *if* we cannot agree about the value of a landscape or a human figure, then its beauty cannot reasonably said to be a property of the thing itself, but must somehow reside in the eye of the beholder. The *object* we intend in the experience of the beautiful is what it is, and capable of being objectively determined beyond our varying aesthetic and moral judgments. We do not disagree *that* there is a landscape or a person *there*, except when we're engaged in abstract epistemological or metaphysical

---

[30] *Ethics: Inventing Right and Wrong*, 15.
[31] Ibid., 18. The distinction between questions of fact and questions of value, worth, meaning, and significance holds even William James in grip. See, for instance, *The Varieties of Religious Experience*, 4–5 and 150.

inquiries; nor do we dispute its objective qualities, but only wonder and come into conflict and argue about its worth.

What is worth noting here, anticipating the argument to be developed below, is that subjectivism and its offsprings, moral skepticism and relativism, are tied to conceptions of what there is in the world, and how the world itself is to be viewed, taken up, and expressed: subjectivism and a certain way of viewing the world (roughly, as an object or as an ordered totality of mere objects) are two sides of the same underlying stance. And it is this way of thinking about what a world is and how we have it that Heidegger persistently and compellingly contests. A large part of early Heidegger's project could plausibly be read as an attack on subjectivism, and an equally forceful attack on the objectivism regarding human value that Mackie finds so troubling. Mackie's view of what there is and how we come to know it is, however, philosophically thin. Once you have reduced the world as the place where things happen to matter to a residual domain of fact, it is certainly not going to contain anything of moral or aesthetic, social or political value. Nowhere does Mackie offer extended analyses of what he means by "subjective" and "objective." We are simply informed, without argument, that subjectivism becomes compelling once we renounce "a fictitious external authority."[32] But we might wonder whether Mackie's world is not itself a fiction. If we grant, with Frankfurt and Heidegger, that we are fundamentally creatures for whom things matter, and with Heidegger that we are necessarily world-bound, then we need to articulate a view of the world that makes room for what matters. And while we should make room as well for controversy, dialogue, and debate about what is important and what we ought to do, we cannot begin the work of criticism and revision unless we begin with a realm of fact "always already" permeated by value. The first task, then, is to get back into a world in which things are allowed to be significant.

On early Heidegger's view, the very distinction between a realm of fact and a realm of value distorts our experience of a world of things that matter. Before the gulf between them opens, and before we begin to wonder where to place our values, if not in a world of mere fact, we already find ourselves in a world of worthwhile things. The world, as Heidegger tells us in 1920, is nothing objective, and precisely because we cannot live in an object: the world is rather the meaningful site of our living and dwelling. And the particular things about which we care come poorly into focus as objects with properties.

---

[32] *Ethics*, 34.

There may well turn out to be circumstances in which it makes sense to ask about an object or a fact, regardless of the value it may or may not be said to possess: that a stone weights six pounds, that Heidegger was born in Messkirch in 1889 *are*, in some sense, matters of fact with a legitimate claim to objectivity (although, even here, one might wonder *why* these examples come to mind). But what about claims like the following: "The world is the objective totality of facts" or "Justice is the rule of those who just happen to be in power"? Is it a mere fact about the moral life that our values are not objective? If it *is* a fact, why so much controversy? Why is it unlikely that we will clear up the confusion or put the debate to rest in the same way that we establish the area of a plot of land?[33] There is hardly an issue of deep philosophical or human importance that resolves itself into a series of questions to which facts will furnish the answers.

There is, to be sure, a sense in which Mackie's critique of objectivism is right, and in a sense anticipated by Heidegger himself: if we eliminate ourselves from our picture of the world (at least in thought), if we strip the world of the *human* element and imagine a world of mere things, we (mere observers) discover nothing like values, ethical concerns, aesthetic characteristics, and moral requirements. But this merely intellectual exercise comes to an end in the face of more pressing claims in human experience. Mattering and worth are not properties, like hardness or color that cling to or define purely physical things. And if our standard of objectivity is an even more elusive view of what there is *an sich*, beyond our capacity to perceive or think or care, we are likely to be as disappointed in the philosophical analysis of value as the disaffected lover of traditional metaphysics, persuaded by the arguments of Kant's first *Critique*. But the Heideggerian conclusion I'm ready to defend in what follows is not that these things are as a result merely subjective, but that they are neither subjective nor objective but *worldly*, where "world" is neither a mere object or state of affairs, nor something to be discovered within the secret hiding places of a worldless subject. Once we spell out the implications of Heidegger's account of being-in-the-world, we will hopefully be less troubled by arguments from the apparent relativity of values and what Mackie calls "queerness."

---

[33] In the *Euthyphro*, Socrates, hardly a subjectivist, asks his interlocutor to consider what sorts of things we quarrel about, and what, when we differ, makes us enemies. Certainly not "which of two groups of things is larger" – a question put to rest in our reliable calculations (or, as we might say, our measuring way of settling fact), but perhaps "these things: the just and unjust, and noble and shameful, and good and bad" (7b–d).

There is one challenge in particular that needs addressing before we move forward. Heidegger's response to the problem, or the lure, of objectivism (or "naturalism" in some sense) might seem to beg the question against such naturalists and quasi-realists as Blackburn who take the natural world at stake in modern science to be somehow fundamental but go on to build up a world of value on top of it. (Searle seems to be of the same opinion, as his quarrels with Dreyfus make clear. Both Searle and Blackburn cannot be said to be indifferent to what Heidegger calls "being-in-the-world."[34] And Blackburn has a moral theory worth contending with.[35]) We shall see in the next chapter that Heidegger, as I reconstruct his early views on *Wissenschaft*, has no real quarrel with modern science. His various accounts of *Vorhandenheit* throughout the period can be read as so many attempts to account for the way in which the objects of science became salient, or objects become relevant in a scientific way. Although Heidegger is not engaged, at least not exclusively, in laying transcendental foundations or "epistemic conditions" for the scientific investigation of nature and, correlatively, elucidating the ontological characteristics of the object of natural scientific inquiry (a task he takes Kant to be doing, among other things, in the first *Critique*), I detect no antiscientific attitude in the early lecture courses and in *Sein und Zeit*. In *The Question Concerning the Thing* (WS 1935–6) Heidegger is even prepared to acknowledge the presence of a *philosophical* significance and dimension in the work of contemporary physics: "the present leaders in atomic physics, Niels Bohr and Heisenberg, think philosophically through and through, and only because of this do they create new ways of posing questions and above all hold out in questionability."[36] Similar views come forward already in the Introduction to *Being and Time*, in Heidegger's discussion of the ontological priority of the *Seinsfrage* and the "immanent crises of the sciences" that tend "to place [scientific] research on new foundations."[37] It is not until much later that Heidegger comes to the more disparaging view that science does not really *think*, at least not in the "essential" way at issue in "being-historical thinking."[38]

---

[34] See, for instance, Searle's *The Construction of Social Reality* and *Mind, Language and Society* and Joshua Rust's interpretation and defense in *John Searle and the Construction of Social Reality*.

[35] Cf. Simon Blackburn's *Ruling Passions: A Theory of Practical Reasoning* and his *Being Good: A Short Introduction to Ethics*.

[36] *The Question Concerning the Thing* (GA 41, 67), tr. James D. Reid and Benjamin D. Crowe (Rowman & Littlefield, forthcoming).

[37] *SZ*, 9.

[38] And already in WS 1935/6, Heidegger is prepared to say: "Does one want science to be even 'closer to life'? I think that science is already so close that it overwhelms and oppresses us" (GA 41, 13–14).

But this implies that projects such as Blackburn's may not be incompatible with Heidegger's. They may just run in the opposite direction: from the world of objective, scientific fact to the world of human significance. (There are Fichtean concerns that such projects are impossible in principle, that, for instance, freedom and self-consciousness cannot emerge on top of a world of brute things, but an interpretation and defense of that position calls for a book-length study in its own right.) This would allow for greater appreciation of the scientific, naturalist worldview. Although I do not think that Heidegger would have shown much interest in various forms of contemporary naturalism, there is no reason to think that *we* should not.

The worry I take Heidegger to be addressing in his critique of certain philosophies that take their start from the fact of natural science concerns the possible *conclusion* that phenomena such as care, significance, and mood are *illusory*. It is true that Heidegger recognizes no "hard problem of consciousness," no more than Nietzsche does. (Both take consciousness to be derivative.) And the problem of "finding meaning in a material world" is already solved, to the extent that we find *that* problem worth our attention. But it does not follow that the problem of the natural world carries no weight in early Heidegger.

Searle, who takes the problem of human consciousness in the natural world quite seriously, does not set off on the right foot in his essay on "The Phenomenological Illusion" when he insists, in a clause embedded in a question, that we *know* that the universe "consists entirely of physical particles in fields of force."[39] He seems to take it for granted, as Heidegger does not, that we *know* this. And the problem, as he sees it, grows out of what we ostensibly know. There is a careless slip in Searle from our knowing that Darwinian evolution is a plausible story about our coming to be in the material world toward our knowing that the basic truths about our condition are physical. Surely the explanatory success of modern physical science is not a sufficient condition of our knowing that the world is fundamentally physical. How would we know such a thing? Not because scientific success in explanation and prediction somehow *makes* it so. And so his idea of "basic reality" is, without argument, a case of begging the question against the Heideggerian thesis that our "basic reality" is one of meaning, anchored in care. If Heidegger is right that care is a grounding condition of our commitment to any project at all – including the project

---

[39] "The Phenomenological Illusion," 318.

of natural science – the conclusion, which Searle simply takes for granted, can rightly be said to overreach.

Searle's "problem of meaning" reduces to the specialized one of explaining "the relation of physics to the utterances of semantics."[40] But that does not come close to what Heidegger means by the "problem of meaning," which embraces questions concerning how the semantics of our speech acts are possible, but also why we should care about such questions in the first place. Heidegger, too, is worried about the relation between mere sounds and meaning (cf. his discussion of sound and significance in SS 1924), but his analyses do not rest upon any presumption, which Searle fails to argue for in any case, that the primary phenomenon of the human voice is its merely phonetic or physical reality. It is sheer dogmatism, as far as I can tell, to insist that the chief problem of human society is how to get from "brute facts" to "social and institutional facts." One might even wonder, just as legitimately, how mere physical facts shake out of a world of socially inflected concern. If Heidegger can be said to dogmatize in his insistence on the fundamentality of social or ethical facts, Searle is even more dogmatic in his dismissals of the Heideggerian account. (Heidegger, like Husserl, does not deny that books, for example, are physical objects, and so that the existence and persistence of literature, for instance, depends upon the existence of the physical objects that make the transmission of literary artifacts possible.) One can only wonder what Searle might mean by his appeal to "brute, observer independent facts" that show apart from any stance or point of view.[41] Color without a perceiver of color? A=A without a creature logically minded? Heidegger is at least worried in the early period that his account of "being-in-the-world" is opposed by theorists who place physical facts and formal, logical truths at the basis of their philosophical concern, and see value as a supervenient problem. Searle is impatient with his adversary. But no amount of swift philosophical argument can decide the question. And if Heidegger is right, the question whether the physical is more primordial than the meaningful, or the meaningful prior to the physical, is, in a way, beside the question. The things of our experience are both at once, if not always at the same time. His project is an ethical, and not an explanatory enterprise.

There is, perhaps, the lingering worry that Heidegger has purchased his commitment to some variety of "meaning-idealism" too cheaply. (Searle, a bit too hastily, in my view, takes questions about Heidegger's version of idealism as a red herring.) But that raises more questions than I can answer

[40] Ibid., 323.   [41] Ibid., 330.

here about what it means to classify Heidegger as an idealist, and whether his own version of idealism means to be incompatible with some variety of realism. (Kant, too, took his "transcendental idealism" to be the best way of accounting for a robust "empirical realism.") This is an important topic in its own right, but it falls outside the scope of the present study.[42]

Heidegger was, in any event, interested throughout the phenomeno-logical decade in the varieties of human cognition and knowledge – practical, technical, scientific, and philosophic. As we argue in the second chapter below, Heidegger is at great pains, following in the footsteps of Aristotle, to show that we should not privilege, say, the scientific over the practical (or ethical) and, just as importantly, that nonscientific insight cannot be reduced to the scientific or dismissed as spurious. Our orienta-tions toward spaces of meaning, what makes it possible for us to get our bearings in practical and ethical situations of action cannot be reduced to the emotive, unless we grant some sort of cognitive aspect to the emotions. If the argument in the fifth chapter below is sound, some distinctions between right and wrong, better or worse cannot be *merely* invented. (In this sense, if not in a sense endorsed by the naturalist, he might be said to be a "realist" in the theory of value.) We should in any case, or pending further notice and compelling argument, take seriously the "phenomenological standpoint" within which they show up, announce themselves, or otherwise make themselves felt. The burden of proof that they are unreal or illusory falls, I think, to the critic or the hard-core naturalist. (We also need to show why or how they can be skirted or suppressed.)

The questions with which we shall be occupied extensively in what follows will, therefore, have to include: What can we be said to know here, when it comes to what concerns us? With what right do we speak of something like ethical *insight*? What sort of knowledge do we have as moral and ethical agents? The denial that we can be said to know anything here is rooted in a family of ontological assumptions that shape what counts as an instance of knowing and what is allowed as an object to be known. And it is here that Heidegger's assault on subjectivism, drawn largely from Aristotle's writings on ethics and politics, makes itself felt. Several basic

---

[42] A recent attempt to challenge an orthodox reading of Heidegger, according to which the theoretical and propositional attitudes are derivative, has been provided by Denis McManus in his outstanding monograph, *Heidegger and the Measure of Truth*. One of the persistent worries facing early Heidegger's phenomenology is that his apparent assault on the "theoretical attitude" is inconsistent with his own practice, that fundamental ontology is itself a distinctively *theoretical* enterprise. I take this problem up explicitly in the final chapter.

insights of the early lecture courses are, I think, worth recovering. And together they offer a compelling assault on some varieties of subjectivism and moral skepticism, even if the moral ontologist has no knock-down proofs to offer the exponent of either to convince him to follow suit.

Ethics With or Without Ontology

The train of thought just sketched draws attention to the importance of ontological assumptions and assertions in our reflections on ethical life. It seems that what distinguishes the subjectivist and the moral skeptic, on the one hand, from someone for whom subjectivism and skepticism are not compelling, on the other, lies in what human beings and their world are considered to be. After what has already been said, there should be nothing surprising in this interweaving of ontological visions and ethical vistas, although there remains detailed work to do. In a sense, Heidegger is merely developing an old Platonic thesis: there is no conception of being without a conception of the good, and no conception of the good to be defended without a conception of what things, including human beings, can be said *to be*.[43]

But one might still object to the ontological interpretation of ethics on at least two grounds: (1) along lines staked out by Hilary Putnam, one might argue that an ethics without ontology is somehow morally to be preferred to an ethics with ontological pretensions; and (2) along a path pursued by Heidegger himself, it might be argued that ontology excludes ethical reflection from the very start, perhaps on the grounds that ethics is not sufficiently fundamental. And so we have to ask: Can ethics do without ontology? And can ontology be liberated from the ethical? In a sense, the argument developed throughout the present study is meant to answer these two questions. But something needs saying by way of introduction.

Hilary Putnam has argued forcefully that ethics not only can exist without ontology, but that it would be better if the ethicist tried to do without it.[44] We do not need to decide what being ultimately means, or what there ultimately is in the world (atoms or quarks, say), in order to begin to clarify our responsibilities as human agents. We should, on this view, just puzzle over how we take ourselves up in the way of being

---

[43] Heidegger works in detail with the good in Aristotle's *Nicomachean Ethics* as an ontological category in SS 1924, on the basic concepts of Aristotelian philosophy.

[44] *Ethics without Ontology.*

obligated. But by "ontology" Putnam means something like what Heidegger calls the onto-theological proclivities of the metaphysical tradition.[45] And while I can't argue in favor of the overcoming of ontology in this sense, I have no quarrel with Putnam and those prepared to follow suit. But can ethics exist without ontology in *any* sense? This is harder to maintain. Even if you have good reasons for disputing or disposing of *some* ontological assumptions, you are likely to make others. Suppose you say that it is in the nature of the human being to have no nature. How are we to understand this, if not as a claim about what it means and is like to *be* human? To *be* condemned to live and act without recourse to a fixed order of nature, say, or in the absence of norms and standards provided by biology? A view of what we ought to do or how we ought to live or what sort of person we should aspire to be commits its holder to a vision of what there is about us that makes it desirable or worthwhile to pursue certain things in a certain spirit. At the very least, ethics requires something like a "metaphysics of morals" or, in Heidegger's preferred manner of speaking, an "ontology of Dasein."

On the other hand, Heidegger has his own weighty reasons for suppressing the ethical dimension of his own ontological labors. He frequently appears to argue that moral concerns fail to get to the heart of the matter and, in a tacit ethical key, that the claims of morality are convenient props that make the conduct of life easier. It is, perhaps, less unsettling to ignore the particular aspects of a relatively unique situation and the potential conflict between two or more worthwhile but incompatible pursuits in favor of a clear set of universal prescriptions, commands, obligations, and duties that define what you consider to be the moral point of view. From this vantage point, the moral life appears evasive and tranquilizing. It is one of Heidegger's earliest (Kierkegaardian) convictions that philosophy itself ought to stir up in us a sense of the difficulty of living well and understanding what sorts of beings we are.

If this seems to transgress the neutral limits of ontology, Heidegger has another reason to disavow ethical intentions; and this has something to do with his convictions on the sterility of academic work in relatively isolated philosophical disciplines. Heidegger repeatedly inveighs against the divide-and-conquer mentality, a mindset he traces back to the Hellenistic era and associates with what Kant calls the "scholastic concept" of

[45] For a fine discussion of Heidegger's conception of ontotheology, see Iain Thomson's *Heidegger on Ontotheology: Technology and the Politics of Education*, especially the first chapter.

philosophy. The swerve toward *Sein*, then, is one way of overcoming this aspect of our intellectual inheritance; for being, as Aristotle argued, cannot be confined to a particular genus or class of entities. If ethics is one discipline among many, distinct from aesthetics, epistemology, metaphysics, the philosophy of religion, and so on, then ontology is nothing ethical.

But it is one of the lessons of Heideggerian ontology that we should not avoid talking about different sorts of objects and experiences, even if our interest in them is ontological. What the young phenomenologist finds distressing in the tradition is, among other things, its tendency to obliterate fundamental ontological distinctions, to treat human beings, for instance, as things with defining properties or works of art as natural objects with other, more "spiritual" values somehow attached. There is an ontological difference between a landscape and a skyscraper, a flower and a human being, a historical event and a natural process, an ethical encounter and a laboratory experiment. To talk freshly about being is certainly not to submerge the diverse objects of our concern in the night in which, as the saying goes, all cows are black.[46] It is not enough to say that ethical life does not matter because being does.

And there is also the fact, stressed by Heidegger himself, that fundamental ontology is rooted in an "ontic ideal" of human life. Even if we wish to argue that the point of becoming authentic is to be better able to do ontology (to perceive being more clearly, to speak about your vision more compellingly), we are still committed to an ethical stance, however slender – call it the ethics of ontology. The implication is that it would be somehow *better* to clarify the ontological nature of our contact with the world, Dasein, death, history, space, and time; and that a life that does not aspire after something like being is somehow deficient. And if a fundamental ontology is supposed to offer a set of conditions or structures that define human existence; and if, because of the sort of being we humans possess, it is possible to avoid or disavow some aspects of our being; and if the being we have to be makes certain claims upon us and carries what we might call normative weight – then an existential analysis of human existence that takes these connections seriously deserves to be called "ethical" under some description.

---

[46] The charge comes down to us from Hegel's attack on Schelling, or his followers, in the Preface to the *Phenomenology of Spirit*.

Heidegger and National Socialism: A Short Discourse on the Method

There is still the now inescapable difficulty of drawing philosophical nourishment from a fundamental ontologist who became a Nazi.[47] Even if an incipient case has been made for the interweaving of ethics and ontology in early Heidegger, and reasons to take seriously the project of grounding moral reflection in ontological insights, nothing has been said to vindicate the sorts of claims made in support of the "ontic ideal" of human life that underwrites the ontological theses defended throughout the 1920s and reworked in detail in what follows. We should ask: How can work on ethics sensitive to the issues that drive some of the best discussions in contemporary moral philosophy derive support from Heidegger, knowing what we now know about the nature and extent of his involvement in the politics of National Socialism, his attempt to cover it up, his disturbing silence about the Holocaust, and the more recent revelations of what Peter Trawny calls "being-historical anti-Semitism" in the *Black Notebooks*?[48] Isn't every appropriation of early Heidegger marred by the well-documented fact of Heidegger's Nazism? It is no longer possible to plead ignorance.

In the face of work by Habermas, Wolin, Bambach, Faye, and a growing number of other philosophical historians and critics, it is not sufficient to distinguish cleanly and without argument between an early and a later Heidegger. For what some of these authors try to show is that Heidegger is moving toward dubious social and political views, dressed up in ontological clothing, almost as soon as he begins to philosophize. The arguments may be thin and the evidence weak, but there are arguments and evidence to contend with, claims to challenge, and counterviews to be developed.

Nor will it suffice to argue that Heidegger's ontology is a neutral theoretical affair. If there is any thread that unites the young Privatdozent in Freiburg, the author of *Sein und Zeit*, and the idiosyncratic National Socialist philosopher of the 1930s, it is the conviction that genuine philosophical work is never conducted from a neutral, merely contemplative standpoint. Nor is it enough to echo Habermas, one of Heidegger's sharpest German critics, and say that Heidegger's is one of the most impressive philosophical achievements since Hegel. For we have to ask:

---

[47] For biographical details, see the work of Ott and, more recently, Safranski.
[48] Cf. Peter Trawny, *Heidegger & the Myth of a Jewish World*.

What are the nature and implications of this achievement, and what political implications does it have?

I have no direct argument to rebut the charge that Heidegger's ontology is already moving toward "reactionary anti-modernism" in the period leading up to *Sein und Zeit*. The proof, if we can speak of proving anything here, is to be sought in the interpretation to be developed in what follows. It is, however, a remarkable fact that Heidegger's work was influential before the facts came fully to light and continues to influence thoughtful individuals who oppose Heidegger's politics. The productive philosophical literature on Heidegger is still growing. Nothing comparable can be claimed for the work of Bäumler, Oehler, and other philosophers of National Socialism, now read mostly by historians interested in German history and by philosophical critics bent on discrediting Heidegger at all costs. Even Wolin is willing to concede that "it would be foolish to claim that Heidegger's political *lapsus*, however egregious, would somehow disqualify his immense philosophical achievement."[49] The proof that there is something that transcends the political – say, a Wittgensteinian insistence on unchosen "forms of life" and background practices or subtle views on the relationship between *Wahrnehmen* and *Verstehen* or a critique of certain features of the detached life of mere theory or an Aristotelian defense of *phronetic* insight – is to be sought out in the body of non-fascist work nourished over the years by *Sein und Zeit*.

To draw from Heidegger's early philosophy is not to exonerate the life of the individual responsible for it, nor is it to defend every aspect of the work itself. The conclusion is hard to avoid that Heidegger frequently behaved like a scoundrel, in his dealings with Husserl, in his detachment from Jaspers, in his politics, in his self-serving retrospective thoughts on his politics, in his notorious silence, in the occasional anti-Semitic remarks of the *Black Notebooks*, and so on. But one can, I think, still maintain that *Sein und Zeit* and the earlier lecture courses contain powerful insights into the limits of the quest for certainty, the nature of tools (how their use reveals something about the world), the fundamental basis of human life in care, the distortions of substance metaphysics, and the temporal and historical constitution of human life. Some views may not be altogether neutral, but still politically thin enough to be worked up and over in a variety of incompatible political contexts. As I argue briefly below, in the second chapter, phronetic ethics will probably not prevent you from becoming a fascist; but it may still

---

[49] *Heidegger's Children*, 9.

capture certain features of a good life within the spaces of liberal democratic politics, as the work of several neo-Aristotelians and good liberal
democrats amply demonstrates.

It is unfortunate that Heidegger came to think that his early views were
preludes to a distinctively Germanic philosophy of the National Socialist
revolution. But we should be suspicious of a hermeneutic principle
according to which a thinker's more recent views are to be taken as offering
definitive perspectives on his earlier achievements, as if subsequent positions were logically entailed by earlier accounts. This is, to be sure, how
philosophizing individuals often perceive their own development. But one
can legitimately consider, for example, Kant's more youthful stances on
human experience and reason to be preferable to his later perspective in the
Critique of Pure Reason. (Recent work on Herder's relation to Kant
[Michael Forster's, for instance] is a case in point.) As it stands, there is
no good reason to think that Heidegger's explicit turn toward the political
is a *necessary* consequence of his earlier ontological insights. There remains
an important gap between Heidegger's early critique of Descartes's
metaphysics, e.g., and the anti-modernist interpretation of Cartesian
ontology in the later period. The latter is one among many possible
interpretations of the former.

It is, in any case, always possible to contextualize a body of work
backward, to trace its perceived concerns back to some widely shared or
eccentric social or political stance, to situate it in relation to other bodies of
work that might have influenced its composition, and to locate affinities
between the language of a text and the language of its social context. This
is what historically oriented and political critics of Heidegger's work are
adept at doing. Everyone is of course free to participate in this sort of
exegetical and critical activity, but often at the expense of the ambiguities
of the work in question.

At times the working assumption seems to be that the meaning of the
work can be decided in light of the non-philosophical circumstances of its
composition. If you discover a parallel between an expression in Spengler
and a turn of phrase in one of the early lecture courses, then Heidegger is
Spenglerian, despite his own explicit attempts to dissociate himself from
the author of *The Decline of the West*. If you find an affinity between
Heidegger's use of *Vorlaufen* and what the word appears to have meant in
some circles during the war, then Heidegger's account of *Sein zum Tode*
(being-toward-death) is a concealed piece of rhetoric in support of military
heroism. But why not see it as a concealed piece of dialogue with a view
voiced by Plato's Socrates in the *Phaedo*? Why not compare Heidegger's

account of death with some remarks by Hegel on death and "the tremendous power of the negative" in the *Phenomenology*?

You can search for evidence of conservative religious or political convictions in Shakespearean tragedy, and praise or condemn the work accordingly. But you may lose sight of the diversity of perspectives that find a voice in *King Lear, Hamlet,* and *Macbeth*. It is remarkable, given the sorts of claims often made on behalf of and in opposition to Heidegger's so-called political ontology, that very few explicitly political comments can be discovered in the early lecture courses, fewer, in fact, than you will find in *Julius Caesar* and in the works of Heidegger's politicizing contemporaries. It is equally noteworthy that political construals of, say, the account of *Geschichtlichkeit* in *Sein und Zeit,* including Heidegger's own in some famous remarks recorded much later by Löwith in Italy, narrow down the range of meanings provoked by the text, and overlook other voices that compete with a single-minded political vision of what it is to be historical. As Heidegger himself had frequent occasion to note, our basic concepts come to voice in words that contain an abundance of meaning, although it will, I suspect, always be tempting to narrow the scope of the sense, in the name of precision, perhaps.

Although I find some of it tendentious and while I do not think that biographical considerations have become central to the evaluation of Heidegger's intellectual worth, as Wolin claims,[50] I don't mean to dismiss retrospective contextualizing interpretations wholesale. They often yield important conceptual constellations and enrich or expand the range of currently available readings. But it is also possible to contextualize a body of work *forward*, to rework its concepts in the light of new prospects, to situate the texts in relation to what matters to some of us *hic et nunc,* and to use them, cautiously, as a resource in your own life and work. It is possible, regardless of what you think the author himself really and truly intended, without the Heideggerian ambition, borrowed from Schleiermacher, to understand an author better than he understood himself, and with little interest in biographical details and settings no longer our own. It might be necessary, however, to draw from the philosopher's toolkit cautiously; some instruments may be more dangerous than others, others less refined, some no longer useful. And you may justly strive to remain sensitive to the global texture of your resource. But it can fruitfully be done, without attempting to defend the work as a whole, and without taking too much interest in the man behind the work. As Heidegger once

---

[50] *Heidegger's Children,* 10.

said of phenomenology in connection with Husserl, we are not interested in Heidegger but in what interested him.

As such, some of what follows is meant to be exegetical, or at least to remain close to the textual detail of Heidegger's early philosophy. Some chapters (especially the chapter on death) are meant to be more reconstructive, or to offer an account nourished by early Heidegger, but not tightly tethered to his official dicta. I aspire to the ideal of a philosophical treatment of early Heidegger, but informed by, or approximating, the historical, even if the historical and the philosophical cannot always be cleanly separated.

A Brief Note on What's to Come

The following chapters proceed for the most part chronologically, beginning with Heidegger's earliest lecture courses, which develop the idea of what I call "ethical criticism" of extant philosophy and science (a precursor to Heidegger's later account of the destruction of the philosophical tradition and a foretaste of further discussion in the present volume), and passing through Heidegger's (ethical) engagement with Aristotle and Descartes and his Aristotelian (and Platonic) development of the idea ontology with a certain conception of the good in view (both during the Marburg period), and his development of the care-structure of human existence in light of Kant's distinction between things and persons, shortly before the publication of *Being and Time*. The final chapters, on death and language, respectively, move more broadly over the entire early terrain, with questions at issue throughout the following study and throughout the period squarely in view – on the competing claims of the universal and the particular, and how to speak, philosophically, about the importance of what we care about.

CHAPTER I

Ethical Criticism

History, Philosophy, and Criticism

In section 6 of *Sein und Zeit,* Heidegger outlines the task of a *Destruktion* of the history of philosophy, on the working assumption that human life, its philosophical articulation and criticism are historical in a fundamental and distinctive sense. If the *Seinsfrage* cannot be formulated without a detour through the history of ontology, and becomes concrete "only when we carry out the destruction of the ontological tradition," it is precisely because the philosopher's past does not merely trail behind the present as a foregone conclusion but "always already advances ahead of it."[1] The past embodied in human understanding conditions the questions it makes sense to ask and lives in the language of philosophical conversation, argument, and debate. Every effort to free ourselves from tradition and to begin with a *tabula rasa* "is pervaded by traditional concepts and ... horizons and ... angles of approach."[2] An understanding shaped and governed by the past plays its enabling role whether the individual recognizes it or not, whether she makes the past an object of study and cultivates an interest in tradition or abandons history to the historian. Individuals and peoples can lack historical consciousness, philosophy of history, and historiography only because the human being is historical "in the ground of its being."[3]

But this indebtedness bears the mark of what Freud calls "ambivalence." If history were not at once obstacle and impetus, there would be no need to dismantle our intellectual and cultural inheritance: the very tradition that makes philosophical questioning possible and stimulates inquiry also "uproots the historicity of Dasein" and inhibits the "productive appropriation" of the past.[4] Human life is both enabled by tradition and entangled

---

[1] *Sein und Zeit* (hereafter *SZ*), 26, 20. See also "Being-There and Being-True According to Aristotle" (December 1924), in *Becoming Heidegger,* 219.
[2] *The Basic Problems of Phenomenology,* 22 (*GA* 24, 31).   [3] *SZ,* 20.   [4] *SZ,* 20.

in what it gives. This holds even when the past has been explicitly interpreted and criticized in a body of written and oral work. A culture rich in historical and philosophical self-interpretation and criticism runs the risk of losing itself in an aimless proliferation of standpoints and opinions, and has to struggle against the seduction of words divorced from serious engagement with issues and, ultimately, with *life*.[5] The responsible philosopher cannot develop a more penetrating understanding of the basic problems of philosophy without critical scrutiny of the traditional prejudices that inform her gaze and separate her from "the things themselves."

*

The train of thought just sketched is plausible enough. But it also verges on one of those "hardened propositions" (*festen Sätze*) that Heidegger frequently invites us to question.[6] Although the relationship between philosophy and its history remains a matter of debate, few would dispute the thesis that philosophical problems, like matters of religious or scientific controversy, are not timeless entities, but puzzles that surface and lose their fascination or continue to provoke thought in the course of human history. Most of us suffer without complaint the burden of history, are happy to criticize outmoded institutions and parochial forms of thought that masquerade as universal and necessary truths, and eager to celebrate the diversity of historical life and the richness of tradition.

That this train of thought strikes such a convincing note should make us uneasy; it gave Heidegger little peace for decades. Although we can applaud attempts to rescue Heidegger from the stigma of reactionary anti-modernism and chauvinism and to develop the seeds of pluralism planted along the way to *Being and Time*, we should question pluralistic appropriations of a body of work that challenges the "panarchy of the understanding" and lax "tolerance of alien views" characteristic of modern democratic and cultural concern,[7] and consistently argues that human life at its best is the undistracted pursuit of the *unum necessarium*,[8] in opposition to the *tentatio* (temptation) of a worldly and historical multiplicity of cares, concerns, and interests that fragments an otherwise self-collected and focused human life. And the verdict on Heidegger's anti-foundationalism and anti-essentialism, two fixtures in the reception of the early writings, has not yet come in.

[5] Philosophy, as Heidegger defines it in WS 1924/5, is a constant struggle against *Gerede*.
[6] *Plato's 'Sophist'*, 9 (*GA* 19, 14).   [7] *GA* 60, 34.   [8] *GA* 59, 169.

There is also a swarm of questions surrounding the practice of phenomenological destruction as Heidegger officially presents it in *Sein und Zeit.*
How does the philosophical criticism of tradition work? Heidegger repeatedly insists that criticism of the tradition is nothing formal, that logic
provides no norms and has itself to be subjected to criticism, and that
philosophy demonstrates nothing in the usual sense. As long as it traffics in
mere concepts and isolated propositions, or merely evaluates arguments for
formal validity, philosophical discourse comes close to being palaver.

In section 6 of *Sein und Zeit,* Heidegger couches the task of *Destruktion*
in the language of experience: destruction loosens a sclerotic and self-
evident tradition and dissolves its concepts in the "original experiences"
that gave them birth. But what sorts of experiences provide the measure?
How are they to be approached and criticized and under what description?
What guarantees their originality? Where does the phenomenologist discover the criteria that guide concrete studies of an extant philosophy? How
compelling or definitive is phenomenological criticism? With what authority does it speak? And what motives come into play?

These questions plagued Heidegger throughout the period leading up to
the publication of *Sein und Zeit.* But none finds an adequate reply in the
programmatic statement of the task of destruction in Heidegger's early
magnum opus or, as far as I can see, in any of the later writings dealing more
directly and at greater length with the canonical figures in the philosophical tradition. We are free to ignore them and to devote our attention to
the subsequent readings of Plato, Kant, Fichte, Schelling, Nietzsche, and
others and, more generally, to later Heidegger's critique of metaphysics;
but we can also read backward in an effort to recover the practice of
destruction and phenomenological criticism in its roots. Thanks to the
publication of the early lecture courses, we have an abundance of material
that sheds much-needed light on Heidegger's developing views on philosophical criticism before they become unquestioned fixtures in the corpus.
Like so many of the concepts and positions that found their way into *Sein
und Zeit,* the idea of destruction has a rather long and complicated history
that deserves more careful scrutiny.

The uniqueness and the difficulty of phenomenological criticism are
consequences of Heidegger's commitment throughout the early period to
an idea of philosophy as a *pre-theoretical* science of human life, where this
means both a science of what comes before theory – a science of everyday
life and what it gives – and a science that is not itself a theory, in a sense
that calls for careful explication. Extant philosophical theories cannot be
measured against another, more adequate theoretical account of human

life or assessed in terms of a fully developed system because for Heidegger, under the influence of Dilthey, life is not an object of possible theory that can be classified and filed away in an ordered network of concepts and propositions. It is something underway in the sphere of what matters and darkly shapes our deliberations. Theoretical reflection and the construction of systems are instances of what in KNS 1919 Heidegger calls "un-living," for the sake of theory divorced from genuine human concern. The measure of phenomenological criticism is to be sought, then, not in a standpoint or detached philosophical or scientific theory or system, but in life itself and the course of its pre-philosophical experience. Phenomenological criticism of the standpoint of epistemology amounts to something like *ethical criticism* of epistemological experience in the name of a life of personal concern (part one). But epistemology is not the only threat to the integrity of human life: the tendency of scientific thought to take over and colonize the understanding of human life is itself the legitimate target of ethical criticism in the name of personal life (part two). If Heidegger's appeals to life and experience avoid the empty gestures and complaints of a shallow romanticism, it is because life is interrogated under a definite description, as something that has a significance that can be understood, interpreted, and criticized. If explicit claims are traced back to their "evidence situation" in experience, experiences, in turn, are construed as expressions of a certain way of life embodying motives and tendencies open to phenomenological scrutiny in the light of a certain paradigm of "genuine life" (the precursor to "authentic Dasein"). This movement back and forth between philosophical claim, experience, and way of life, guided by an ideal of human existence – the very practice of phenomenological destruction as early Heidegger understands it – is another, extended version of the practice of ethical criticism (part three).

Against Indifference

How to criticize a philosophical standpoint as a whole? How to criticize a project that has not merely to be refined or completed, but dethroned? How is rebellion justified? And with what authority does the critic speak?

These questions come especially into play when the authority of a global style of thinking and questioning is contested. Epistemology is in question throughout the early lecture courses as first philosophy, as the basic discipline that establishes the normative framework of all other philosophical disciplines and guarantees the reality of their respective objects and our ability to know them. Works of art, religious beliefs, ethical claims, and scientific theories can come forward as legitimate objects of philosophical knowledge only after we have at our command a definitive, well-grounded account of the norms and principles of knowledge as such, and a theory of the object of knowledge. Arguments against the presuppositions of the epistemological project that rest upon epistemological assumptions are ruled out in advance. Formal and immanent criticism, the detection of invalid inferences, arguments targeting the specific claims of an established theory, and other common strategies of philosophical criticism remain tied to the standpoint under attack and fail to reach the terrain upon which battle can be fruitfully waged. Phenomenological criticism of epistemology is, in Heidegger's hands, essentially external.[9] The point is not to play a defective game better or to alter the rules of play but to stop playing and to persuade others to do the same.

Heidegger's strategy is anchored in the phenomenological assumption that epistemological claims are essentially experiential, that the epistemological standpoint can be best understood and criticized on the soil of experience. To ask "Does the world out there really and truly exist?" – to ask the basic question of epistemology, as early Heidegger understands it[10] – is to experience the possible unreality of the external world or at least to occupy a experiential standpoint from which it appears to make sense to ask about and to demonstrate its reality. As Heidegger writes in SS 1919 in an effort to clarify the practice of phenomenological criticism of an extant philosophical position, "A phenomenological criterion is just the understanding evidence and the evident understanding of experience, of life in and for itself in the *eidos*."[11] This isn't to deny that some epistemological claims are about objects that cannot be directly experienced. That epistemologists often traffic in abstract propositions and constructions is beside the point: abstraction and construction are themselves motivated experiences ("acts" in Husserl's sense). Heidegger's point of departure is an invitation to consider what it might be like to ask about the reality of the world, or to question our pre-philosophical involvement in the world of human concern.

Heidegger's early lecture courses take aim, then, at a target made answerable to experience and made over in the image of phenomenology. To those who distance themselves from phenomenological reflection and

---

[9] Although, as we shall see, the criticism turns out to be *internal* to a certain form of life.

[10] GA 56/7, 79. An argument for the primacy of epistemology in the economy of philosophy is offered and criticized in section 16 of KNS 1919. Taken together, sections 16 and 17 form the prototype of a phenomenological argument that reappears in section 43 of *Sein und Zeit*.

[11] GA 56/7, 126.

criticize the myth of experiential givens, this phenomenological makeover might seem to beg the question.[12] It is true that Heidegger shows little interest in the details of various epistemological theories,[13] spends little time responding to the specific arguments of his contemporaries, and reduces a rich variety of epistemological theories to the experience of a driving question amenable to phenomenological criticism. But the point of construing epistemology as an account of experience or, more plausibly, as an account that rests upon a certain description of or set of assumptions about experience, is to locate the aspirations of epistemology on a human terrain where the project becomes more fully intelligible, and fruitful non-theoretical scrutiny and criticism first becomes possible. Phenomenological criticism assumes that philosophy is a thoughtful and critical way of life.

Heidegger's strategy is first deployed in KNS 1919, in a compact but suggestive contrast of two very different accounts of experience that illustrates what we are calling "ethical criticism," and contains *in nuce* a rich variety of theses Heidegger will develop more fully and defend over the next decade and into the later years. In the wake of a detailed presentation of the methods and basic concepts of neo-Kantian theory of knowledge, accurately construed as an effort to extract from the contingent material furnished by psychology and history the set of timelessly valid norms, basic principles, and axioms that make knowledge possible, Heidegger invites his students to reflect upon the fundamental experience that motivates the search for a *theory* of human knowledge of the reality of the world. How do matters look when the question concerning the reality and knowability of the world is earnestly raised and lived? And what is there in or about it to criticize?

Epistemological reflection is responsive to the conceivable unreality of the external world, a world that includes physical things, plants and animals, tools, works of art, religious and secular institutions, individuals and peoples, and the objectifications of human thought (diaries, published memoirs, fictional narratives, manuscripts, philosophical essays and scientific articles). The world is also the place where these things meaningfully interact, where natural forces contend with natural forces, and where agents struggle and strive, work and play, domesticate animals for work and pleasure, read books, use tools, contemplate aesthetic objects, wonder

---

[12] We should, however, be careful not to confuse reflection upon experience with introspection, as Wayne Martin reminds us in his complex account of the phenomenology of judgment.

[13] This claim needs slight qualification. In KNS 1919, Heidegger devotes an entire chapter to the critical-teleological method of neo-Kantian epistemology.

about the laws of nature, run for political office, make friends, and – demonstrate the reality of an external world that somehow contains each of these things. Finally, the world embraces its own past: evidence of a long natural history of the earth, traces of life lived before me and my generation; monuments and records of significant historical persons and events all find a place in the external world.

Epistemological consideration of the world begins where the interweaving of significant things and events in human experience ends. The epistemologist replaces concrete interest and participation in the arena of natural phenomena and human activity with the seemingly simple demand that the reality of the container of all these ostensibly real things be demonstrated. She invites us to reduce the rich diversity of our world to the sheer presence of something real, stripped of all internal qualitative differences and devoid of every aspect that fascinates or repels, facilitates or impedes, and to place even this insignificant and bloodless presence in question. And she encourages us to consider ourselves as little more than the abstract locus of doubt and the theater where the resolution of doubt plays itself out. She invites us to live, at least for the time being, the simple question, as Heidegger phrases it in KNS 1919, "Can anything be said to be?"[14] "It is not asked whether there are tables or chairs, houses or trees, sonatas by Mozart or religious powers, but whether there is *something as such*."[15]

What sort of experience is this? What remains to be said about an experience that appears to place everything in question because it presupposes nothing? In fact, there is almost nothing that can be said about this mere "*living toward something*," an experience that has, strictly speaking, nothing before or behind it, neither world nor history, that runs its course in detachment from anything recognizably human. The question asks about nothing particular and the one who questions is no one in particular. We cannot say that the questioner occupies a questioning *standpoint* or lives in a situation; for standpoints and situations are possible only where the gaze can single out something definite against a background and a possible course of action is able to come up for deliberation, in something like what we ordinarily mean by "world." And it is precisely world in the concrete sense that stands in question.

---

[14] This is a slight paraphrase of Heidegger's '*Gibt es etwas?*' ("Is there something?" or "Does something give?").
[15] *GA* 56/7, 67–8.

How to persuade someone to adopt another stance, to detach herself from this utterly detached experience, and to consider (her own) experience otherwise? The experience itself, stripped of every questionable presupposition, gives nothing to think, nothing to understand, and nothing to criticize. Heidegger's solution is swift and decisive, and amounts to an ethical argument against impersonality and indifference: "What is decisive: simple inspection finds nothing like an 'I.'"[16] This anonymous stream of questioning comportment leaves us indifferent: the subject who makes an earnest attempt to identify with the standpoint of epistemological reflection fails to find itself as a center of possible care and concern. At this point, the lecture course takes a personal turn:[17] "Is there in [this experience] anything like a meaningful reference back to me, the one who stands here at the lectern, with this name and this age? Examine for yourselves. Does there lie in the question 'Can anything be said to be?' a for me (as a student of philosophy), a for me (Dr. X), a for me (as a student of law)?"[18] If the experience can be said to belong somehow to me, "it is still so detached from me in its sense, so absolutely *Ich-fern*" that I, as this particular individual, philosophizing in an elusive but productive historical situation, with a rich set of concrete concerns, cannot properly care about it.[19] The question leaves me cold and indifferent, relates at best to an indifferent "I," and fails to touch me in any vital concern. Epistemological reflection begins where significance ends, and nothing can be said to matter. And from the standpoint of life, where *I* am at stake in what I fully and vitally experience and question, where the mattering of things matters to me, the only fitting reply to the account of epistemological experience is: *Who cares?*[20] The only appropriate response is to leave the standpoint of epistemology and the question concerning the reality of the world alone, as matters of indifference.

But to leave impoverished and unworldly accounts of experience alone is just to leap back into the world. If epistemological reflection gets stranded in an experience that borders on unintelligibility, it makes sense to ask about the world from which the epistemologist detaches herself.

---

[16] *GA* 56.7, 66.

[17] KNS 1919 is filled with references to the person and personal life. In the *Vorbetrachtung* on "Science and University Reform," Heidegger defines science as "the *habitus* of a personal life." And in the Brecht transcript of the same lecture course, genuine phenomenological insight is the fruit of "honest and uncompromising immersion in the genuineness of life as such, in the end only through the genuineness of *personal life* as such" (*GA* 56/7, 4, 220).

[18] *GA* 56/7, 68.   [19] *GA* 56/7, 69.

[20] *Sorge* serves as the criterion of philosophical criticism in the early lecture courses before it comes into focus as the basic structure of factical life or Dasein.

Heidegger invites his students to throw themselves into and to consider[21] another experience, one that resides squarely in the world and calls for the density and movement of a finely wrought narrative: "*You* come *as usual* into *this* lecture-hall at the *customary* hour and go to *your* usual place. Focus on this experience of 'seeing *your* place.'"[22] Each of the words stressed is significant and indicates a phenomenon that will be taken up, articulated more fully in the ensuing years as a structural moment of being-in-the-world.[23] (1) *You*: not an impersonal center or empty *Ichpoll* of an impersonal flow of experience, but someone with a meaningful past concerned about her future, someone, in short, with a *history*. (2) *As usual*: as you, in the context of university life, working on a degree, with certain interests, motives, and aims, are *accustomed* to do, have grown into the *habit* of doing. (3) *This* lecture-hall: not a region of homogeneous or empty (physical or phenomenal) space, but a place where something might be learned, where Smith gave a stirring lecture two weeks ago, where interests are alive, a place, in short, with a communal significance and the environment of a rich array of partly interweaving stories. (4) The *customary* hour: a time also significant, determined by or embodying the rhythms of a certain way of life, a pregnant and "lived" time that fits obscurely into the overarching time of a life. (5) *Your* usual place: again, not a point in indifferent, insignificant space but the owned space where someone in particular prefers to sit.

The point of this argument against indifference and in defense of a significant world of concern is not only to persuade those tempted by epistemological pseudo-problems to return to the pregiven soil of concernful life, but to re-introduce the very same world from which epistemological reflection has excluded and alienated itself as a philosophical problem. The pre-objective world that "worlds," and has to be protected from the reifying and "un-living" tendencies of *Dingerfahrung* and scientific theory in KNS 1919, will be divided into *Umwelt*, *Mitwelt*, and *Selbstwelt*, each *Sorgenwelt* examined in relative isolation, in WS 1919/20, and the moment of significance inherent in it subjected to more exacting phenomenological analysis. In the ensuing years, Heidegger will go on to shape and refine his account of the world as the *Gehaltssinn* of

---

[21] Both the immersion and the (reflective) consideration are essential to Heidegger's method. Phenomenology is not a simple return to life, as Kisiel suggests in his gloss on Heidegger's response to Natorp in *The Genesis*, but a reflective consideration of pre-reflective life that strives to remain in the closest possible proximity to its object.

[22] GA 56/7, 70. With the exception of the final 'your' the emphases are mine.

[23] Kisiel rightly ascribes breakthrough significance to KNS 1919 in *The Genesis*.

factical life without rehearsing the ethical argument of KNS 1919.[24] The note of personalism that resounds throughout KNS 1919 will fade away and be replaced by the seemingly neutral language of Dasein. But these growing silences shouldn't blind us to the ethical weight of the concepts of "world" and "personal life" introduced in KNS 1919 and developed more fully along strictly ontological lines in subsequent lecture courses. If anything, the ethical resonances of their earliest appearance should alert us to the dangers of construing ontology as an abstract account of being. The world retains its sense throughout early Heidegger as an ethical category, as the place where everything that directly concerns us happens, where each of us is vitally implicated, and where it makes sense to speak of reliable human character (*ethos*) exposed to social and historical vicissitudes.[25] World is introduced in the lecture courses of the first Freiburg period not as a mere transcendental condition of human knowledge and *praxis* but as the inescapable site of meaningful personal life; and epistemology is taken to task for eliminating those features of the world that make it possible to live, for presenting before the philosopher's gaze a picture of the world as an *object* that encourages us to adopt a standpoint that intensifies indifference as it diminishes our capacity to care. "'World,'" as Heidegger concisely remarks in WS 1920/1, "is that in which one can live (one cannot live in an object)."[26]

The argument against indifference, the argument that encourages a leap of sorts into the world of concrete life-experience, is nothing like a refutation in the usual sense: it takes aim at no definite proposition or thesis, passes no judgment on the alleged coherence of a theory, and establishes no fixed conclusions from which other propositions might happily be derived. The train of thought terminates in factical life and *Umwelterlebnis*; but these can hardly be called conclusions that follow from epistemological premises. KNS 1919 simply invites us to compare two very different accounts of experience, to find one of them culpably remote from anything of real human concern, to redirect our attentive regard to

---

[24] In the short account of significance as the reality that belongs to factical life in WS 1919/20, Heidegger curtly dismisses the question "whether the world exists in itself" or is dependent on my thought as "senseless" (*GA* 58, 105). Epistemological theories do not inhibit life "as long as it lives in factical relations of significance."

[25] It retains its sense as my home in *Sein und Zeit* (*SZ*, 54). But in the later work, we find nothing like the urgent plea that finds expression in KNS 1919: "We stand ... before an abyss: either into nothingness, i.e., absolute reification, or we leap into *another world* or, more precisely: for the first time into the world as such" (*GA* 56/7, 63).

[26] *GA* 60, 11.

experience, and thoughtfully to consider the world in which life runs its course. It is, in short, a persuasive invitation to *change the subject*.

But arguments of this style have their limits. If they are not definitively persuasive, if the epistemological project continues to fascinate and forge ahead, it is precisely because the success or failure of ethical criticism depends upon a certain construal of experience that will always remain questionable; because life and experience are always *owned* and appropriated in a plurality of distinct ways of life and styles of philosophical thought; and, perhaps most importantly, because detachment from life, intensified in epistemological reflection, is an essential possibility of human life. The epistemologist remains free to deny the fidelity of Heidegger's portrait of epistemological experience, to accuse Heidegger of doing battle against a straw man, to offer her own, competing account of the basic experience that drives her project, or simply to insist that phenomenological considerations and questionable appeals to life and experience are irrelevant.

If we are convinced of the sterility of epistemology in early Heidegger's sense, we are still left to wonder what comes next. The argument might be an invitation to change the subject, but it is not clear what the new subject is and what, if anything, it has to do with philosophy. Heidegger's anti-epistemological beginnings are admittedly humble, the experiences evoked and opposed to the refined standpoint of traditional philosophical reflection almost trivial: taking hikes, climbing mountains, watching the sun set, listening to a teacher at the podium, browsing for books, conversing with fellow students at a local café. At first we scarcely know what to do. Should we write poems or tell stories? Become politically active? Join a religious order? Pursue concrete scientific work in a specialized field of study?[27] Ethical criticism of epistemology along the lines just sketched offers no direct reply. Life expresses itself in a bewildering variety of ways. Novels, poems, plays, political and devotional tracts, abstract paintings, diaries and working journals – each in its own way lends a voice to experience, and is a way in which life comes expressly to itself. If experiences themselves also already embody an interpretation of life, life comes to itself and expresses itself simply in being lived.[28] If Heidegger went no further than this, there would be little of enduring philosophical value in

---

[27] Heidegger names each of these possibilities (art, politics, religion, and science) as an example of a "genuine form of accomplishment and life" in the *Vorbetrachtung* of KNS 1919 (*GA* 56/7, 4).

[28] Life's inherently self-expressive tendency is a *Leitmotiv* of WS 1919/20. The *Selbstwelt*, *Mitwelt*, and *Umwelt*, e.g., are introduced in Part One as *Bekundungsgestalten* of 'factical life,' and science is taken up in the second part of the course as a *Bekundungszusammenhang* of life.

the appeal to personal, "self-worldly" life;[29] the argument against indifference would be an argument against philosophy itself. Philosophy – or at least Heidegger's own philosophical development – would be at an end. Is there a philosophical intention alive in the *Rückgang* to life and experience?[30] Can this intention be divorced from ethical motives, or is it a matter of drawing our attention to something we ought, in the name of objectivity, to pay more careful heed, in order to get right our picture of what human life is and what its world has to give?

Against Scientism

KNS 1919 might be the place to search for Heidegger's breakthrough, but phenomenological criticism continues in the following semesters and swells beyond the limits of KNS 1919 into a large-scale, powerful assault on certain scientific approaches to human life and the hegemony of theory in phenomenology itself. Epistemological theory now lies behind Heidegger as a philosophical and personal dead-end, as something that no longer vitally resonates with life and experience, and as an obstacle that no longer inhibits the phenomenological quest for the "absolute *origin* of the spirit in and for itself – 'life in and for itself.'"[31] But the non-philosophical sciences and the ideal of objectivity that guides concrete scientific inquiry and research are different matters. The pursuit of scientific knowledge emerges largely unscathed from the phenomenological criticism deployed against a certain style of epistemological reflection in KNS 1919. In contrast to epistemology, the sciences are not paralyzed by exaggerated doubts about the reality of their objects, do not run their course in a vacuum of sterile self-reflection, and grapple concretely, methodically, and securely with a world of things that matter. If the solution to an epistemological problem strikes some as irrelevant and leaves the world of everyday life alone, the appearance of a novel scientific theory often deeply interests us and, in its concrete technological application, can visibly alter the contours of our world. If epistemology is no true way of life, but something that occupies the mind at leisure, alongside other, more pressing concerns, a passion for science and scientific research can develop into the productive shape of a life responsive to perplexity. The sciences also present us with powerful

---

[29] Crowell makes this point in opposition to 'personalist' and mystical readings of early Heidegger in *Husserl, Heidegger, and the Space of Meaning.*

[30] Heidegger employs the term *Rückgang* in WS 1919/20 (*GA* 58, 160) to name the movement away from theory toward factical life lived in a world, and it plays an important role in SS 1924 (*GA* 18).

[31] *GA* 58, 1.

norms of objectivity and rigor that command our respect, frequently serve as measures of philosophical insight, and, precisely because of their unclarified but incontestable power, cry out for careful phenomenological scrutiny. It comes as no surprise, then, that Heidegger devotes the bulk of a lecture course on the *Basic Problems of Phenomenology*, held in the winter semester of 1919/20, to the phenomenon of science and its relation to the world of everyday life.

The philosophy of science developed in WS 1919/20 is peculiar. Heidegger pays no attention to the scientific theories of his contemporaries, has nothing to say about well-established scientific methods, and offers nothing comparable to a history of scientific problems and solutions. Science is introduced in the first part of the course almost casually, as neither the passion of a concentrated life's work nor a potent and inescapable historical force that transforms nearly every aspect of modern life, but as something we just happen to encounter, with no greater importance and emphasis at first than anything else we happen to experience in the course of daily life.[32] We encounter science in the same Heideggerian setting within which we experience everything else that commands our attention or leaves us indifferent

But science is more than just an object of passing everyday concern. It insinuates itself into the modern life-world pervasively and offers itself as a global way of disclosing, grasping, and progressively determining the objects we experience in prescientific life. Science shows up for early Heidegger as an *Ausdruckszusammenhang*, as a distinctive context (*Zusammenhang*) in which life discloses and expresses itself, and struggles to make sense of itself and its world. If science is singled out for detailed consideration, it is precisely because it leaves nothing untouched, but "appears to seize . . . all areas of life and world."[33]

Heidegger's account of science, developed in sections 15–17 of WS 1919/20, is essentially genetic and experiential, an account "from below" of the appearance of theoretical science as an exceptional way of life. Although it might superficially resemble a psychological analysis of scientific experience, the phenomenology of scientific comportment has nothing to do with the psychology of science, and sheds no light on the personal reasons that account for the choice of subject matter. Heidegger takes it for granted that aspects of our world stimulate an interest in cognition and that the choice of a field is largely a matter of individual concern. The account more closely resembles a piece of intentional analysis

[32] *GA* 58, 35.   [33] *GA* 58, 55.

in Husserl's sense: it explores the sense of intentional comportment, analyzes the content *as intended*, and considers both in the light of an intelligible nexus (*Zusammenhang*) or neglected soil of experience. And it is centrally preoccupied with the initial upsurge of the scientific attitude rather than its more elaborate and subtle development in a sustained way of life. Its questions include: How does science emerge as an expressive context of life on the basis of the *Lebenswelt*? What is the "relational sense" of scientific comportment? How is experience modified in the direction of scientific inquiry? How does science transform the life of the individual who pursues theory? How does science show up as a life-stance? And what does science necessarily leave behind?

The objects of scientific thought, the targets of explanatory efforts, are just those things we experience and understand as we get around in the world of everyday life.[34] A flower-strewn path encountered on a walk in early May arouses a desire to know, and finds its way into the "expressive context" of a botanical monograph. A Rembrandt in the Kaiser-Friedrich-Museum can become the subject of art historical research. In each case, we meet with the same things, under different descriptions and in different contexts shaped by different aims, in scientific inquiry and in the course of ordinary life. This overlap is no accident. In a move pregnant with far-reaching implications, Heidegger suggests that scientific thought is somehow made possible by the manners in which things display themselves, are pregiven (*vorgegeben*) to an emerging science in prescientific life. Things can become objects of scientific thought only because they are already somehow there, given in advance and disclosed and expressed in a certain way in the life of prescientific involvement.[35] If life can live in the "motivated tendency" of scientific comportment, if science can carve out a "sector" (*Ausschnitt*) of the surrounding world and disclose its objects methodically, this is because things display themselves in the *Lebenswelt* of prescientific life.[36] Every science has "*a certain pregiven soil*," grows out of

[34] The formal sciences are another matter. Heidegger has little to say about them in WS 1919/20.
[35] Cf. *GA* 21, 153.
[36] As Philipse correctly notes, Heidegger's conception of science and its specialized domains is broadly Husserlian (*Heidegger's Philosophy of Being*, 38). Every science has a domain of objects open to 'regional' phenomenological and ontological research that can develop without reference to or dependence upon specific scientific methods, claims, and theories (*SZ*, 9). Philipse goes on, however, to oppose a Kuhnian strand in early Heidegger to his official commitment to a 'static' Husserlian account. But the tension Philipse detects in Heidegger's philosophy of science rests upon a failure to appreciate that the special sciences are *at once* rooted in domains carved out in pre-scientific life and capable of revolutionary development. There simply is no 'static account' of science in early Heidegger. On Heidegger's view, pre-scientific life and scientific theory are equally historical.

the familiarity life has with itself and its world, and draws constantly from a wellspring of experience.[37] However elusive and difficult to formulate it might be, the understanding embodied in the comportments of everyday life is highly differentiated and wonderfully discerning. We know, performatively,[38] so to speak, the difference between animal and plant, tool and painting, foodstuff and metal, historical artifact, person and mere thing, and distinguish between the various domains taken up and developed in the special sciences, without the highly developed and explicit conceptual and methodological resources of scientific thought.[39] To adapt a pregnant expression from the *Nicomachean Ethics*, the grounding discernment lies in understanding. This does not entail that Heidegger thinks of human experience as non-conceptual (in this respect I agree with Sacha Golob that Heidegger is not "a pioneering nonconceptualist"[40]), but it does mean that concepts behave differently in life, on the one hand, and in explicit thought, on the other.

Science takes shape within, and to some extent against, this diffuse familiarity at work in the experience of the life-world. The longest stretch of the account of the "Stages and Moments of the Apriori Genesis of the Expressive Context of Science" is devoted to the scientific reshaping of prescientific experience. As we might expect, experience (*Erfahrung*) is not the bloodless *Erlebnis* of mere sense data disengaged from the environing world, but having insight into possibilities of human existence. Experience is "earning from the journey of life," getting to know something by delving into it.[41] Experience includes knowing what is available, knowing what can and cannot be done and what it would be good to do – forms of knowing that develop over time out of concrete engagement with unique situations of thoughtful action. A "man of experience" is someone who knows his way around in the world or practical life. Someone who has political experience in this sense is not only acquainted with the data of political science or conversant with the history of political thought, but has spent time *in* politics and is at home in the contemporary world of political

---

[37] *GA* 58, 66. Although science takes up its domain freely and develops its methods somewhat autonomously, "the structures of its concept-formation are predelineated in the sense of its subject matter" (*GA* 58, 74).

[38] By 'performatively' I mean that the understanding *works* these distinctions into its concrete, practical dealings with things. On Heidegger's view, the distinctions are *in* the performance before they develop into clear and exact concepts.

[39] As Heidegger puts the matter in *Sein und Zeit*, "The elaboration of the area in its fundamental structures is in a way already accomplished by prescientific experience and interpretation of the domain of being to which the area of knowledge is itself confined" (*SZ*, 9).

[40] *Heidegger on Concepts, Freedom and Normativity*, 2.   [41] *GA* 58, 67–8.

life. Political experience is earned by *living* politically. Experience is the primal phenomenon of knowing: to know in the first sense is not to possess information but to have insight that grows in a rich field of encounter, to know how to do certain things well, to be accomplished.

While the competent scientist must be experienced and continues to dwell understandingly in a familiar world, science itself is not experience in this ostensibly primitive sense. Although the objects of science are the same as the items encountered in daily life, the situations of encounter are not. Scientific thought might be rooted in the rich weave of the "carpet of life," but the carpet must be pulled away or, to adopt a better figure, individual strands must be torn out of their native and vital context and pursued in relative isolation. The diffuse milieu of everyday experience must be concentrated *as* an experiential soil (*Erfahrungsboden*) from which "a unified *Sachcharakter* can be lifted" and posited as a *Sachgebiet* for scientific determination.[42] On the noetic side, situated, holistic *Umwelterlebnis* must yield to detached, analytic *Dingerfahrung*. It is at this point, for instance, that we attempt to *explicate* the concepts we have of things or to define objects in terms of their essential marks (*Merkmale*, as Kant would say).

Fragmentation of the life-world and reification of experience are two sides of the same process, and together they form the basic accomplishment of scientific thought that interests early Heidegger. The growth of scientific exposition and explanation is a continually advancing synthesis that rests upon a fundamental, ongoing analysis.[43] To say that science fragments the world of everyday life is to say that every special science is essentially abstract: its objects are drawn out of the life-world, detached from their surroundings, and set up in a *Sachgebiet* ("material domain") as themes for ongoing investigative inquiry. The experiences themselves are equally abstract: only certain experiences matter, and those that have cognitive import are torn out of the context of a personal history, assembled around the theme in question, and directed toward a purely cognitive aim. Although we live in relation to various regions of things and perceive a swarm of differences in everyday life, the boundaries are permeable, the differences embedded in a relatively unaccentuated practice, and the situations allowed to interpenetrate and absorb their contents in a vital rhythm of comportment. We move effortlessly from social situations to the

---

[42] *GA*58, 69.

[43] These are not Heidegger's terms in WS 1919/20, but they capture fairly well what is at issue in the 'genesis of the theoretical.' While the account is brief, the process itself is a highly protracted *historical* affair.

privacy of domestic space, distinguish between the car we drive home and the pedestrian to be avoided on the sidewalk, relate differently to a painting on the wall in a gallery, the bench strategically placed in front of the canvas, and the stranger who invites us to comment on the Rembrandt. We do all this without having to dismember the situation and to thematize discrete contents, in the absence of any theory.[44] Each thing comes into view in a tangled flow of living participation. In the context of science, however, the vital unity of the situation, lived in an otherwise uninterrupted advance (*Fortgehen*) that draws its past tacitly along without looking back, is extinguished, its contents externalized, hardened, and scattered in a heap of ruins (*Trümmern*) that serves as building material for scientific construction.[45] Every non-philosophical science is essentially decontextualizing: the productive work of scientific thought begins where the elusive whole and the sense of being surrounded by and entangled in it end and, in Heidegger's own suggestive phrase, things fall apart (*fallen auseinander*).[46]

The phenomenological account of the genesis of science just outlined is admittedly schematic. Heidegger says nothing about the growth of mathematical thought and its application to *res extensa* comparable to Husserl's discussion of Galilean science in section 9 of the *Crisis*; offers nothing like Dilthey's detailed hermeneutics of the construction of the historical world in the *Geisteswissenschaften*; and provides only a laundry list of five "structural forms" developed in the productive and "concrete logics" of the special sciences. While he often mentions in passing that the account ought to be worked out more fully, and returns to the topic in the ensuing years, Heidegger, unlike Husserl, never really gets around to developing a comprehensive phenomenology of scientific cognition.[47] His interest and intention clearly lie elsewhere.

Both the interest and the intention come clearly to the fore in the culminating account of scientific objectification as another instance of *Entlebung* in section 17; and it becomes equally clear that, on Heidegger's view, science (or at least those sciences with explanatory intentions) risks constructing an "iron cage" from which phenomenology has to free itself. Although science is a more respectable and vital pursuit than

---

[44] On the view just outlined, it would be misleading to say, as it is often said, that every experience or perception is 'theory-laden.' It would be closer to the truth to say that every theory is charged with an understanding embodied originally in practice, that theory is, in short, *practice-laden*.

[45] *GA* 58, 121.   [46] *GA* 56/7, 209.

[47] WS 1924/5 is the only possible exception, but it plays out as an interpretation of the opening chapters of the first book of Aristotle's *Metaphysics*.

epistemological theory, the scientific life involves roughly the same modi-fication of experience we encountered in the phenomenological criticism of epistemology in KNS 1919. The argument trades upon the familiar antagonism between absorption in and detachment from the life each of us lives both before and, to some degree, after we take up the scientific tendency to disclose the world methodically, a life that satisfies and expresses itself in a familiar world of interweaving situations, lives out of the rich soil of history, and enacts itself concernfully toward an open and uncertain future. If this flowing life comes to a halt and turns back upon itself, if it pauses to consider its own motives and tendencies, perhaps in response to an incipient crisis or simply in order to clarify and reorient itself, it normally does so in a way that preserves the rhythms and textures of vital experience, in conversation, for instance, and in narrative, or in a sort of dialogue with itself in the chambers of memory.[48] It is driven by an interest that has at first nothing to do with scientific cognition. Aspects of the life-world are singled out and moments of past life accentuated (both show up under a certain description, are taken *as* something definite), but what steps out of the background shows up precisely as significant, as something that still bears the traces of its prior involvement in a personal *Selbstleben*.

It is just this involvement that scientific comportment puts out of play. The break with spontaneously flowing life that Heidegger places at the threshold of the scientific attitude is far more decisive and estranging than the temporary pause that makes possible reflective efforts to make sense of ourselves and to render our lives coherent. To enter a scientific context of expression is to construct a situation in which the self-world (roughly: the world of personal concern, the world in which I am at stake in what I care about, do and suffer) no longer plays a productive role but is bracketed in the name of an impersonal objectivity (*Sachlichkeit*). "All the rich relations to the self-world are severed [*unterbrochen*]: in the scientific context of expression, living flowing life is 'somehow' hardened [*erstarrt*] or stands in a completely different form of life."[49] Again: "*Science takes up life-worlds in a tendency of unliving* and in this way factical life is robbed of its authentic living possibility and . . . vital enactment."[50]

---

[48] "The explication [of life] is the *kenntnisnehmend erzählende* [explication] of the full participation in life, but in the basic style of factical encounter" (*GA* 58, 111). Heidegger's account of self-explication closely resembles and is probably drawn from Dilthey. See my "Dilthey's Epistemology of the *Geisteswissenschaften*" in the *Journal of the History of Philosophy*.

[49] *GA* 58, 77.   [50] *GA* 58, 77.

But what more precisely does it mean to say that scientific comportment lives in a tendency of *Entlebung*? What becomes of us when we adopt a scientific attitude and pursue theory? What qualities of experience are left behind as scientific objectification advances? What is the cost of scientific objectivity?

Prescientific life is ever in pursuit of something (an ideal, an aim) that grants importance, meaning, and direction to the fleeting awareness of environmental things, is a continual advance of the present toward the future in active and hopeful expectation of something worthwhile.[51] But the object of desire actively pursued is, *as* desired, present in the mode of absence, as the target of a practical intention that can fail to reach its goal. The present is not only the temporal site of an awareness of objects, but the fulfillment of previous expectations and the point of departure for further anticipations of experience.[52] Experience in the robust, vital, and temporally thick sense delineated earlier in this chapter is not only "earning from the journey of life" but spontaneity, adventure, and risk. It is not only living out of the past but reaching actively, concernfully, and expectantly toward an open and uncertain future, is, in short, exposure to what the ancients called *tuchê*. The urgency and anxiety that attend our plans and encourage us to make calculations and predictions are deeply rooted in a pervasive, unsettling sense of contingency, of being at the mercy of forces and circumstances that frustrate our expectations, mock our hopes, thwart our best intentions, and make the difference between success and failure, *eudaimonia* and disaster.[53]

But experience is also trained upon a tangled world of concrete particulars encountered in unique situations of thought and action. However superficially similar two or more situations might appear, there is always something incomparable in each. While each particular is taken up and construed in a certain way,[54] and invites comparison with other particulars, and although every utterance is universal in form, as Hegel rightly

---

[51] For the 'continual advance of the present' as a counter-concept to a conception of time as an objective *Ordnungsform*, see Dilthey, *Gesammelte Schriften* 19: 211.

[52] The notion of the present as 'fulfilled self-consciousness,' as the satisfaction or frustration of a prior (practical) intention, is also Dilthey's. See *GS* 19: 221.

[53] Negation is lived before it becomes an object of logical reflection. In WS 1921/2, the experience of 'nothingness' is said to include "the nothingness of uneventful history, the nothingness of failure, the nothingness of futility, the nothingness of hopelessness – and all this in factical ... situations, contexts, and life-worlds" (*GA* 61, 146).

[54] See Husserl's account of perceptual *Auffassung* in the Fifth Logical Investigation and the study of categorial and sensible intuition in *LU VI*. Perceptual life itself is categorially structured and endowed with something like logical form.

insists in the opening section of the *Phenomenology*, we deal concretely with and care chiefly about particular things. A close friend is not an instance of *homo sapiens* with a definite anatomical structure, physiology, and natural history, but an individual with a uniquely significant past tied in numberless ways to my own life in a shared history of particular interactions and encounters. To care about her is never to care about a species. I care about her as the one who went with me *that time there*, who helped me through that painful ordeal, who often read my work in progress and whose comments are incomparably insightful. Someone else could have done these things with and for me (substitution is possible), but the experiences would have played out differently.

Being surprised, taking risks, caring about unique particulars: these and a large array of kindred phenomena are possible only for a being that has or realizes itself over time as a history, that not only occupies a place before, alongside, and after other beings in an abstract order of time, but lives in a peculiar and knowing relation to time.[55] A creature thoroughly smitten by the pleasures and pains of a dislocated moment, and so unable to situate the contents of present experience in relation to previous encounters and future prospects, could never be taken by surprise, would remain deaf to the rich language of the unexpected, and would be incapable of sympathizing with the plight of others. Like Nietzsche's cattle in the second Untimely Meditation, such a creature would be "neither melancholy nor bored" but simply "contained in the present, like a number without any awkward fraction left over."[56] Its experience would lack the continuity, attentiveness, and engagement that sustain and nourish an active concern for particular things. But more importantly still, its experiences would be not only immune to the unexpected, self-enclosed, carefree, and trivial, but meaningless, less even than a dream. Although we (normal socialized adults) can grasp in a fleeting instant an arrangement of meaningful things, things themselves are meaningful, not because they occupy a slice of mere awareness or are the targets of isolated acts of consciousness, but because they are woven into the fabric of historical life, because each of us *becomes* familiar with things and what they mean, or can mean, and uneasily at home in a significant world.[57] In the absence of any meaningful historical

---

[55] Life has unity, according to WS 1921/2, in the form of *Erstreckung* (*GA* 61, 84). Life is not stretched or suspended between two points on a time-line but "stretches itself" along.

[56] *Untimely Meditations*, 60–1.

[57] This is to say nothing about the ultimate origins of meaning. Early Heidegger takes it for granted that meaning is "always already" there, that each of us finds herself cast into a meaningful world and compelled to get oriented in it.

context, things become, at best, mere clusters of sensible qualities distributed over distinct fields of sensation. The falling snow visible through a
window in my study becomes wet, white flecks moving about soundlessly
in a multicolored but dimly perceived background. But for a vision
entangled in and guided by a history of experience, it is also an obstacle
to be faced during the morning commute to work; the promise of good
skiing; an inhospitable climate to the homeless; a chance for children to
make sculptures and snow-huts, perhaps a reason for the authorities to
cancel school; an example of perspectivism in the thoughts of a university
professor; a symbol of emptiness in the poetry of Wallace Stevens; a
wonderful manifold of geometrical forms; a natural object subject to the
laws of physics; a cluster of atoms for the physical chemist; a mystery of
God's creation in the mind of the pious. It is each of these things because
experiences accumulate in a history of experience, because I have com-
muted, gone skiing, know something about the plight of the homeless,
have read Wallace Stevens, studied chemistry and physics, and so on.
A gaze cleansed of everything past does not see things as they truly are;
it sees precisely – nothing.

We are now in a position to understand more concretely and precisely
the sense in which science lives, in Heidegger's phrase, "in the tendency of
unliving." Human experience in its undeflected course is at once open to
the unexpected, concerned presently about particulars, and indebted to the
past. In the rich world of human affairs, things take us pleasantly or
painfully by surprise, concrete and unique particulars are valued and
esteemed at the expense of other equally concrete and unique particulars,
and the unruly lives of individuals and communities unfold, interact, and
have meaning in the knotted shapes of personal and overlapping histories.
This largely unpredictable world of human activity, a world of surprising
and meaningful things valued and scorned in work and play, loved and
hated in the complex and intertwining lives of unique individuals, leaves
no permanent trace in the world of natural scientific objectivity.[58] This
second world, the world of theoretical objects that explain or account for
the world of things experienced naïvely, is one in which the objects of
everyday life have been denied their capacity to surprise; particulars show
up and matter only as examples of some universal law or property or
species, and the past is reduced to an irrational force or (more charitably) as
a sequence of partly successful attempts at scientific enlightenment, and is
eventually stripped of its significance.

---

[58] This is obviously not the case in the world of the *Geisteswissenschaften*.

Of course, there is surprise, selective concern, and historical significance in the lives of individual scientists. Scientific experience itself retains the aspects of human experience just sketched, provided the work of science remains unfinished and individuals go on caring deeply and passionately about scientific knowledge of the world. But these phenomena have no strictly scientific import. The world just is as it is and has come to be; and the scientific aim is to know it as it is and has come to be. If the scientist is surprised by an unanticipated experimental result or discovery or cares about the fate of her own theory or takes an interest in the rich history of scientific thought, that is *her* personal, extra-scientific affair. If science is risky business and has a history, if it knows something like the drama of personal life, it remains a *human* pursuit estranged from a certain conception of its own ideals. To approach the scientific world of rigorously determined objects divorced from uncertain human concern is to leave behind human life, as we (perplexed, striving, concernful, needy) human beings know it.

The point of all this is lost if we construe Heidegger's ethical criticism of scientific thought and experience as the work of an anti-scientific mentality, as just another instance of dissatisfied reactionary thought trained upon modern intellectual culture in order to rehabilitate some pre-modern vision or way of life untainted by the evils of scientific objectification. There are many things that can and should be subjected to rigorous, natural scientific analysis. I might not know what is causing this pain in my back, but however indefinite or fuzzy my awareness of it is, there is something quite definite going on that deserves to be objectified by someone who knows the structure and function of the human body, and how best to treat it as a material object better than I do. To persist in ignorance and to avoid the doctor in fear of an unpleasant diagnosis or to justify the use of tobacco because life cannot and should not be objectified is not to protect the sanctity of prescientific life but to live in what Sartre called "bad faith."[59] Phenomenological criticism of scientific objectification is not rejection of but *reflection* upon the scope and limits of an essential – for us necessary and important – way of life. The path of objectification and unliving that leads to genuine scientific knowledge of a reified fragment or specialized domain of the life-world is hardly an egregious and culpable error of Western civilization. Although it has a history and plays out in a field of contingency, scientific thought is nothing accidental but anchored in a permanent possibility of human life.

---

[59] On this point see Sartre's *Truth and Existence*, 33–43.

It involves what we might call the "necessity of the possibility" of detachment from contingent circumstances and particular objects, development of the longing to know, cognitive ascent to more general principles and laws, and reduction of the multiplicity of phenomena to the unity of scientific concepts. We are the sorts of creatures who can always detach ourselves from the local and particular in search of an impersonal but reliable objectivity, creatures for whom everything experienced is a possible object of scientific thought. "Everything . . . *is able to be reified [hat die Chance der Verdinglichung].*"[60] Everything is able to become a mere (indifferent) thing. To deny this is not to win radical independence from scientific thought, but to remain blind to an essential dimension of human life, to substitute another abstraction for concrete experience, and to narrow the scope of human potential. In short, it is to deny, or suppress, what we are and can be, and what the things themselves are and can be.

The real target of Heidegger's criticism in WS 1919/20 is not science *tout court* but an extreme interpretation of life that (in intention at least) doubts the value of our particular attachments and attacks the understanding embodied in our prescientific concerns, that condemns the knowledge or insight we have of ourselves and our world as engaged agents because they fail to measure up to scientific standards of rigor and evidence. It is not the exact knowledge of, say, the human body in the science of medicine or the psychiatrist armed with a plausible theory of human development and neurosis, but the attitudes of the doctor who only sees statistics and laws rather than persons who care about their own health or the Freudian who sees her patients above all as publishable case studies rather than suffering human beings with a tenuous hold on the world around them and complex personal histories that resist simple analysis and often challenge the official dogmas of the profession. In the language of KNS 1919, the target is the *primacy* and *absolutization* of a theoretical attitude that reverses the proper relationship between scientific theory and human life and sees in human experience only a path that leads to rigorous scientific knowledge and a world of significance better off left behind and alone.[61]

In order to avoid the construction of a straw man, we have to distinguish, as Heidegger does not (at least not very clearly in sections 15–17 of WS 1919/20), between legitimate and hard-earned scientific knowledge and the pernicious ideal of total scientific objectification, between science as an earnest cognitive pursuit that discloses important aspects of the

---

[60] *GA* 58, 127.   [61] See *GA* 56/7, 59 and section 17; also, *GA* 58, 127–8 and 149–50.

life-world and the set of convictions that coalesce in *scientism*. Scientism – roughly, the view that physical science knows all there is to know and to care about, that prescientific experience is just bad or incipient science, that the rich language of prescientific life is destined to yield gradually to the precise language of mathematical thought – is guided by an ideal that undermines the conditions of our own active and meaningful lives, fails to do justice to us *human* knowers, and makes the scientific desire to know unintelligible.[62] At a certain level of detachment from human life, we no longer have ourselves in view, are not really living any longer, and cannot tell ourselves a coherent tale about how we got there or why we ought to go on. Motives, tendencies, and directions of thoughtful *scientific* engagement with and discourse about the world are in life or nowhere. To the extent that the scientist herself is *moved* to study something and cares about the fate of scientific knowledge, her own life falls outside the scope of object-ification, and the integrity of her experience in the sense articulated above is preserved.

Life against Itself

At this point we have a clearer sense of Heidegger's views on the bank-ruptcy of traditional epistemology and the dangers of self-undermining scientism, and a vague sense that something like the personal life bracketed in epistemological and scientific thought is at stake in Heidegger's develop-ing phenomenology and ethical criticism. The critical engagement with epistemology and science as instances of *Entleben* in KNS 1919 and WS 1919/20 leads back to the concernful life already underway before epi-stemological reflection and scientific thought come on the scene. Philoso-phy begins and ends with the materials of daily life and a concernful relation to a world of significant and unique particulars: the situated, flowing experience of the tables and lecture halls, bookstores, libraries, gardens, automobiles, friends, relatives, and strangers that constantly sur-round us is the soil philosophy is given to cultivate. If personal life is the proper theme of phenomenology, then it must possess a meaning or sense. Life is "nothing dark or chaotic" but something that has a meaning which calls for interpretation.[63] Interpreting the shape and significance of life cannot be divorced from actually living it.

But simple appeals to personal life and immediate lived experience run the risk of being dismissed as too easy and guilty of *Kitsch*. Too easy: talk of

---

[62] See also Nagel's *The View from Nowhere*.   [63] GA58, 239.

"life" is vague, the sense of human experience diverse, and the philosophical problems embedded in life far from obvious.[64] There is rich diversity in even the most monotonous of personal lives. Each life has its rhythms and its ruptures, its joys and sorrows, its moments of intense engagement and passionate involvement with the world and its periods of dryness and apathy. If phenomenology begins with absolute sympathetic immersion in life, we have a right to ask: under what description? If life comes to itself in a variety of expressive contexts and is always somehow making sense, philosophy is called upon to make sense of life's sense-making capacities in a roundabout way. As Heidegger notes in the review of Jaspers' *Psychology of Worldviews*, philosophical problems show up for us because the understanding in which we live is not as spontaneous as it seems, is loaded with traditional concepts and theories that must be questioned and criticized.[65] "The path leading to the things themselves is a long one."[66] Our sense of the problems, the puzzlement that gives rise to philosophical thought, is awakened not by empty gestures toward personal life and lived experience but by way of *reflective* engagement with our own experience in dialogue with the tradition underway in it.

Kitsch: life, on Heidegger's own view, is always difficult. Finding our way in it is never as easy as surrendering to the mysterious play of *Ereignis*. Although we are occasionally at one with ourselves and at home in some pressing and clearly defined task, we are also in conflict with ourselves and at sea in an unstable world of human possibilities. Life is not merely passive surrender to unruly events but self-shaping deliberation and choice. The world is also not only the place where each of us is comfortably at home and at peace, but a field of conflict, misery, and disappointed expectations. Coming to be uneasily at home in the world is learning how to make difficult choices, caring for some things at the expense of other, equally important things, being painfully divided about what we ought to do, coming to grips with loss, privation, aging, infidelity, and death.[67] Coming to terms with life might involve something like surrender to what it gives and *Hingabe* to its currents, perhaps even resignation in the face of what it takes away; but these are the ends of life, not its unquestioned beginnings.

---

[64] In WS 1921/2, Heidegger warns against the dangers of a *Lebensphilosophie* taken up by "those philosophers who would rather gush with enthusiasm than think" and calls for a rigorous *conceptual* elucidation of the basic sense of life (*GA* 61, 79–83).

[65] *Supplements*, 96.   [66] *Supplements*, 74.

[67] For the "difficult" in Heidegger's early work, see *GA* 58, 33, *Supplements*, 113, and WS 1921/2 on "the Easy."

"Kitsch: inadmissibly simplifying the task of life in every situation."[68]
Heidegger rescues himself from *Kitsch* in Musil's sense, almost as soon as
he begins to work out the implication of taking "life in and for itself"
seriously. Life comes to itself, *objectifies* itself, for better or for worse, in a
variety of shapes and situations; and because some expressions of life more
fittingly capture what it means concretely to live, life is called upon to
criticize its manifold expressions of itself. The point of doing philosophy is
not to recover a lost sense of home or to construct a worldview in which
every question finds a fixed and abiding answer, but to make life and
philosophy difficult. "If it is the case that factical life authentically is what it
is in … being hard and being difficult, then the genuinely fitting way of
gaining access to it and truly safekeeping it can only consist in making
itself hard for itself."[69] If life is set in opposition to epistemology and
scientism in KNS 1919 and WS 1919/20, life is finally set against itself,
and becomes the target of a peculiar sort of ethical criticism in the ensuing
lecture courses.

But ethical criticism or evaluation of life is clearly no undivided class of
activities. It involves a diverse body of reflective practices shaped by an
equally diverse set of interests and undertaken from a variety of philosophical and non-philosophical perspectives. There are profound differences in
form, content, and level of generality between the rejection of certain ways
of life and the defense of philosophical contemplation in Book IX of
Plato's *Republic* and the tenth book of Aristotle's *Nicomachean Ethics*, on
the one hand, and bumper-sticker opposition to abortion. All three
versions of ethical criticism appear to differ from the skeptical and probing
practice of Socratic *elenchos* depicted in Plato's early dialogues. An ethical
critic might assume widespread disagreement among her interlocutors or
she might assume general consensus about what really matters, and shape
her speech or conversation accordingly. Not every instance of ethical
criticism is moralizing or concerned with moral values in the narrow sense
worked out by Kant and his descendants. Some varieties take aim at
particular aspects of human life, while others take issue with ways of life
as a whole. Some ethical critics offer positive pronouncements, articulate
and defend a concept of the good life, while others are content merely to
argue against existing ethical norms and standards. Ethical criticism can be
transparently partisan and divisive or, like recent legal and philosophical
defenses of human rights, undertaken in the name of something held to be

---

[68] Musil, *The Man without Qualities*, Volume II, 1766.   [69] *Supplements*, 113.

universal and in a spirit of reconciliation and mutual tolerance, as direct as a religious tract or as indirect as Kierkegaard's pseudonymous writings, as simple as Rilke's appeal to an archaic torso of Apollo or as complex as Kant's defense of human freedom and dignity in the *Critique of Practical Reason*. In light of Heidegger's interest in what he calls "facticity" we might expect something like detailed reflection upon the concrete concerns of particular ways of life and a comparative analysis of various shapes (*Gestalten*) of life guided by a more or less explicit philosophical or religious *Weltanschauung*.

The phenomenologist is neither moralist nor prophet nor proponent of a definite worldview. Heidegger's opposition to the very idea of "worldview philosophy" is pervasive, and runs through the period leading up to *Sein und Zeit*, and beyond. Ethical criticism of life is, at least in Heidegger's development in Freiburg, something fundamental and philosophical, something like the task of reconceiving what it means to be a human being. The ontological turn of WS 1921/2 does not preclude ethical reflection for the simple reason that ontology comprehends and grounds ethical life: to rethink what it means to be human is to reconsider what it means to live a human sort of life.

A fundamental construal of life is never ethically neutral. If I grasp human life as the life of a pleasure-seeking and pain-despising animal, I will live it differently than I would if I believed that the human being is an immortal soul temporarily imprisoned in a body that corrupts its vision of the good. Both ways of life will differ from a life lived in terms of a Cartesian ontology that takes the soul as the place where knowledge of and power over the world of *res extensa* unfolds. It makes an *ethical* difference whether I see human life as active or passive, potentially free and self-determining or fruitfully modified and shaped by a world of complex interactions between persons and things and persons and persons. More to the point of Heidegger's phenomenology: it matters whether I see myself as a thing among things with certain tasks shaped by certain properties and faculties in a relatively fixed world (Aristotle) or as a self-interpreting animal living its life in a world of shifting significance. An ontology of human life is no mere theoretical enterprise: we are at stake in the categorial analysis of human life. Changing the way we understand the being of human life (and being as a whole) is not like discovering that water is hydrogen hydroxide or that Napoleon was defeated at Waterloo or that a famous painting in the Louvre is a forgery. At a certain level of analysis, a fundamental concept of life and the way of life it expresses are the same.

The ontological and ethical self-criticism of life is, then, a deliberate, conceptual or categorial self-interpretation of life. Categories are not concepts that classify and determine objects, but construals of the sense of a phenomenon. They are not imposed upon life from the outside, but live in a definite shape of life itself, are basic ways in which a life comes concernfully to itself and interprets itself. They express a fundamental and holistic understanding of life and announce a possible way of life.

The hermeneutics of facticity, or categorial self-interpretation of life, is concerned about fundamentals and oriented toward the whole of human life, but a fundamental and holistic interpretation of life is not necessarily a universal account of every conceivable life. Categorial self-analysis is not simply a matter of making the general sense of life explicit and unifying the diversity of lives in a complex concept that captures the fixed essence of *homo sapiens*.

Categories interpret *divisively* in the light of a certain ideal of human life, are guided by a sense of what life *ought* to be like and give expression to a certain paradigm. They tell us something about what life is like when it owns up to itself, when it lives in a manner consistent with the sort of being it is. And they tell us something about what life is like when it fails to be itself. It is a remarkable fact about us that we can fail to live up to the human condition, that we can fail somehow to be our*selves*. Categorial self-interpretation serves to awaken a sense of what it means to be a human being, not merely to record some important information about human life or to develop a theory that holds life at a distance from itself, but ultimately in order to become, in Gadamer's words, "keenly aware of one's being-there and [to make] it one's own."[70]

WS 1921/2 is a puzzling text: nominally devoted to phenomenological interpretations of Aristotle and officially devoted to philosophy as a philosophical problem, the course offers nothing of interest on Aristotle and no definitive concept of the philosophical enterprise. Although the object of philosophy finally receives the name of *Sein*, Heidegger's first explicit account of the categories of human life comes perilously close to moralizing criticism of worldly life cloaked in the finery of ontological analysis. In many cases it is difficult to distinguish between those structures that are essential to any and every human life and form the neutral ontological keyboard upon which the authentic and inauthentic alike must play, and those categories that capture features of a culpably self-alienating, evasive, and "ruinant" way of life. On the other hand, WS 1921/2 allows us to see

---

[70] "Martin Heidegger's One Path" in *Reading Heidegger from the Start*, 25.

more clearly just how closely intertwined ethical criticism and ontological interpretation are, to understand better why phenomenology is essentially critical or destructive, and to grasp more directly the sort of life or "ontic ideal" that underwrites Heidegger's more mature and formal ontological insights.

As Krell observes, WS 1921/2 offers something like "a genealogy of masquerade and ruinous self-deception."[71] Heidegger no longer pits detached theories of life against the facts of life occluded by theory but sets life against itself. The unliving of total theoretical detachment from life is just one of several ways in which life manages more or less successfully to distort and escape from itself; and it has to be accounted for in terms of motives and tendencies that operate in the life of everyday concern. Life is already avoiding itself, masking, concealing, and reifying itself, before epistemological reflection and scientism come on the scene. If phenomenology becomes destructive criticism of everyday life, it is because life has what we might call *architectural* tendencies: life tends to build secure shelters for itself that immobilize, protect, reassure, and tranquilize.[72]

World might be the place where significant things happen, interact and matter, but it is also the place where significance fades and yields to banality, concern degenerates into indifference (*Unbekümmerung*), and life gets *set in its ways* and entangles itself complacently in trivial pursuits.[73] If WS 1919/20 offered a phenomenological genesis of scientific unliving and a critique of life-denying scientism, WS 1921/2 provides a categorial snapshot of the complacency, conformity, and *rigor mortis* of everyday prescientific life. The danger of unliving receives a variety of names: *Verfestigung, Mitgenommenwerden, Zerstreuung, Verhärtung,* and so on. But we can discern throughout the account an overarching moral interest in life's inner propensity to reify. As Heidegger will claim repeatedly in *Sein und Zeit*, in the formal language of fundamental ontology and *Seinsverständnis*, Dasein has a natural inclination to understand itself in terms of the world of things taken care of and manipulated in everyday life, to interpret and, as a Kantian might say, to use itself as a thing among mere things. In WS 1921/2, however, this insight is conveyed in terms that are

---

[71] "The 'Factical Life' of Dasein" in *Reading Heidegger from the Start*, 376.

[72] This, I take it, is what Heidegger means by *Praestruktion*.

[73] The world of *Kultur* is singled out repeatedly in the early lecture courses as the target of venomous criticism for reasons that are not always clear, but that seem to have something to do with the tendency to security and indifference that marks "a life of care for cultural assets" (See *GA* 61, 119–20.).

more overtly ethical.[74] If the world reflects back the light of a caring self that reaches out toward it in its "neediness" (*Darbung*), it is also the theater of life's masquerading misadventure: life is *relucent* and *larvant* in the world.

This is not the place to work out a detailed interpretation of the account of *Ruinanz* developed in this "verbose, baroque, and turgid" course of lectures composed during a period of transition in Heidegger's rapidly developing conception of philosophy and the life it questioningly serves.[75] But a cursory glance at the categories of relation (to the world) developed in the first chapter of the third part of the course – *Neigung, Abstand*, and *Abriegelung* – is enough to dispel the illusion that we are dealing with ethically neutral concepts of human life comparable to the concepts and principles that structure scientific discussions of life in the non-philosophical sciences: *Neigung* is not only the primitive thrust of life toward a world but the tendency to become dispersed, fragmented, and self-satisfied. *Abstand* is not the tendency to acknowledge the difference between the trivial and the important, but a culpable refusal to see the distance that separates the noble from the base, motivated by a pernicious self-preoccupation that blindly elevates at the expense of others and cares chiefly about rank, success, position in life, and worldly advantage, that struggles, in short, to get ahead. *Abriegelung* is the self-sequestering loss of myself in chance opportunities to live at ease mapped out in advance by the public world. And *Neigung, Abstand*, and *Abriegelung* coalesce in a quest for worldly certainty, ease, and *securitas* that brings life to a dogmatic and tranquilizing standstill and fixes the world in a rigidly determined pattern of unquestioned possibilities for mindless work and thoughtless recreation. Together, the categories paint an extremely unflattering portrait of a distinctive way of coming to grips with and caring about the world. Although they might be neutral in the sense that they capture tendencies that live in each of us, the tenor of the account is quite clear; and it is difficult to avoid concluding that these tendencies ought to be vigorously *resisted* in the name of another, less rigid and unsatisfying way of life.

The ethical criticism of life in WS 1921/2 does not bear on any particular content (*Gehaltssinn*) of worldly concern but targets a global way of being in and toward the world in terms of what Heidegger calls the

---

[74] Or one might agree with Grondin that in the early lecture courses Heidegger philosophizes more honestly and "ingenuously on the issues that preoccupied him without a philosophical system in his back pocket" and more openly about the ethical intentions that inspired the project of fundamental ontology (*Reading Heidegger from the Start*, 347).

[75] The assessment is Kisiel's in *The Genesis*, 235.

"relational sense" (*Bezugssinn*) of human life as it lives in, out, for, with, and against the world of everyday concern. In this way, it manages to avoid petty moralizing and partisan support of a particular worldview. But it also raises serious questions about Heidegger's ethical and ontological intentions and the coherence of the ethical criticism of everyday life. If epistemological reflection and scientistic theory were attacked as forms of escapist detachment from a world that matters to and deeply affects each of us, the world itself, under a certain description, provides life with an escape hatch from its own uncertain, insecure, and unsettling being that has to be dismantled with the same dogged and merciless persistence. What the right hand of KNS 1919 and WS 1919/20 offered to the unhappy epistemologist and disaffected scientist as a refuge from the desert of mere theory divorced from life the left hand of WS 1921/2 seems to be taking away.

So what is wrong with caring deeply about the world and building a secure life and playing a clearly defined role within its relatively fixed boundaries? The world appears to be all there is to care about; and our identity seems to be bound up precisely with the roles we play and the tasks we undertake for the sake of ourselves, both in and for the sake of the world. Every serious commitment to a definite project appears to place us in an area of worldly concern and to assign us a role in the drama of human life. Philosophy has its place in the university, the religious life finds its home in a church, political life has its reliable institutions and time-worn procedures, the artist who cares about the fate of her work cannot afford to avoid important exhibitions or to ignore the verdict of her more trustworthy critics. And each of these activities is motivated and driven by a rich variety of interests in the world. A political anarchist detaches herself from *this* world of social and political life for the sake of what she takes to be a better, less constraining and repressive world in which traditional authority and fixed social and political principles no longer have any legitimate binding force. To separate ourselves from the world of earthly and embodied human interest is not to win the blessed life, but to detach ourselves from the soil that nourishes our deepest and most abiding thoughts and concerns, to estrange ourselves from the conditions of meaningful individuation, and to deprive ourselves of the only field of thought and action. In terms of Heidegger's own compelling account of life as inescapably worldly, as *essentially* "being-in-a-world" and caring for the world, escapist flight from the world and refusal to play a definite role in it prove incoherent. Culpable: if this is the only world of life we *can* know, if life in the world is, in Dilthey's phrase, the "*prius* of thought" and the objective correlate of our cares, we are partly responsible for and should not remain indifferent to what happens and fails to happen in it. Incoherent: every attempt to flee from the world will be just another way of being (double-mindedly) in it. Is Heidegger trying to force us into the unfortunate and incoherent predicament of having to care about something that in our better and more enlightened moments we can only see as a contemptible shadow that ought to leave us indifferent?[76] Or is he just confused about what he has to say? Is the mood that permeates this early account of a life burdened with possibilities not of its own choosing and subject like the hero of an ancient tragedy to the inscrutable powers of *Schicksal* "dour and even dire" or does it envision another possibility that avoids the extremes of self-forgetful absorption in and ascetic detachment from the world in which each of us unavoidably finds herself uneasily at home?[77] Is Heidegger's earliest ontic ideal essentially ascetic? What sort of life *is* under critical scrutiny here?

The short answer to the last (most important and grounding) question is: a life so thoroughly absorbed in and taken by the interpreted world that the sense of alternative possibilities and the capacity to envision *another* life and *another* shape of the world have withered to such an extent that the current state of affairs becomes the only one conceivable and the ways of life it offers the only ones that are allowed to make sense. To live contentedly in the world of the obvious is to know in advance what each thing is and where it has its proper place, what life has to offer, what counts as success or failure, and how best to manage one's public and private affairs. It is to treat life as a business affair and to dismiss every question that touches upon the elusive whole of worldly life as it stands in the present as idle speculation or romantic dissatisfaction.[78] The world of this life is one in which everything is in order and the only task that remains is to find a secure, compartmentalized place in it and, once that is done, to adjust and make one's calculations accordingly.[79] There is very little to criticize because the critical faculties have been put to sleep. There is less risk, to be sure, but the sense of uncertain adventure that grants to life its relish has atrophied. The categories that interpret factical life in WS 1921/ 2 in relation to the world capture the very being of a life on the verge of losing the vital sense of possibility that inhabits everything actual. "Higher

---

[76] Philipse argues along these lines in *Heidegger's Philosophy of Being*, 346–52.
[77] Krell, "The 'Factical Life' of Dasein" in *Reading Heidegger from the Start*, 368.
[78] "'Life' is a 'business,' whether or not it covers its cost" (*SZ*, 289).
[79] Rejection of the normative ideals of a calculating and manipulative way of life that knows where it stands is at the heart of the phenomenology of conscience in *Sein und Zeit*.

than actuality stands possibility" – if this serves as an aphoristic apology for phenomenological rebellion against fixed schools and traditions, it applies just as well to the life that finds itself reflected in phenomenological concepts.

There is a studied ambiguity in the concept of the world in early Heidegger: on the one hand, it signifies the *interpreted* world that each of us "always already" inhabits before we begin to reflect upon our involvements, a world of unquestioned paths marked out for us in advance that we find ourselves traveling as soon as we begin to ask questions about what we see and do.[80] This is the world of clearly delimited tasks, prohibitions, duties and obligations, a world to which we are at first called upon to submit. On the other hand, world is the space of flexible significance from which we cannot turn away without losing ourselves, a world open to re-vision and reinterpretation in the light of inchoate experiences that find no settled home in the interpreted world of everyday life. ("World" in the latter sense places constraints upon the critique of "world" in the first sense. We can distance ourselves from the interpreted world but never from the world as such. It is not the world that has to be left alone but a certain construal of what is possible and meaningful in it. In truth, these are not two separate worlds but the same world under two very different descriptions corresponding to two very different ways of life, one complacent, the other skeptical, but both shapes of *Sorgen*. To detach myself from the *interpreted* world is just to find myself better placed in *the world*.)

The categories articulate or indicate indirectly and by contrast another, less dogmatic, more flexible and uncertain way of life that finds expression in the final pages of the course. It becomes clear in the culminating discussion of objectivity and questionability that what has been at issue all along in this "dour and sour" account of a life too absorbed in the world to pay attention to itself, too caught up in the quest for certainty and security to notice just how strange things can be, and too knowing to be capable of approaching each concrete situation openly and with an eye responsive to the uniqueness of things, is nothing less than the *immediacy* and obviousness of the nearest world that grips and fascinates everyday life. As Heidegger begins to clarify his train of thought, we begin to see that the categorial self-interpretation of ruinant life is not at all a Gnostic account of some egregious fall into the material world but something like a genealogy of the so-called "objectivity" of the world of a life on the verge of complacency and stagnation: "we cannot assume, without further

---

[80] See *Supplements*, 116.

discussion, that the immediacy of the world of care, as what is most directly over and against, constitutes the paradigm case of self-given-ness."[81] In a Hegelian turn of phrase, Heidegger warns his students that the immediacy of the world is "formally speaking" something *mediated* and as such worthy of being questioned.[82] The account of *Ruinanz* is a sort of Husserlian *epochê* in reverse, an attempt to explain how we come to be fascinated and taken by the world of the natural attitude in the first place.

But every account of this sort presupposes some sense of what is missing in the natural attitude and must at least indicate a way out of the iron cage of the rigidly interpreted world that stands in the way of a more vigilant and careful philosophical life.[83] It is also remarkable that Heidegger offers nothing comparable to the Husserlian reduction to the uncorrupted space of a transcendental subject standing before a field of absolutely certain data.[84] The break (*Bresche*) in the fabric of immediate life is nothing less than the initiation or renewal of life's *dialogue* with itself in relation to tradition. "Precisely insofar as it is factical, the factically interpretive dialogue [*Zwiesprache*] residing within the factical enactment of life is a breach [*Bresche*] in the coherence of immediate life."[85] Heidegger says, unfortunately, precious little about this dialogue that dwells in the heart of human life. But it is revealing that he grants here that to be my*self* is not to sequester myself from the world, but to participate in an ongoing conversation about my life and the world that surrounds me. WS 1921/2 poses a sharp contrast between a life lived slavishly in relation to the world of public concern and a life that takes responsibility for itself in living and questioning conversation. To be drawn mindlessly into the gray world of everyday life is just to put an end to what Plato in the *Sophist* called a "dialogue of the soul with itself."

Human life comes back to itself, cares properly for itself, and achieves its "genuinely developed self-givenness," not by plunging blindly into the world, "seizing, laying hands on things that appear to be urgent," and not by standing aloof from the world in an attitude of cynical contempt or mystical devotion, but in questioning and "living in the answer[s] . . . in a

[81] *GA* 61, 150.   [82] *GA* 61, 149.
[83] 'Vigilance' or 'wakefulness' is not mentioned in WS 1921/2, but in SS 1923 the 'hermeneutics of facticity' is claimed to develop a "radical wakefulness" in human life and to open "a possibility" of Dasein's "becoming and being for itself in the manner of an *understanding* of itself" (*GA* 63, 15–16).
[84] The Husserlian (and Cartesian) quest for certainty is addressed explicitly in another version of 'ethical criticism' in WS 1923/4.
[85] *GA* 61, 151.

searching way."[86] The life that stands on this side of the (interpreted) world (as we know it) is not an unworldly or ascetic life, but a *skeptical* life devoted to questioning what we tend to take for granted, and not in the name of another life on the other side of the world, but for the sake of this life in this questionable world. The point of doing philosophy is not, as one American thinker would have it, to leave the world alone,[87] whatever that might be, but to get back into it and to learn how to care for and cope with it in a fitting way.

Ethical Criticism and the Philosophical Life

I have tried to make the case for a reading of Heidegger's early views on phenomenological criticism and ontological interpretation as the embodiments of an ethical interest in human life guided by a certain ontic ideal of human existence. While I avoided a neat definition of ethical criticism in the opening pages, for reasons that are consistent with Heidegger's own views on the limits of isolated propositions and theses, the reader should by now be in a position to understand, perhaps better than any isolated statement could convey, what is meant by these terms. A philosophical claim can be construed as ethical insofar as it bears ultimately upon the way in which human beings attempt to live and to understand and interpret themselves, for the sake of living a better way of life. A species of philosophical criticism deserves to be called "ethical" insofar as it questions and evaluates certain positions, attitudes, and theses in terms of an ideal of human life at stake in the critical practice.

But the interpretation is still infected by some lingering doubts that ought to be confronted. For one, Heidegger explicitly denies that he is doing ethics throughout the Freiburg lectures. In WS 1919/20 Heidegger cautions us not to look to philosophy to provide "practical propositions and norms" that might guide ethical life, and suggests that every genuine philosophy is born out of a certain "fullness of life, not from ... basic ethical question."[88] Time and again, as we noted in the Introduction, Heidegger denies that philosophy knows anything like disciplines. Moreover, the early lecture courses are centrally preoccupied with the problem of *method*, a term that suggests a scientific interest of some kind. Finally, ontological claims themselves can always be taken up and construed as

---

[86] GA 61, 153, 149.
[87] Cf. Jonathan Lear's essay by this title, which echoes a pronouncement of the late Richard Rorty.
[88] GA 58, 149–50.

propositions that capture the neutral structure of human life, or the basic constraints placed upon any meaningful way of living, regardless of one's ethical or moral interest. Fundamental ontology can always be construed as another *theory* of human existence. On this view, the discussion of factical life in WS 1921/2 would be little more than a necessary stage in the philosophical articulation of the philosophical life.

I think it is possible to agree with each of these claims and still insist that phenomenological ontology and criticism are concerned about the ethical, or capture something of the sense of ethical life. To say that philosophy knows no disciplinary boundaries is just to say that the object of philosophy is nothing that can be cut into pieces that can, in turn, be analyzed in total isolation from the whole. A phenomenology of the work of art, for example, will have to take a stand on or attempt to clarify the nature or being of language, history, human life and experience, scientific thought, human knowledge, and so on. An epistemological project that doesn't ask questions like, "What sort of knowledge comes to language in a poem?" or "What are the historical conditions of human cognition?" or "What do I know as an ethical being?" runs the risk of distorting the phenomenon of knowing and leaving behind contexts that fruitfully shape the way the problems show up and help to map out nuanced responses to the question concerning *epistêmê*. If the phenomenology of ethical life offers no concrete norms and practical propositions, this is because it probes the texture of ethical life more deeply and comprehensively than moralizing language and moral philosophy in the narrow sense can reach and moves in a dimension of life in which detached propositions and simple rules of conduct, divorced from concrete situations of thought and action, no longer have a place, are removed from what Heidegger in WS 1921/2 calls a *living morality*.[89]

Furthermore, method, on Heidegger's view, is nothing divorced from the subject matter but simply the way in which the "things themselves" show up and develop in a philosophical understanding. To say that phenomenology or philosophy is a discourse on the method of philosophy is just to say that ethical criticism and interpretation of life are essentially philosophical criticism and interpretation. There is a tight link in the early lecture courses between method, subject matter, and way of life: the method is the way of life that secures access to itself and the subject matter is the way of life at issue in every search for the method. As Heidegger observes in SS 1923, "The relationship between hermeneutics and facticity

[89] *GA* 61, 164.

is not a relationship between the grasping of an object and the object grasped, in relation to which the former would simply have to measure itself. Rather, interpreting is itself a possible and distinctive how of the character of being of facticity. Interpreting is a being which belongs to the being of factical life itself. "[90] Claims about Dasein do not capture the fixed properties of an object from which total detachment is possible. The linguistic similarity between a claim about some object (s is p) and a fitting expression of human life conceals an ontological difference between entities with fixed properties, and that being "has its being to be" (as a task) in ongoing dialogue with itself and others.

The *Seinsfrage* is not an ethical question and the ontologist does not ask *about* ethics because the question concerning the meaning of being already reflects the deepest ethical determination of Dasein. Ontological questioning embraces the ethical from the very start. Philosophy is not, on early Heidegger's view, detached inquiry, an attempt to get things right, at least not in that (objectifying) way: the philosophical attitude is a *life-stance*, and philosophy itself a paradigmatic way of life.[91] Ontology is the self-explication and critical self-evaluation of life, for the sake of life.[92] To become a philosopher in early Heidegger's sense is to come to live in a certain way, not merely to think at a distance about certain objects, not to fix life in an abstract system of concepts to be admired, but to *own up* to what it means to be a human being and to speak out in a manner consistent with what has been discovered along the way. To ask about "being" is to ask what being must mean in order for a certain way of life to be possible. The sort of ontology one does, cribbing from Fichte, depends upon the sort of life one aspires to live.

---

[90] *GA* 63, 15.

[91] "Philosophy is a *Grundwie* of life," as Heidegger observes in WS 1921/2 (*GA* 61, 80).

[92] In WS 1921/2 Heidegger replies to the question 'Why do we philosophize?', tersely enough, "For [the sake of] factical life" (*GA* 61, 39).

CHAPTER 2

Ethical Truth and the Quarrel between the Ancients and Moderns

Heidegger's "Anti-Modernism"

As we noted in the Introduction, there seems to be a consensus emerging in certain circles that Heidegger was consistently hostile to all things modern, lured away from an enlightened view of the world by an idealized image of life in the earliest days of the Greek *polis*, before the pernicious influence of Socrates and his followers began to take root, and before reason and its concepts surfaced as the unyielding "adversary of thought."[1] In the work of a growing number of historians and philosophical commentators and critics, a picture is taking shape of a philosopher ill at ease with the conditions of modern life, troubled by newspapers and technology and liberal democratic institutions, engaged, under the baneful influence of Spengler, in a Quixotic struggle against what he misunderstood to be "the decline of the West," and unable to appreciate the general values of autonomy, rationality, and universality central to the overarching spirit of the European Enlightenment. A thinker, in short, more at home among peasants plying their trades in the Black Forest than in conversation with the rootless cosmopolitans haunting the bustling cities of New York, Paris, and Berlin.[2] And more disquieting still, the evidence for this construal is ostensibly not confined to the speeches, essays, and lecture courses written or delivered during the period of Heidegger's involvement in the politics of National Socialism, but can be discerned in the work leading up to the publication of *Sein und Zeit*: the seeds of the stance worked out more fully

---

[1] "The Word of Nietzsche 'God Is Dead'" in *The Question Concerning Technology and Other Essays*, 112.
[2] See, for example, Richard Wolin's *The Politics of Being: The Political Thought of Martin Heidegger* and, more recently, *Heidegger's Children: Hanna Arendt, Karl Löwith, Hans Jonas, and Herbert Marcuse*, and Charles Bambach's *Heidegger's Roots: Nietzsche, National Socialism, and the Greeks*. Mention should also be made of Habermas's attack on Heidegger's critique of Western rationalism in *The Philosophical Discourse of Modernity: Twelve Lectures*, and the provocative and disturbing biographical studies of Victor Farías and Hugo Ott.

by the rector who admired Hitler's hands[3] and called for pledges of allegiance to the leader of the German *Volk* were planted in the earliest lecture courses and manuscripts of the young *Privatdozent* in Freiburg and the associate professor at Marburg.[4] Heidegger seems to have been a born and baptized a reactionary anti-modernist.

There may be a few good reasons to accept this unsettling vision of early Heidegger's philosophical trajectory and its deepest and most enduring ethical and political concerns. As early as 1919, Heidegger voices dissatisfaction with the idea of universal history, moral progress, technological advancement, and the growing solidarity of mankind, declaring his own kinship with a partisan reading of the more parochial writings of Hamann, Herder, and Schleiermacher.[5] An early course of lectures on the phenomenology of religion held in Freiburg takes issue with the "secularization and self-sufficiency" of modern life and the "tolerance of alien views" we tend to associate with a more humane and enlightened approach to the diversity of religious beliefs and customs and non-religious forms of life.[6] And in a number of lecture courses and manuscripts from the same period, Heidegger inveighs against the very idea of universal humanity and every cultural or historical interest in what binds us together as members of *homo sapiens*, despite every difference in particular values and interests and ways of life.[7]

This is probably sufficient reason for many to leave Heidegger well enough alone. But there are other reasons to doubt that Heidegger has anything important to say to those of us who still care about the fate of philosophy in contemporary life. Throughout the early 20s Heidegger flirts with the idea that the philosophical tradition as a whole has somehow exhausted its vital possibilities. As he informs his students dogmatically in 1920: "We philosophize not in order to show that we need a philosophy, but precisely in order to show that we need none."[8] And again three years later: "It is my conviction that philosophy is at an end. We stand before completely new tasks that have nothing to do with traditional philosophy."[9] And so we have a thinker not merely averse to what he took to be the Cartesian roots of our deracinated modern lives but a philosopher who

[3] Mark Lilla, *The Reckless Mind: Intellectuals in Politics*, 24.
[4] This is in a nutshell the argument developed by Wolin in *Heidegger's Children*.
[5] *GA* 56/7, 129–36.   [6] *GA* 60, 33; *The Phenomenology of Religious Life*, 23.
[7] "Factical Dasein always is what it is only as one's own Dasein and never as the Dasein in general of some universal humanity. Expanding care on the latter could only ever be an illusory task" (*Supplements*, 114).
[8] *GA* 59, 191.   [9] *GA* 17, 1; *Introduction to Phenomenological Research* (hereafter, "*IPR*"), 1.

denies that he is doing anything importantly philosophical; and now two good reasons to let Heidegger and his disciples be.

So why should anyone interested in that strange discipline we call philosophy and eager to defend what is best in modern life under some description also care about the polemical writings of an unhappy *Schwarzwald* redneck who became a Nazi? If we scrutinize the landscape of early Heidegger's dissatisfactions and denials, we discern, among other things, a dawning philosophical interest in the nature of truth and its convoluted intellectual history, a subtle and careful examination of the Cartesian quest for certainty and its limits, and a brilliant appropriation of Aristotle's account of *alêtheuein* in Book VI of the *Nicomachean Ethics*. We discover no blind hostility to the modern and no slavish adherence to an antiquated form of life, but a powerful interpretation of ancient and modern ways of conceiving truth, and an invitation to participate with Heidegger and his historical interlocutors in the ongoing conversation that constitutes every vital intellectual tradition. I hope to go on to show in the present chapter that we discover no small dose of what most of us are prepared to embrace under the auspices of philosophy: for it is partly thanks to the discovery of the ethical problem of truth that the Christian theo*logian* and *Antiphilosoph* became a philosopher.[10]

Dismantling the Cartesian Quest for Certainty

It is the business of philosophy to care about the truth in at least two ways. We expect the philosopher to take an interest in the truth of what she writes or says. Sometimes we expect her to say something important about what truth itself is, and where properly to locate it (in propositional assertions, for instance).

We may eventually decide that nothing general and nothing fruitful or non-circular can be said about what truth itself is. Or we might come gradually to believe that truth is just a property of certain sentences made possible by a contingent language game, and no more puzzling than a

[10] The literature on Heidegger on truth is already too large to survey. I've benefited the most from three outstanding book-length studies: Daniel Dahlstrom's *Heidegger's Concept of Truth*, which includes helpful surveys of early Heidegger's engagement with Aristotle and occasionally takes up the ethical dimension of Heidegger's ontology, Mark Wrathall's *Heidegger and Unconcealment: Truth, Language, and History*, which focuses on the direction Heidegger's early account of truth assumes in the later works, and Denis McManus's *Heidegger and the Measure of Truth*, a work that has unsettled more than anything else I've read to date a few of my views on Heidegger's relation to philosophical theory and the theoretical attitude.

naturalized view of language, as one of several biological capacities that defines *homo sapiens*. Or we may be inclined to embrace the more troubling view, endorsed in some contexts by Nietzsche, that what we call "truth" is just a certain sort of error without which we would be unable to live. We might be led to deny that "truth" has any meaning and reference at all and espouse some variety of unqualified skepticism. But we earn the right to these philosophical conclusions, if it all, only after we have made the effort to puzzle over and consider what we think we mean when, on various occasions and in diverse settings, we use the expression "true." Philosophy comes into its own on Heidegger's emerging view as the search for the meaning(s) of truth *itself*.

If there is a *philosophical* quarrel between the ancients and the moderns revisited in early Heidegger's confrontation with the Cartesian legacy and its roots, it is staged as a fundamental and consequential controversy over the very idea of truth, and in a register we do well to consider *ethical*. There may very well prove to be disturbing political implications of Heidegger's critique of the Cartesian tradition and its enduring grip on contemporary life and thought in the early lecture courses. But before we rush to political judgment on the basis of superficial similarities between ontological analysis and social commentary, we would do well to linger over the details of Heidegger's subtle and patiently developed *philosophical* account of the quest for certainty and its limits in the winter semester of 1923/4. In this pregnant course of lectures delivered in Marburg, the newly appointed associate professor defends a series of specific assertions about the nature and driving force of the search for *cognitio certa et evidens*, and equally precise claims about what the Cartesian determination of *scientia* and *verum* necessarily leaves behind. He offers compelling reasons to think that what the various philosophers of consciousness fail to consider, under the acknowledged or unrecorded influence of Descartes, makes no small ontological and, as we shall see, *ethical* difference.

Although the account is polemical,[11] Heidegger's earliest sustained meditation on the roots of Cartesian thought pays surprising respect to

---

[11] In section 20, Heidegger tells us that the account of Descartes is essentially a *Kampf* with the past. (See *IPR*, 88; *GA* 17, 122.) Already, in the way Heidegger sets up the contrast between Aristotle and the Cartesians in the opening discussion of the etymology of "phenomenology" (drawn largely from Aristotle), he seems to be nudging his students toward the conclusion that Descartes and his heirs, unlike Aristotle, overlook the *world* of what we encounter, in favor of the certainty of what can be grasped within it and, more often than not, against it. See, for example, the discussion of Aristotle's account of perception (in *de Anima* II.7) in section 1a, where Heidegger interprets *en phôti* as "being in daylight" and being visible as standing in the illuminating presence of the sun.

the historical figure of Descartes and the intellectual possibility his work represents. Far from dismissing the *Regulae* and the *Meditationes* as expressions of a debased conceptual and scientific ideal or, as the subsequent chronicler of *Seynsgeschichte* is wont to do, as the symptoms of inevitable historical decline, Heidegger frequently reminds us that the Cartesian tradition stands for a genuine possibility of human thought: the philosophy of consciousness inaugurated by Descartes is no parochial (French) affair, but "is grounded in distinctive *possibilities* that [human] existence bears within itself."[12]

The rise of an ideal of absolute certainty as the sole mark of truth might signal the reversal of a more ancient paradigm by "an intelligence gone mad," but the madness is nothing foreign to human life.[13] Its history is nothing less than a record of our own intellectual struggles and spiritual anxieties. To confront this tradition philosophically is to shed light on the historical and conceptual roots of an outlook that has come to seem self-evident to some, to cultivate "something like a *respect for the history* in which we live out our own" lives,[14] and to criticize the tendency to adopt a stance we no longer fully understand and to work with philosophical paradigms and conceptual resources we might in the long run discover good reasons to renounce. But fruitful criticism comes only after the possibility in question has been faithfully explored and thoughtfully motivated.[15] "Care about knowledge known," Heidegger observes, "has a dominance that is *uprooted*, no longer aware of its origins." And so, he suggests, we are called upon to return to "a *genuine being of care in its primordial past*. To return to the genuine being of care . . . is to return to a *context of research* that bears the name 'Descartes.'"[16]

So, Heidegger invites his students to ask: What do the Cartesian texts have to say about a certain shape of cognitive desire and fulfillment? What sort of aspiration finds a voice in the *Regulae* and *Meditationes*? And what drives it? In short: What does Descartes care about and why?

The reference to "care" and its motives is neither arbitrary nor imprecise. As we began to argue in the Introduction, care is at once an essential

---

[12] *IPR*, 35; *GA* 17, 47.

[13] *IPR*, 33 (*GA* 17, 43). Heidegger even grants (in section 4) that the possibility worked out by Descartes is prefigured in Greek philosophy, despite the fact that the Greeks possessed no concept of consciousness.

[14] *IPR*, 86; *GA* 17, 119.

[15] ". . . the history that offers us such possibilities and transformations is nothing contingent and remote that lies behind us . . . but in the *transformations of history* we encounter nothing other than *our own existence* [Dasein]" (*IPR*, 36; *GA* 17, 47).

[16] *IPR*, 84.

ingredient in Heidegger's gradually emerging picture of what it means for human beings to be, and an operative concept that shapes the Heideggerian evaluation of diverse philosophical stances and cognitive strivings. Care is neither an accidental characteristic of human existence, as though we could imagine ourselves in every other respect the same but no longer or not yet caring, nor a merely subjective feature of experiential life that forces us to project contingent and unjustifiable values on a neutral screen of objective facts, but a grounding condition of meaningful human activity in general. "Care," Heidegger notes early on, "is nothing subjective and does not feign what it takes care of; care allows [what it pursues] to come into its genuine being."[17] Care announces itself wherever significance and intelligibility become visible in a ruling way of life. Insofar as philosophical visions and projects are grounded in some variety of care, it should be possible to evaluate them in terms of the concernful and illuminating way of life they embody. However remote from the cares, concerns, and insights of everyday life Descartes' arguments appear to be (the worries they address are, by Descartes' own admission, slender metaphysical doubts), the Cartesian aspiration itself takes shape in the humble field of human interest and behavior and apparent human need. It is ultimately as a motivated *human* pursuit that the quest for certainty and the "care for knowledge known"[18] have to be analyzed and criticized. What we are interrogating, then, is the human terrain upon which the search for *cognitio certa et evidens* rests, what it embraces, and what soil it leaves uncultivated, by design or innocent neglect.

The quest for certainty is neither unintelligible nor unmotivated from the standpoint of everyday life and concern. In the *Discourse on the Method* and in the opening paragraph of the first of his six *Meditations on First Philosophy*, Descartes sketches a picture of dissatisfaction that at once resonates with some of the intuitions we identify with a more reflective stance on our own cognitive interests and, importantly, helps to motivate the search for "one firm and immovable point" in our knowledge of what exists and the pursuit of stable and enduring convictions about what we ought to do. We often give our *assensus* to untested assertions and embrace views that have no better support than the consent of our contemporaries and peers, or rest upon the unchallenged authority of the past. When Descartes says that he discovered in the various writings of antiquity more confusing diversity of opinion than settled truth, he gives voice to a genuinely philosophical experience, something like what Hilary Putnam

---

[17] *IPR*, 34.   [18] See, for instance, *IPR*, 53.

calls "reflective transcendence."[19] We do not have to endorse the argument
for the existence of God in the Third Meditation or to assent to Cartesian
claims about the independence of body and mind in order to appreciate
the philosopher's skeptical anxieties about untested opinion and the slavish
adoption of traditional stances and unquestioned beliefs that drive the
search that gave birth to Cartesian epistemology and metaphysics. As we
argued in the previous chapter, Heidegger himself often takes issue, in the
spirit of Descartes, with our tendency, in philosophy as well as in everyday
life, to accede to tradition, at the expense of posing questions more
originally. It is this tendency toward radical insight into what things are
and how best to appropriate them that Heidegger finds initially appealing
in Descartes's enterprise, despite the obviously critical intentions of the
lecture course.

There might be good reasons to renounce in theory and in practice the
very idea of absolute certainty and unshakable conviction, and good
reasons to embrace a more flexible and open *fallibilist* stance toward what
we believe and desire and hope to accomplish.[20] But an enlightened
willingness to acknowledge the importance of what cannot be known with
absolute and unassailable certainty begins with an earnest consideration of
the pragmatic grounds of the desire to know more certainly and securely
than we often do. In this way, the Cartesian point of departure is the
opening move of what we often associate with the enduring practice and
beneficial habits of a more reflective and examined way of life. The
incipient Cartesian stance is the burgeoning enemy of intellectual complacency, unwarranted self-confidence, and dogmatism. To be moved by its
beginnings is to begin questioning what we've so far taken for granted. If
Heidegger finds the Cartesian project threatening, it is partly because
Descartes's anxieties are the fundamental ontologist's own. As Heidegger
notes in SS 1920, philosophy has the task of making us *uncertain* (or
insecure), a project that clearly overlaps with the opening moves of the
Meditationes.

But if the point of departure just outlined were the whole of what we
associate with Descartes's name, there would be little to criticize, but even
less to remember in the body of work he left behind. We would have, at
best, an eloquent protest in the first half of the seventeenth century against
intellectual tendencies and inveterate habits of mind that Socrates opposed

---

[19] See *Ethics without Ontology* (Cambridge: Harvard University Press, 2004), 92.

[20] Putnam attempts to dissociate fallibilism from both skepticism and the dogmatic certainty of what
he calls "inflationary metaphysics" in *Ethics without Ontology*.

forcefully at great risk to his own life and to the chagrin of his contemporaries in the fifth century BCE, in the service of an examined and self-critical way of life, and that Montaigne, among more recent others, vigorously but humanely rejected. We would have a powerful literary expression of the rudiments of a philosophical attitude, but nothing like a distinctive metaphysical or theological system and nothing comparable to the epistemological quest for absolute *certainty* elaborated in the *Regulae* and *Meditationes*. But Descartes is clearly not merely an early modern counterpart to Socrates and no simple heir to the ancient skeptical and cynical traditions. His work is far removed in style and execution from the probing intellectual and practical uncertainty and highly personal self-scrutiny of a Montaigne. The "I" that survives unscathed from the crucible of Cartesian doubt and affirms only its own existence and the sheer fact that it is a *res cogitans* is nothing like the humble seeker and eager conversationalist of Plato's early Socratic dialogues, and unlike the restless author who constantly examines himself and his concrete convictions in the *Essays*, leaving his reader in doubt about what he is ultimately willing to affirm.

The differences between Cartesian and non-Cartesian varieties of skepticism hinge on precisely how one responds to the situation of perceived uncertainty, where the response to possible doubt eventually leads, and what sort of self-consciousness, or *Selbstbesinnung*, serves to found a more stable and reliable, or at least a better, view of the world. There is more than one way to come to grips with the uncertainty and apparent insecurity of human life and thought. One might embrace some version of skepticism as the most fitting response to our cognitive situation, perhaps in the manner of the ancient skeptics who argued for the equipollence of every argument for or against any particular stand on an important philosophical or moral issue;[21] one might espouse some version of absolutism, as Plato and, in some contexts, Aristotle appear to do; or one may simply refuse to get involved in metaphysical and moral controversies and recommend enlightened acceptance of what we already believe, and affirm the previously unexamined standpoint of everyday life and the language in which it finds itself uninhibitedly expressed, as Heidegger himself, on some readings, appears to argue. The differences between one philosophical or unphilosophical response and another lie in the

---

[21] See Michael Forster's account of ancient skepticism in *Hegel and Skepticism* and Martha Nussbaum's discussion of the tradition in *The Therapy of Desire: Theory and Practice in Hellenistic Ethics.*

concrete *path* one travels in answer to our initial disorientation and perplexity, and how one manages to overcome painful hesitation and initially paralyzing uncertainty in the name of what we call knowledge or truth. They lie, in short, in what one is ultimately willing to affirm, on what grounds, and with what degree of confidence and self-assurance.

In Heidegger's view, the driving questions of Cartesian thought are: What should the will assent to in the explicit shape of judgment, in what (purified) intellectual circumstances, and on what cognitive grounds?[22] When are we justified in giving our voluntary assent to the various propositions our mind holds freely before itself?[23] The path mapped out in the *Regulae* and traveled in the *Meditationes* is designed to lead, in a strictly regimented and ordered sweep of thought, away from error and ungrounded judgment and toward "the perfection that lies in the *assecutio veritatis*."[24] If the power of judgment were not subject to a self-posited rule, if the mind in its freedom could not bind itself rigorously to a method worked out in advance of every particular cognitive pursuit, we would be more likely to wander and go astray than to discover the truth; and more likely to hit the truth, if at all, by *chance* rather than design. The vagaries of an inattentive and unregulated mind, free to roam and affirm or deny as it wills, must consequently be subdued if the sciences are to be built on a stable conceptual foundation and the search for particular truths is to have some measure of success.[25] We need a method that can serve as "the measure for the [mind's voluntary but rational] *assensus*."[26] Where a clear and trustworthy method or *regimen* is still lacking, we cannot say whether

---

[22] "Insofar as Descartes in his entire investigation has his eyes on knowledge and views a human's being accordingly, he must determine *knowing's being*, hence a human's being, fundamentally as *judicium*. For only then is a human's being, in keeping with the way it is, related to the summa perfectio insofar as the *judicium* exhibits a *modus volendi*. Judicium is equivalent to assensionem praebere" (*IPR*, 151).

[23] The references to "will" and "freedom" are not merely decorative. On Descartes' view, the power to judge is always free. In the Fourth Meditation, it is the freedom of the will, taken as the unrestricted ability to affirm and deny, pursue or avoid, coupled with the limited range of our understanding, that explains the human mind's propensity to go astray. As long as I refrain from making judgments "in cases where I do not perceive the truth with sufficient clarity and distinctness, then it is clear that I am behaving correctly and avoiding error" (*The Philosophical Writings of Descartes* (hereafter "*PWD*"), Volume II, 41; *Oeuvres de Descartes*, ed. Adam and Tannery [hereafter "AT"], Volume VI, 59). Error, then, is a perversion or misuse of free will. And as Heidegger observes, were we not free to give our assent to things poorly perceived, or to judgments that fail to capture what is clearly and distinctly perceived, we would have no need of a regimen.

[24] *IPR*, 149; *GA* 17, 196.

[25] "But it is far better never to contemplate investigating the truth about any matter than to do so without a method. For it is quite certain that such haphazard studies and obscure reflections blur the natural light and blind our intelligence" (*PWD* I, 16; AT X, 371).

[26] *IPR*, 153; *GA* 17, 202.

the truth about anything is truly in our grasp or not: we may not be mistaken in our affirmations and denials, but if we are not in fact deceived, mistaken, or misguided, we have yet to *know* it. For this very reason, the method must tell us not only how to conduct the search for truth, but what conditions must be met in order to satisfy our cognitive aspirations. The method is not only a logic of discovery[27] but a tissue of *regulae* that clarifies what generally *counts* as true and worthy of our assent, and specifies those formal characteristics that jointly determine the very nature of *scientia* or *sapientia*, "which always remains one and the same, however much it may be applied to different subjects."[28] The delineation of the method of inquiry and the formal account of knowing and its proper objects belong to one undivided philosophical enterprise.

"Every *scientia*," Descartes tells us in the Second Rule, "is *cognitio certa et evidens*."[29] Whether our ideas hook up with something beyond the propositional content of our own mind is, at least at first, less important than *how* those very ideas are given to us. As Descartes argues in the last two *Meditationes*, the truth about external reality is to be properly measured by what can be clearly and distinctly perceived. As Heidegger notes, what is at issue is nothing less than the very *being* of the thing in question, made over in an image of being-certain. It matters less *that* there really is an apple on the desk in front of me, containing within itself each of the qualities I attribute to it, than *whether* my initially confused conception of an apple can be resolved into an interconnected cluster of clear and distinct *perceptions* of the object I mindfully intend.[30] "The rule under which Descartes places [all] knowing is the *clara et distincta perceptio*."[31] For an idea to be clear, it must be grasped explicitly by a *mens attendens*; and its object, if we can speak of it here, must be fully present, "*lying there in the open*" and in no way concealed or indirectly given to the attentively perceiving mind.[32] In order to be distinct, a perception must be clearly

---

[27] For the idea of Cartesian method as a logic of discovery, see Garber's *Descartes' Metaphysical Physics*, 59.

[28] *PWD* I, 7; AT X, 360. In Heidegger's terms, what is at issue in the *Regulae* is the very "being" of knowing and "*the sense of verum's being*" (*IPR*, 148; *GA* 17, 195).

[29] *PWD* I, 10; AT X, 362.

[30] For a brief discussion of the inward turn of Cartesian epistemology, see Taylor's "Overcoming Epistemology" in *Philosophical Arguments*, 4–5. I disagree with Taylor, however, when he tells us that the Cartesian seeker after science "is not directed away from shifting and uncertain opinion toward the order of the unchanging" (Ibid., 4). Descartes is, as much as Plato, interested in opinions that do not wander; but he places the order of the unchanging within the mind rather than somewhere else. Descartes's arguments often terminate in what cannot be thought away and remains the same despite the shifting circumstances of its givenness.

[31] *IPR*, 154; *GA* 17, 203.   [32] *IPR*, 154–5; *GA* 17, 204.

separated from every other perception, "cut off from other *perceptiones*."[33] Where our cognitions are confused and their objects cloaked in darkness and ambiguity, we cannot be said to know anything, although we might be vaguely familiar with something. What cannot be given with utter clarity and distinctness to an attentive and discriminating *mens*, or reliably assembled out of clear and distinct perceptions, falls outside the scope of what can possibly be known and should not be given our assent.[34] This is no mere epistemology, if Heidegger is right, but what we might call an "epistemologically motivated ontology."

But what sort of intellectual requirement is this? Why hold ourselves to such strict cognitive demands, refusing to yield, at least in theory but in the long run, hopefully, in practice as well, to any representation or thought, proposition or opinion that contains anything obscure, unclear, or uncertain? Where does the Cartesian ideal of clear and distinct, certain and evident *cognitio* originate? Is there a class of objects that satisfies the ideal purely and simply and that Descartes embraces and endorses as the measure of all the others? And if so, why single it out as the privileged example of what we can in general know? As Heidegger asks, "Where does Descartes get the right to pre-judge, according to what is set forth in the *regula generalis, every* possible knowledge that might surface?"[35] Why not grant that we can, and indeed in some cases *should*, find reasons of a sort to assent to ways of seeing or construing the world of human life that cannot be reduced to clear and distinct perceptions of the truth about particular items or aspects of what appears to us to be?

The rules, Heidegger notes, tell us nothing about what in particular we can reasonably hope to know. As a formal set of principles, the method is indifferent to the concrete and diversified subject matter of human inquiry: "Nothing is said in the rule about the specific object-character of what is supposed to be grasped by the rule."[36] As we saw, human knowledge and wisdom are everywhere the same, like the indifferent beam

---

[33] *IPR*, 155; *GA* 17, 204–5. The two criteria really go hand in hand: I cannot clearly distinguish between one idea and another if I don't have a clear perception of each. To achieve clarity in my perceptions is to distinguish sharply between them.

[34] "... we reject all ... merely probable cognition and resolve to believe only what is perfectly known and incapable of being doubted" (*PWD* I, 10; AT X, 362).

[35] *IPR*, 156; *GA* 17, 206.

[36] *IPR*, 156. This Cartesian view cuts against the grain of Heidegger's views on method and matter throughout the early period, and beyond. In the spirit of Aristotle, Heidegger maintains tirelessly that the proper concepts of method grow out of long familiarity with the sort of object one is trying in thought to grasp. As Heidegger complains, "The sense of being-related [to the object] ... is a purely formal, indeterminately general sense" (*IPR*, 156).

of light that illuminates everything it happens to light upon without the partisanship and strife we usually associate with fruitful philosophical dialogue and debate. We are consequently not told how to make progress in our knowledge of, say, history or the principles of ethical and political life; we are not told how to develop a science of living beings or what distinguishes knowledge of mathematical objects from knowledge of the properties of and causal relations between physical things. Cartesian epistemology does not distinguish between gods and insects, numbers and logical relationships as objects of rational inquiry. There is no difference between the context in which we ask about the nature, power, and influence of a divine being or inquire into the characteristics and behavior of a flea; and no reason to think that our answers ought to embody what we have individually experienced or tentatively come to believe about the objects in question; we have even less reason to think that the status of a scientific claim might reflect the social and historical circumstances of the scientist and the beliefs she has been bred or led to accept as the natural starting point of her research. In every case, we have merely to deal with the contents of our own ideas and to ask whether the idea in contention is given in the right (disembodied) way. As Descartes notes in the Third Meditation, setting up the strategy of his first proof for God's existence, the task is to explore only the content of one's own mind, to consider the idea, internal to the mental landscape, we have of something. If it presents itself clearly and distinctly or can be derived from what is immediately evident, we ought to affirm it, and if not to deny it. The question is always only: How can we frame solid and true judgments concerning everything we have to consider, regardless of the specific kind of thing we normally or naturally and unreflectively take it to be, and regardless of the specific situation of our encounter with the objects of *scientia*?[37] In opposition to the ancients who considered things as falling under natural kinds and investigated them accordingly, Descartes is concerned merely with the order of our knowledge of things: "all things can be arranged serially in various groups, not in so far as they can be referred to some ontological genus ... but in so far as some things can be known on the basis of others."[38]

As Heidegger observes, however, Descartes has a body of established doctrine and a species of knowledge tailored to a particular set of objects in mind; and it is this general intellectual orientation and confidence that provide the concrete paradigm of what is allowed to count as legitimate

---

[37] *PWD* I, 7; AT X, 359.   [38] *PWD* I, 21; AT X, 381.

cases of knowledge and insight.[39] This is to say that the Cartesian attempt to lay out the rules for knowledge of the object *as such* only allows certain sorts of objects to come forward for scientific treatment: "What is characteristic is that a *completely determinate region of objects* is prefigured on the basis of the sense of the idea of science, objects that alone are such as to come into consideration at all as possible objects of scientific research."[40]

That body of knowledge and the source of Descartes' assurance is mathematics, specifically *arithmetica* and *geometria,* the only disciplines established so far that satisfy the general rule of assenting always only to the *clara et distincta perceptio.* Already in the fourth rule, in echo of the second, we are told that arithmetic and geometry "are far more certain than other disciplines, for these alone meditate on an object so pure and simple that they plainly suppose nothing which experience might render uncertain."[41] It follows from the commitment to the purity and simplicity of mathematical objects, not that we ought only to pursue arithmetic and geometry, but "that those seeking the right path to truth should not occupy themselves with any objects besides those that have a *certitudo equal to these objects.*"[42] The mathematical disciplines offer up examples of the sort of object the fledgling Cartesian scientist is seeking. "They are therefore the easiest and clearest of all the sciences and have just the sort of object we are looking for."[43] When we formalize them, in a manner that admittedly remains obscure in the *Regulae,* we get nothing less than a general science (*mathesis universalis*), which deals solely with pure connections of order and measure, beginning with the simplest elements, given with absolute certainty in a clear and distinct *intuition,* and advancing slowly and serially toward every possible object that "can be known on the basis of others."[44] And it is this *Urmathematik* that tells us what we can legitimately affirm and on what grounds of certainty and evidence we are entitled to give intellectual assent to an *ens* or class of entities as objects of *scientia.* In this respect, the *mathesis universalis* is, as we suggested above, something like a *formal ontology* that determines what counts as an object of scientific thought and, given Descartes's conception of the role of *scientia* in disclosing what

---

[39] "Hence, what is characteristic is that a *completely determinate region of objects* is prefigured on the basis of the sense of the idea of science, objects that are alone such as to come into consideration at all as possible objects of scientific research.... Although the rule contains nothing about objects in terms of content, it nonetheless passes a judgment on the entire realm of possible experience in such a way that it prefigures definite objects, those corresponding to the sense of the rule" (*IPR,* 157; *GA* 17, 207).

[40] *IPR,* 157.   [41] *PWD* I, 12; AT X, 365.   [42] *IPR,* 159; *GA* 17, 210.

[43] *PWD* I, 12; AT X, 365.   [44] *PWD* I, 21; AT X, 381.

is, that simultaneously determines what can be said meaningfully *to be*.[45] As Heidegger tersely observes, "the *ens* reaches its task [or its very being] only through the *detour over the certum*."[46] But this is to say that the quest for certainty *mistakes* the possibilities that are truly its own, possibilities, we might say, of mathematical cognition, by expanding the rule to a *regula generalis*: "And indeed, this mistaking takes place in such a way that it *exceeds itself*."[47]

We find comparable views in the *Meditations on First Philosophy*. The ditch separating the *Regulae* and the *Meditationes* is at once wide and narrow: wide insofar as the metaphysical views published in 1641 are without precedent in the *Regulae*, although they find terse expression in 1637, in the fourth part of the *Discours*; narrow because the quest for certainty that expands into Descartes's metaphysics or first philosophy is clearly delineated in the obscure outline of the method in the *Regulae*.[48] The path traversed in the Cartesian meditations on *prima philosophia*, the path that leads to the discovery of the *cogito sum* as the *certum aliquid*, is set in motion by the *regula generalis* and guided by the earlier reflections on the method of scientific inquiry. Here, too, the question concerns what the mind ought to affirm and on what grounds our cognitive assent can be most assuredly based. Everything that comes before the mind's inquisitive eye is questioned only "in regard to whether it satisfies the rule" of clear, distinct, and indubitable perception.[49] What sort of thing something happens to be – a table, a tool, a number, another embodied mind, and so on – hardly matters, as long as its givenness satisfies the criterion of strict certainty, now construed explicitly as perception beyond every conceivable doubt. What cannot be given in this way is to be supposed false, which is to say: a *non ens*, not really a "being" at all, but only the shadow of what can be demonstrated to be.[50]

This is not the place to rehearse in detail the well-worn path of the first two Meditations or to consider the various objections raised against the arguments and Descartes' own, often ingenious replies. I would like simply

[45] This is not to claim, as Marion does in sections 12–13 of *Sur l'ontologie grise de Descartes*, that order is somehow *created* by the knowing mind, as though the subject were somehow responsible for generating the world; it is just to say that every science involves the *objectification* of an *ens* by the rule-governed *mens*.

[46] *IPR*, 169; *GA* 17, 222.

[47] *IPR*, 170. What it misses in its expansion will be discussed toward the end of this section.

[48] For a helpful discussion of the metaphysics within the *Discours*, see Marion's "What is the Metaphysics within the Method? The Metaphysical Situation of the *Discourse on the Method*" in *Cartesian Questions: Method and Metaphysics*.

[49] *IPR*, 175; *GA* 17, 230.   [50] *IPR*, 176.

to mention two key points that surface in Heidegger's reconstruction of the path and, finally, to discuss briefly what the Cartesian quest for certainty overlooks and why it ought to matter to the otherwise sympathetic interpreter of Descartes.

It is often said that Descartes is partly responsible for the subjective turn in the early modern era, and as an abstract claim this is certainly true. The first truth, which we discover in the Cartesian order of knowledge, is an unassailable truth about ourselves as thinking and doubting beings. But it is easily overlooked that the author of the *Meditationes* does not care about the subject *as such* but only that the *ego sum* survives the crucible of doubt and serves as the epistemic point of departure for unshakable knowledge, first, of the divine being whose restored and reassuring presence overcomes the situation of hyperbolic doubt and, secondly but just as importantly, of the world of *res extensa*, in the end reduced to what Dan Garber nicely calls "the lean, spare objects of geometry."[51] When he has to determine the nature of the *ego* that thinks, he considers as an essential characteristic of the entity "only what satisfies the rule." Everything the *human* ego associates with itself obscurely, everything merely suggestive or probable, is rigorously excluded; and all that remains is an empty point of reference in the intellectual life of the *cogito*. The truth about the *ego* is the bare fact that it is the *certum aliquid* and the desired *fundamentum* of Cartesian science. It happens to be the case that the *ego sum* satisfies the formal requirements of the search, defined by those rules that specify what can count as a legitimate object of cognition, and so a "being" in the relevant sense. Even this matters to Descartes only insofar as the ego certain of itself in the act of thinking itself can be captured in the form of a universally binding proposition from which other propositions can somehow be derived. As Heidegger observes toward the end of his account of the nature of consciousness and the *res cogitans* in Cartesian thought, "the horizon of my own existence now falls prey . . . to the *remotio*."[52]

We have already had occasion to note that the Cartesian description of rigorously scientific *cognitio* is *formal*. Although it is drawn from a particular class of privileged objects, it offers itself as an account of the rudiments of human reason's properly guided and well-grounded activity as such, regardless of the particular objects the reasoning mind might be variably moved to consider and heedless of the particular circumstances of intellectual inquiry and assent. It is an account that reduces the diversity of objects given in diverse ways in untutored experience to a single, all-embracing

[51] Garber, op. cit., 75.   [52] *IPR*, 187; *GA* 17, 243.

cognitive standard, ignores what with Wittgenstein we might call our shared *Bezugssystem*, and sets aside as confused and uncertain the obscure but pregnant Background of our explicit propositional attitudes and beliefs and the rich diversity of objects they encompass. And it does so not by mere oversight but self-consciously and by design: the concrete surroundings (*Umwelt*) we inhabit and the concrete assumptions and insights that, though fallible and revisable, make it possible for us successfully to cope within just these particular circumstances provide no *fundamentum certum* and have, therefore, to be laid aside.[53] For they can give us nothing like the stable intellectual foundation the Cartesian inquirer desires. Even the various *acts* of consciousness – loving and hating, sensing, willing, thinking, desiring, doubting, despairing, and so on – are treated as so many modes of a single, all-encompassing *cogito*, certain merely of itself in the performance of thinking and indifferent to *what* it normally intends and in what (everyday) sort of way. In every case, whether we have to consider a series of numbers or a physical object or a suffering human being, what matters is always only whether a certain sort of *scientia* can be grounded and developed.[54] As Heidegger succinctly observes: "The diversity of content does not interest [Descartes] at all."[55] That we might be said to *know* something about the past or have intimate knowledge of the concrete texture of our *Lebensform* and the commitments embodied in it – although we cannot know them with rigorous certainty or divide what we know into a series of discrete propositional assertions – is inconceivable from the Cartesian standpoint. Where genuine knowledge is concerned, there is no middle ground between complete illumination and darkness.

We have now seen why one might be initially moved to embrace the Cartesian quest for certainty, what speaks for the intellectual asceticism of the *Regulae* and *Meditationes*, and where the project leads. We have offered a brief reconstruction of the path the Cartesian must travel and a brief but, I hope, illuminating account of what, on Heidegger's view, one can expect to discover as legitimate objects of voluntary intellectual *assensus* along the way. But it is now time to catch at least a passing glimpse of what the project leaves behind and to consider why we cannot afford to remain indifferent to the soil neglected by Cartesian science and its philosophical foundations.

---

[53] See *IPR*, 179; *GA* 17, 236.
[54] As Jean-Luc Marion argues in chapter 6 of *Cartesian Questions*, the *alter ego* is never restored in the *Meditationes*. "The *Meditations* renders conceptually impossible the acknowledgment of another person – at least as another *mens* – who would function as an *ego*." (*Cartesian Questions*, 129)
[55] *IPR*, 167; *GA* 17, 220.

Heidegger, like Dewey in his Gifford lectures, frequently associates the philosophical quest for certainty in Descartes (and Husserl) with an anxious and fantastic longing for *security* and the desire to escape from the perilous circumstances and vicissitudes of human life, exposed as it is *in practice* to uncertainty, contingency, unexpected change, and unanticipated danger and disaster.[56] The "care for knowledge known," Heidegger observes, "provides itself a quite specific tranquility and the certitude of an objectively binding accountableness."[57] In the end, there might be good reasons to wage intellectual war against some forms of uncertainty and to shield ourselves from the unsettling reversals that the ancients associated with the fickle forces of *tuchê* and the obscure designs of the gods. This project is, for us fragile, embodied minds, inseparable from the task of becoming the "lords and masters of nature."[58] The more we know with certainty about the way the world of *res extensa* works, the less likely we are to be surprised by what it brings and the readier we will be to respond to encroaching physical threats to life and limb. To know the precise composition of our own bodies, the functions of its organs, and the causes of what afflicts it is to be better placed to care for our mortal coils, perhaps even to free ourselves from preventable disease and to combat the dreaded "infirmity of old age." These aspirations are the worthwhile but *abstract* legacy of the Cartesian project. As noted in the first chapter, if we can know with some measure of certainty and in opposition to the rhetoric of Philip Morris that smoking causes cancer, so much the better for us.

But the anxious quest for certainty also threatens to blind us to other, equally important circumstances, questions, experiences, and even truths. Throughout WS 1923/4, Heidegger mentions in passing a variety of phenomena that come, if at all, only perversely within the limited purview of the various philosophies of consciousness inaugurated by Descartes. What we but dimly understand and call by the name of "love"[59] and its uncertain and shifting targets, but also history and tradition, works of art, ambivalent, everyday life, religious concern, and (of course) *Sein* itself, as something "said in many ways," cannot be fruitfully discussed and articulated if the certainty of human cognition is our only aim: most of these objects cannot be known with absolutely binding certainty at all, and not

---

[56] For the idea of the quest for certainty as fantastic detachment from the real world, see *The Quest for Certainty*, 185.

[57] *IPR*, 61.   [58] *PWD* I, 142–3; AT VI, 62.

[59] In a rare reference to love in the early lecture courses, Heidegger writes, against Husserl and the theoretical appropriation of intentionality, "In itself, it is, indeed, monstrous to designate love a 'consciousness-of-something'" (*IPR*, 44).

merely because we temporarily lack the relevant standpoint or empirical data. They fall under the class of objects that Descartes claims we can know with *moral certainty* or have to accept on the basis of mere custom, and dismisses as philosophically or scientifically impertinent. What can we say with absolute certainty about, say, the meaning of an amorous encounter and commitment or the life and historical importance of Napoleon and his wars or the significance of Kandinsky's artistic experiments or the legitimacy of Christ's religious and moral reforms? And what can we say even about the validity of evolutionary science or neurobiology, if absolutely certain intuition and infallible deduction are our only available criteria of scientific progress and success? The Cartesian standards of scientific *cognitio* and the rule of voluntary assent seem to rule out most of what we consider worthy of our deepest and most sustained philosophical thought and scientific attention.

But in what is perhaps the most provocative stretch of the *Introduction to Phenomenological Research*, Heidegger suggests that the Cartesian quest neglects the truthful connection between what one experiences and values in everyday life and "what one designates as *bonum*" and traditionally associates with the philosophical discipline of *ethics*.[60] If there is one central phenomenon the Cartesian philosopher is ill equipped to handle, it is the nature, scope, and rationality of concrete ethical life and the things we variously pursue as creatures to whom things uncertainly but often passionately matter.[61] As Heidegger observes early on, anticipating what comes into focus more clearly toward the end of the course, the Cartesian tendency "reaches so far that the possibility of a concrete ethical life is made dependent upon the presence of an ethics, as an absolutely binding science."[62]

The Cartesian cannot account, first, for the very choice, or binding force, of a *Lebensform*. We might come to doubt that a particular way of life is valuable or confidently to affirm the vague conception of a better way of life, but this is more likely to be in the light of reasons internal to a certain overarching and still unquestioned *Lebensform* than by way of radical doubt about the validity of every uncertain lifestyle and ethical commitment.

---

[60] *IPR*, 212; *GA* 17, 276.
[61] But see John Marshall's valuable account of Descartes' moral philosophy in *Descartes's Moral Theory* for an appreciative look at the philosopher's contribution to ethics.
[62] *IPR*, 62.

The Cartesian is also poorly placed to understand how concrete deliberation within a particular form of life works: for it is pretty clear on both Aristotelian and Kantian models that the moral agent never enters ethical situations naively.[63] We come to certain circumstances with a robust but often tacit sense of what is likely to be salient in them and what in general ought in similar circumstances to be done and what, from a Cartesian point of view, can only look like untutored confidence in what we uncertainly experience. This sort of trust in what cannot be clearly and distinctly perceived is not an intellectual or moral defect we may hope eventually to overcome, but a constitutive feature of concrete ethical life itself, trained upon relatively unique and shifting circumstances of thought and thoughtful action and, as we shall see, concerned about particulars. If we had to wait for clear and distinct perceptions to surface, we would hardly begin to act. The Cartesian quest for certainty is *in ethical practice* a recipe for paralyzing *uncertainty*.

Cartesian thought also makes little room for the concrete perception of *suffering* others as the targets of moral concern.[64] For we can never be absolutely certain *that* the experience of another is as we consider it to be: it remains perpetually open that what we call pain is really pleasure and what we take to be a reason to respond with sympathy or philanthropic action is just a perception of the mechanical movements of *res extensa* and not evidence of an embodied mind in need. And so, adhesion to the salient characteristics of ethical life, the existence of others and ourselves in what Heidegger calls the *Mitwelt*, roughly, "the world shared," like the commitment to the senses and the bodies they reveal, falls prey to the *remotio* and, to judge by the train of thought worked out in the *Meditationes*, is never to be restored with Cartesian confidence and self-assurance. In short, and bringing each of these suggestions together in a "formal indication" of Heidegger's topic, what is neglected in Descartes and his descendants is nothing less than "*the genuine object of concern: human existence.*"[65] This is also to say: the truth embedded in a life of human concern, beyond the quest for (mere) certainty – call it ethical truth.

---

[63] See my "Morality and Sensibility in Kant" and the fourth chapter of Barbara Herman's *The Practice of Moral Judgment*.

[64] This is not a conclusion Heidegger reaches in WS 1923/4. But it is consistent with what he has to say elsewhere about the shared world of our concern.

[65] *IPR*, 66. A few pages later, "*Care about knowledge known has excluded human existence as such from any possibility of being encountered.* History is degraded down one more level as a fund of material and collection of examples for philosophical notions. The tendency to get a grip on human existence is severed" (*IPR*, 68).

Recovering Ethical Truth in Aristotle's Ethics

In *Ethics without Ontology*, Hilary Putnam shrewdly reminds us that the criticism of tradition is an easy matter when we refuse to accept the responsibility to work out viable alternatives to the ideas and practices we attack.[66] Heidegger's dissatisfaction with "the modern" is not a reactionary protest: we have seen that it rests upon an acknowledgment of the power of the Cartesian project in general, a compelling account of its origins, and a precise interpretation of its nature and scope. We shall see that, in the long run, it involves the qualified rehabilitation of a richer conception of truth worked out by Aristotle, and tailored in part to the concretely situated and variable life of the ethical agent, interested in the good (*agathon*) toward which all human endeavors strive.

It is hardly surprising that a thinker in search of an alternative to the Cartesian restriction of truth to what can be known with unqualified certainty, and as historically informed as the author of *Sein und Zeit* clearly was, would look for philosophical inspiration and nourishment to Aristotle's account of the varieties of *alêtheuein* in the sixth book of the *Nicomachean Ethics*.[67] For it is precisely Aristotle, good scientist though he was, who recognized the limits of theoretical inquiry and situated the truth of *epistêmê* in the larger field of human life and *praxis*: if we ought in science to be satisfied with nothing less than infallible insight into eternal verities, in the finite life of human action and social intercourse, the quest for certainty is naturally bound to come up short. Nothing prevents us from thinking we've got it; but Aristotle argues persuasively that we will be mistaken. To look for Cartesian certainty in the world of everyday life and action is to make an egregious category mistake. The grounds of ethical commitment and confidence are to be sought elsewhere, in a sort of insight that has little in common with the results of mathematical reasoning, infallible intuition and deduction.

Heidegger lectured on Aristotle for the first time at length and in real depth in SS 1922 and again in SS 1924,[68] in a course devoted to the basic

---

[66] *Ethics without Ontology*, 113.

[67] Heidegger's debt to Aristotle is discussed extensively throughout Kisiel's *The Genesis of Heidegger's "Being and Time"* and by Franco Volpi in *"Being and Time*: A 'Translation' of the *Nicomachean Ethics*?" and Walter Brogan in "The Place of Aristotle in the Development of Heidegger's Phenomenology." Both essays appear in *Reading Heidegger from the Start: Essays in His Earliest Thought*.

[68] See *GA* 62, *Phänomenologische Interpretationen ausgewählter Abhandlungen des Aristoteles zur Ontologie und Logik*, and *GA* 18, *Grundbegriffe der Aristotelischen Philosophie*.

concepts of Aristotelian philosophy and the experiential roots of philosophical concept-formation; but the most extensive engagement with
Aristotle's account of truth comes in the expansive opening chapters of a
lecture course held in WS 1924/5 on Plato's *Sophist*. It is from this well-
known text, published in 1992 as volume 19 of the *Gesamtausgabe*, that
I would like somewhat freely to draw.

If we look to WS 1924/5 for evidence of blind hostility to the modern
and nostalgia for more ancient philosophical paradigms, comparable to
Heidegger's later infatuation with the world of the pre-Socratics and its
surviving fragments, we are likely to be disappointed. There are two closely
related intentions that animate this important stretch of the course. The
first is to offer an appreciative interpretation of Aristotle's subtle analysis of
the five ways of *alêtheuein* in the sixth book of the *Nicomachean Ethics* and
to draw out some of the implications of taking seriously what Aristotle calls
phronêsis, a human sort of wisdom that deals with matters and circumstances that can always be otherwise. It is here where Heidegger discovers a
powerful alternative to detached Cartesian *cognitio* and more recent conceptions of knowing, in a model of pre-theoretical truth – call it *alêtheia*, or
veritas embedded in *vita*[69] – he will qualify and reinterpret considerably
over the years, but never abandon.[70] In this respect, he is an important
precursor of more recent and contemporary virtue ethics in America
and abroad and a compelling voice in the debate over the nature of
practical reason and the sort of truth we can expect to win in the context
of practical life.

The second aim is to place in sharp relief a troubling *tension* in
Aristotle's account of *eudaimonia* between the demands of phronetic
excellence and the competing claims of *sophia* or contemplative
excellence in the pursuit of the *human* good. It is here where Heidegger
discovers an ancient anticipation of the detached stances of modern
scientific and ethical theory (canvassed in the last chapter), and the
dubious predilection for stability, unalterable necessity, and a mummified
eternity that Nietzsche and Dewey, among others, associate with the
escapist tendencies of the entire philosophical tradition; and it is as a critic
of the Aristotelian stance on the nature of human life at its best that he
shows himself to be no slavish admirer of antiquity.

---

[69] For the (Augustinian) relation of *veritas* and *vita* and the task of embedding the former in the latter,
see *IPR*, 87.
[70] In "Being-There and Being-True According to Aristotle," Heidegger observes, tersely, "What we
shall find is that truth is not a characteristic of judgment but instead is a fundamental determination
of the Dasein of human beings themselves" (*Becoming Heidegger*, 220).

Toward the end of our Heideggerian account of the Cartesian quest for certainty and its limits we recorded the inability of the demand for clear, distinct, and absolutely certain perceptions and ideas to respond with intelligence and sensitivity to the agonizing difficulties of finite deliberation and concrete human choice. If we hold ourselves at arm's length from the circumstances in which we find ourselves concretely situated and withhold our voluntary assent from everything we discover to be uncertain, we are not better and more "impartially" placed to deliberate and decide, but deprived of the fruitful perspectives and tentative assumptions that make ethical life, commitment, and reflection possible in the first place. We are deprived of the sustaining Background and context of our active lives, and ill equipped to converse about the practical alternatives we routinely face. For conversation and deliberation about the requirements of our social practices require at least a tentative intellectual commitment to appearances that cannot be known with certainty and can always be determined otherwise. Practical life itself demands our assent to certain truths that fall outside the scope of scientific understanding. As Cartesians, we might be better able to explain the complex behavior of an animal or to analyze the eccentric path of a planet or to clarify the circulatory function of the heart (although this is itself debatable); but we will remain ethically immature and politically inept, great theoreticians, perhaps, but blind and stunted moral agents. Or we will simply borrow our ethical orientation and convictions uncritically from the uncontested customs and habits of our contemporaries and blindly follow suit. This is the cost of our refusal to acknowledge something like the irreducible truth of *praxis*. It is a price Aristotle and Heidegger are unwilling to pay.

What Heidegger finds compelling in the Aristotelian account is not merely that it captures and embodies the moral point of view or argues abstractly for the primacy of practical reason over its theoretical counterpart, but that it is willing to acknowledge that "the ways in which the world is uncovered [in human life] are not all indifferently on the same plane."[71] In the sixth book of the *Nicomachean Ethics*, Aristotle distinguishes between two broad modes of *logon echon*, having reason, language, or thought: the *epistêmonikon* is the *logos* that contributes to the cultivation of rigorous knowledge and infallible insight, while the *logistikon* concerns "the development of deliberation" in uncertain circumstances of making and doing.[72] Under the former heading Aristotle places *epistêmê* and

---

[71] *Plato's "Sophist"* (hereafter *PS*), 21.   [72] *PS*, 19.

sophia, under the latter *technê* and *phronêsis*.[73] Both *epistêmê* and *sophia* deal with matters eternal and necessary and traffic among the unalterable *archai* of the non-human world of plants and animals, stones and gods, a world of things we discover to be what they are prior to and without the help of human making and doing.[74] What we long to know must always be what it is, regardless of whether we happen to know it or not: for if something alters after we have come truly to know it, if it changes *exô tou theôrein*, our cognitive view becomes false and our knowledge unreliable. But acquired knowledge cannot turn into ignorance. If our cognitive aspirations were in danger of running into the unlimited or indefinite and failing to hit their stable targets, we could not be said to know anything at all, but to arrive at best at relatively settled *doxai*, to be replaced by other, temporarily stable opinions. When it comes to knowing in the most rigorous and proper sense, we rightly seek the safety and reliability of the unchanging.

In Aristotle's account of the nature of cognitive striving, philosophy, like any other reflective activity aimed at understanding something better, originates in *aporia* (impasse, puzzlement, perplexity).[75] The search for knowledge, as opposed to mere *doxa* (opinion) and *pistis* (belief), is a response to the recognition that the well-worn tracks of a once-reliable understanding can no longer be traveled in the naïve manner of pre-reflective life.[76] The growth of *theoretical* understanding is, or eventually involves, the replacement of a potentially unruly conception, or opinion, of the proper objects of *epistêmê* with a stable and reliable awareness of the way things really and truly are, an awareness grounded in simple perception (*noein*) of eternal and unchanging first principles, and developing in the steady advance from what lies closest to us and appears at first to be intelligible without further ado to what lies furthest from the gaze of common sense but is intelligible in itself.[77] Inquiry reaches its fitting end when the mind discovers the *archê* or "first principle" of the matter in question.[78]

---

[73] I am leaving out of account, for the moment, Aristotle's puzzling remarks on *nous*.

[74] For an account of Aristotelian science and its relation to the *archai*, see Irwin's *Aristotle's First Principles*.

[75] "Now the one who is at an impasse and wonders feels that he is ignorant" (*Metaphysics* I.2).

[76] A brief account of the origins of *epistêmê* in the experience of puzzlement or impasse, and the idea of scientific progress as being released from perplexity, is given in Aristotle's *Metaphysics*, Book Three, chapter 1.

[77] Aristotle, *Nicomachean Ethics*, Book One, chapter 4.

[78] For definitions of *archê*, see the first chapter of *Metaphysics*, Book Five.

An account that passes for scientific or philosophical truth can, of course, be false, and for a variety of reasons. We might be mistaken about what constitutes an *archê* (the result of *epagôgê* might, for instance, be based upon limited experience and hasty generalization); the derivation of one proposition from a set of propositions might prove upon closer examination to be faulty, a risk that increases as our arguments grow in bulk and complexity and the observations upon which they rest fade from memory; and judgments based upon insufficiently examined perceptions might be mistaken. We are neither beasts, whose perceptions lack "discourse of reason," nor gods, who simply perceive the truth immediately; and so our knowledge is discursive and thereby fallible.[79] But the ideal of perfect cognition, of knowledge without remainder and a knower no longer groping restlessly after objects cloaked in darkness, persists as the guiding aim of any serious scientific pursuit. As Socrates observes to Euthyphro, it would be better for our speeches to stay still and to be placed unmoved (*akinêtôs*).[80] The risk of movement diminishes as the object of thought becomes better illuminated and clarified. To know in the fullest sense is to see things without shadows, to bring *ta phainomena* fully into the light of day (*phôs*); and this means to come finally to relate to what "cannot be other than it is."[81] Even perception, which relates to particulars, is a primitive stage of knowledge, precisely because it is no mere flux of sensations, but a first grasp of the differences between things. To know an object of perception is to bring the swarm of things to a standstill, to see the *katholou* in the particular, and eventually to pin down the multiple lines of causation that intersect in each thing according to its *genos*.[82]

Ideally nothing should escape the comprehensive vision of the philosopher whose gaze embraces nothing less than "the whole of being."[83] Those fortunate souls gifted with a nimble intelligence, a reliable and capacious memory, sharply differentiating perceptual organs, and a susceptibility to wonder can, provided they diligently cultivate that part of human nature that is best and most akin to the gods, reasonably hope for a life no longer, or at least less, constrained by the cares and concerns and competing

---

[79] For the same reason, Aristotle insists in the *Politics* that human beings require the *polis* in order to realize their full potential. See *Politics*, book one, chapter 2.

[80] *Euthyphro*, 11d. This is Socrates' reply to Euthyphro's complaint that each of his suggestions "somehow always keeps going around for us and isn't willing to stay where we place it" (11b).

[81] *Posterior Analytics* I.2.

[82] For the image of bringing the flux of particulars to a stand in a process that terminates in the genuine universal, see the final chapter of the *Posterior Analytics*.

[83] *Metaphysics* IV.3, 1005b.

spheres of value that burden the untutored slave of necessity. As the pursuit of wisdom draws closer to genuine *sophia*, the knowing individual draws as near as possible to the untroubled insight of the gods,[84] whose tranquil gaze takes in nothing less than the eternal and unchanging order of things.[85]

But it is the mark of a defective education to seek the same sort of *akribeia* and *alêtheia* in every area of human life and thought. *Technê* and *phronêsis*, unlike *epistêmê* and *sophia*, disclose the salient features of everything that *endechomen allôs echein*, both things we have to make and what we have variably to do. The table we wish to fabricate has to be brought into being out of materials lying more or less to hand: the world of *technê* is a world of things we have to shape and produce in the light of a certain *eidos* that captures in advance the object's form and function. The thing we are about to do (*prattein*) has variably and contingently to be done: the world of *praxis* is a world of things we have to accomplish in the shifting light of a *phronetic* awareness of what is possible, desirable, or demanded, not in general but in *this* particular circumstance, on *this* particular occasion, in *this* particular way, and for *this* particular purpose. To measure each of these activities in terms of a single, overarching standard of knowledge and truth is to do violence to the differentiated world of human life and experience: knowing, making, and doing are three irreducible ways of relating to and disclosing features of the world of human concern. Our various activities are *truthful* in more ways than one.

This short rehearsal of the modes of *alêtheuein* is already enough to distinguish generally between an Aristotelian approach to truth, which allows considerable diversity among our truthful experiences and their various objects, and its Cartesian counterpart. But what is the specific alternative to the Cartesian stance Heidegger discovers in the Aristotelian explication and defense of *phronêsis* as the *aretê* of practical life?[86] The short answer is: *phronêsis* is the knowing ability or developed intellectual capacity to live and act well and to deliberate effectively within the diverse

---

[84] For the "divinity" of *sophia* or the science that exists for its own sake and knows the ultimate *aitiai* of things, see *Metaphysics* I.2.

[85] According to *Metaphysics* I.2, the acquisition of knowledge puts an end even to the experience of wonder (*thaumazein*). The mind that understands why things are as they are is no longer puzzled or perplexed and finds nothing wonderful in things.

[86] I leave *phronêsis* untranslated here and in what follows for the (unsatisfying) reason that I'm not sure how to translate it. "Prudence" certainly won't do, for reasons that should become clear below. "Practical insight" is better, but *phronêsis* doesn't include any reference to practice or the practical. And "wisdom" (Rowe's choice in the recent Oxford edition of the text) is the only term we've got to translate *sophia* (which Rowe translates as "intellectual accomplishment").

settings of human life, to realize something like the *human* good over the course of life as a whole, and to help others as far as possible to do the same, all the while acknowledging the limits of what one individual can do for another and knowing that one might fail to hit the intended target, for a variety of unpredictable reasons. But this reply will not get us very far.

From an initially compelling point of view, *phronêsis* seems to resemble the expert knowledge of the competent technician, skilled in a particular craft and conversant with the reliable qualities and characteristics of her material. For the *phronimos* seems to know something that the unskilled does not, namely, how to act well and to deliberate about what ought to be done; and she seems to know better than her imprudent counterparts what means to employ in the pursuit of certain ends. This is why Aristotle classifies "practical wisdom" as a species of intellectual virtue. Her materials are just the conditions and various circumstances of human action and the diverse goods toward which her life moves; she apparently knows these things as well as the good craftsman is acquainted with the salient characteristics of wood, stone, and metal. The *phronimos* and the technician are both competent where the rest of us are frequently confused or at a loss to know what to do: like a good doctor, the person of practical insight knows her way around in an important area of human concern (living and acting well) and both are routinely able to realize the *telê* (aims, purposes, or ends) of their intentions, health in the one case, human flourishing and success in various specialized pursuits in the other. It is natural to expect someone who knows what to do and how best to act in her own setting to be able, in a moment of contemplative detachment, to tell the rest of us what to do and how to deliberate and choose well in comparable circumstances. It is natural also to think that the successful should be able to detach themselves from their success and inform the rest of us how it was achieved, not contingently and uncertainly but *in principle*. A good novelist should be able to teach the fledgling writer how to compose the best and most interesting plots and how to render human character and circumstance in a captivating and compelling way. The successful politician should be well placed to help the novice get elected. A couple about to celebrate fifty fruitful years of marriage ought to be able to provide a recipe for the happily married life. If they cannot do this for us, we are likely to find fault with their own expressive powers, as if to say: a more eloquent success story could be told by someone with greater verbal skill. The industry of self-help books feeds upon the expectation of and hope for a teachable vision of *eudaimonia*. Living well certainly *seems* to be a technical and teachable affair.

But in Heidegger's Aristotelian view, how best to respond to our unsettled predicament and how far we can be led by the teachings of others is a fantasy. If the fantasy were our reality, we would probably idolize the unruly and longingly imagine another, less certain and predictable world, where some fail and others manage somehow to succeed: for part of the thrill and excitement of doing something well stems from the initial uncertainty of the outcome. We do not really have a coherent picture of what we want when we attempt to make our lives over in the image of a technical affair. We can, at best, deliberate together; but this is not equivalent to taking the other's place, when his own life is at issue, or saying something that would apply to anyone, anywhere.

Phronêsis and *technê* are comparable only to the precise extent that each concerns matters that are not invariable. *Phronêsis* cannot be taught as a subject of technical consideration and skill for the simple reason that the object of practical insight is not, like the object of artful activity, an *object* that has to be made in accordance with reliable rules but a *life* that has to be lived in relation to values that have uncertainly to be pursued in obscure situations of thought and thoughtful action. As Heidegger makes the Aristotelian point, "we call *phronimos* the one who deliberates in the right way *poia pros to eu zên holôs*, regarding 'what is conducive to the right mode of being of Dasein as such and as a whole.'"[87] The object of *phronêsis* is something that can be otherwise, but the insight bears always upon the deliberator herself, as someone seeking some good and having her own action in view. "On the other hand, the deliberation of *technê* relates simply to what contributes to the production of something else, namely, the *ergon*, e.g., a house."[88] We may not be able to ensure that just anyone will be able to make a decent table as well as a master craftsman and there might even be something like *phronêsis* in the development of technical skill, but the technician can provide reliable insight into how *in general* good tables are to be made, what sort of material will best serve the purpose of production, and what concrete steps should be taken in the work of fabrication. The ability to formalize technical insight into a series of relatively discrete and certain bodily movements is what allows for machines to make tables and chairs as well as, if not better than, the most skilled of human artisans. For the object of *technê* is a physical object that stands *para* the technical activity that brings it reliably into being. The know-how may be the fruit of our own explorations and experiments, but the movements of the body can be faithfully imitated by a non-human

[87] *PS*, 34.   [88] *PS*, 34.

artifice. Well-designed machines are often better able to manipulate the material world than their merely human prototypes.

But no mechanical device will inform us about what constitutes the good life and how best to live. For this insight requires time and patience and a rich experience of the various possibilities of human life: it demands, in short, the development of a space of inwardness that reflects what we have come gradually to think about the shape of the good *for us*. Even if a machine could calculate the best course of action in any given circumstance, it would still be up to us to act in relation to concerns and matters of human interest that no machine could possibly reach or register on its own. No mechanical contrivance can serve as a surrogate for the hard work of everything we richly associate with the difficult task of living out our lives in a world where we are often confronted with stark alternatives in competing spheres of value and concern.[89] The *phronimos* cannot offer a reliable formula of successful practice simply because deliberation about human life *as such* and as a potentially integrated *whole* has no stable object or *eidos* in view. Deliberating well must take into account a diversity of human "materials" and interests and competing values, and always concerns concrete circumstances and shifting conceptions of the good, the point of which is to best realize what we take to be worthwhile in our concrete and reflective practices. The *phronimos* might have to retrace her steps or retract a previously settled conviction: the person of practical wisdom is no infallible ruler or guide. But to revise one's plans or to alter a course of life insightfully and not haphazardly is also the mark of unteachable *phronêsis*.

But in what sense can *phronêsis* be said to embody some *truth*? Once we have acknowledged that the *phronimos* has no absolute standards or infallible and general insights to communicate to the rest of us, we might be inclined to attribute her success to raw talent combined with fortunate circumstances or to exclude even talent from the equation and simply ascribe happiness in life to sheer good luck, distributed blindly and randomly like success in some cosmic lottery. But this is not how *phronêsis* looks from the inside, so to speak. If we truly believe that living well is a matter of behaving as the wind appears to blow, *eikê*, as Jocasta unconvincingly advises her husband to think and live in Sophocles' famous play, there is no room in our view of life for anything like experienced practical

---

[89] The critical implications of Heidegger's (Aristotelian) views for the project of artificial intelligence have been explored by Hubert Dreyfus in his commentary on the first division of *Being and Time*, *Being-in-the-World*, 117–119.

insight. A considered view of practical success should make *some* room for the blind workings of mere chance, operating in a world where the talented and insightful often sadly fail; but even the lucky sometimes make poor use of the opportunities fortunate circumstances bring, and the *phronimos* often succeeds *despite* obvious misfortune. If good luck were a sufficient cause of happiness and success, there would be happier and more successful individuals in the observable world than there are. Those who succeed robustly and routinely must be on to something like a truth about themselves and the world in which they have to live.

If we locate truth in the isolated assertion or statement, as Descartes, Frege, Lotze, and Quine, among many others, are wont to do, there is little truth to be discovered in phronetic insight.[90] Or if there is propositional truth in *phronêsis*, it collapses into the teachable truths of technical skill or scientific knowledge and *phronêsis* itself is just another name for *technê* or *epistêmê*.[91] If, however, truth is something like the way some things become concretely visible in the finite life of human action, then *phronêsis*, too, can be said to be true, if not certain, despite our inability to convey what we know in abstract formulas and atomic assertions. In the moment of phronetic awareness, something like the concrete and relatively unique situation of our engaged and embodied agency becomes apparent; and the agent herself becomes transparent to herself as the one for whom something important is at stake, not as an object of disinterested contemplation but precisely as something to be accomplished that depends on what she is prepared to do and is able for now to see *within* the clarified setting of her involvement. "Hence the task is to uncover ... the concrete situation, which is at first hidden, and in that way to make the action itself transparent."[92] The truth of *phronêsis* "is not an autonomous one, but rather one that serves to guide action."[93] It is always somehow tied to what in particular and concretely the agent is attempting to do – to write a play, to make a speech, to choose a mate, to convince a friend to adopt a view, to complete a doctoral dissertation, and so on. "That is, the disclosure of *phronêsis* is ... carried out with a constant regard toward the situation of the acting being, of the one who is deciding here and now."[94]

---

[90] See Quine's *Pursuit of Truth* and Dahlstrom's account of Heidegger's rejection of "the logical prejudice" in *Heidegger's Concept of Truth*.

[91] Heidegger's commitment to the truth of *phronêsis* partly explains his long-standing opposition to the reduction of truth as such (or what he subsequently calls "primordial truth") to the truth captured and conveyed in the *Satz*, the truth of detached propositional assertions.

[92] *PS*, 102.   [93] *PS*, 37.   [94] *PS*, 96.

Its disclosures are also always in some sense new: however much one situation might resemble another in content and general structure, the passage of time, the accumulation of insight and experience, and the difference between one person and another ensure that no two situations are in every respect the same.[95] "Everything directly experienced is," in the words of a famous American pragmatist, "qualitatively unique; it has its own focus about which subject-matter is arranged, and this focus never exactly recurs. While every such situation shades off indefinitely, or is not sharply marked off from others, yet the pattern of arrangement of content is never exactly twice alike."[96] *Phronêsis* reveals "an *eschaton* which at every moment is always different."[97] This is why every genuine situation poses a problem to be tackled: if every situation were like every other, "there would be no such thing as a situation which is problematic."[98] Every situation would be grasped in a detached, aesthetic vision, its object a completed whole, and the spectator left with nothing to do save to look on and admire. There would be no risk of failure, but no promise of possible achievement.[99] We would know with certainty what we ought to do, with the finality of divine providence.

But this is not our world. The gods can be assumed to know infallibly what will be, but the rest of us have to wait for what the future has to bring, and ought to expect to be unsettled. Every genuine discovery in the uncertain life of *praxis* has something novel and surprising about it.[100] We are always free to classify situations as instances of a general type, involving "the standardized objects of reference designated by common nouns,"[101] and to act accordingly in a stereotyped world; but as long as we remain

---

[95] To say that phronetic truth is always somehow new is *not* to endorse a conception of truth that makes no room for learning and experience, as Lafont, among others, argues in *Heidegger, Language, and World-Disclosure*. We may not be able to experiment with ourselves in controlled circumstances, but we can certainly *develop* practical insight and learn more about ourselves along the way. As Heidegger notes, *phronêsis* is a *task* and a *praktikê hexis*, not a given, and its cultivation in relation to the *prakton agathon* requires time, patience, and practice (*PS*, 95).

[96] *The Quest for Certainty*, 187.

[97] *PS*, 109. Again: "*Phronêsis* is the inspection of the this-here-now, the inspection of the concrete momentariness of the transient situation. As *aisthêsis*, it is a look of an eye in the blink of an eye, a momentary look at what is momentarily concrete, which as such can always be otherwise" (*PS*, 111–12).

[98] *The Quest for Certainty*, 187.   [99] Ibid., 195.

[100] This is one reason why Heidegger associates *phronêsis* with "the phenomenon of conscience" (*PS*, 39). In *Sein und Zeit*, conscience is said to be always in each case *mine* and to bear always upon myself and the unique situation in which I discover myself to be called upon to act. In Plato's *"Sophist"* and in *Sein und Zeit*, conscience or *phronêsis* is what makes the situation of action accessible, concretely and uniquely and as my own.

[101] *The Quest for Certainty*, 189.

attuned to the peculiarity of our circumstances and their unfinished objects, we will be suspicious of every hasty generalization and "averaged set of properties and relations" and reluctant to form unthinking habits.[102] And because action aims always at something good *for us*, the failure to respond to fresh situations with flexible insight and attunement and to give our assent to the contextualized truths we discover in practice "is a personal shortcoming."[103]

On the Aristotelian view Heidegger seems prepared to accept, then, that there is a truth in practice and ethical deliberation as well as in scientific theory and contemplation; and the former cannot be reduced to an obscure, deficient, or temporary variation of the latter. There are some truths that only show up for the thoughtfully engaged agent, sensitive to her own situations and concerns, willing to live with and to act on fallible insight, and happy to revise her plans and convictions as circumstances alter; and some truths that can be detached from the contingent circumstances of their discovery. Once we come to know that two and two make four, we can always return to this stable truth: our enduring knowledge of it is in no way affected by the further course of experience. As Kant observes in the first *Critique*, there is no room for mere opinion in some branches of mathematics. But knowing that it would be good to pursue a career in law or medicine and knowing how to argue for a particular stance on a particular legal case cannot be detached from how things currently and circumstantially appear to be.

Our ethical and practical awareness and concerns might be roughly guided by invariant principles and relatively certain and stable truths, as Kant, Rawls, Putnam, and others insist, but our ethical intentions move toward particular individuals encountered in unique situations of thought and thoughtful action. There is something that it is like to inhabit a particular ethical space of reason and truth, and there is something that it is like to pursue scientific understanding. Every effort to eliminate the uniqueness of the forms of reason and truth that give limit and shape to our ethical and practical lives, whether in theory or in practice, is probably a misunderstanding. If the reform is limited to the spaces of mere theory, it is a harmless philosophical aberration; if it is translated into practice, the consequences are not always so benign.

Aristotle's account of the varieties of truth and the diversity of its objects can be interpreted as an ancient protest against the hegemony of the theoretical and scientific understanding of practical life and developed

---

[102] Ibid., 189.   [103] *PS*, 38.

for our purposes as a compelling alternative to detached and uniform Cartesian insight; but as we know, the author of the *Nicomachean Ethics* makes an abrupt shift toward the end of his account of the structure of human flourishing that resembles the Platonic commitment to a detached life of theoretical contemplation, a swerve that, if taken seriously, alters the meaning of the work as a whole and transforms how we view and evaluate ethical life itself. For Aristotle seems to suggest in Book Ten that if we could choose between a life of uncertain practical activity and a life of untroubled, leisured, and autonomous contemplation, we would be fools to choose the former over the latter: at best, the life of practical excellence serves the interests of a superior and more divine way of life that occasionally transcends the conditions of mortal activity and realizes our cognitive aspirations more purely and securely than the life of ethical excellence is able to do. A life of merely practical activity is carefully weighed and found to be deficient and second-rate; the truly happy human life is contemplative, is more like the life of the gods, at once continuously active, loved and pursued for its own sake, leisurely, self-sufficient and complete, and more in keeping with "the best thing in us" than merely practical activity can ever be. If the bulk of the work is meant to valorize and explicate the structure of a virtuous life of practical activity, political collaboration, and the close ties of *philia*, the account of *eudaimonia* in the final chapters of the tenth book unsettle our confidence in the ethical life and point to another organized way of life (*bios*) that stands somewhat scornfully aloof from ordinary human action and its humble circumstances. *Phronetic* excellence and the engaged life of *praxis*, while superior to a life devoted to sensual pleasure or the hollow accumulation of wealth, finally give way to the untroubled life of *sophia*. Other modes of human knowing are more necessary and urgent than *sophia*, but none is better.[104] The virtues of practice remain in place only in order to support the detached, contemplative pursuit of something that lies just beyond the merely human and belongs most properly to the gods. "With regard to *alêtheuein* ... *sophia* has the priority."[105]

Ethical truths may not be reducible to theoretical insights, and *phronêsis* is certainly weightier than mere theory, "the gravest and most decisive knowledge,"[106] but the truths of contemplation are more satisfying than the truths of mere *praxis*. If we wish to know our place in the *kosmos* as a whole, beyond the contingent *circumstances* of life in the *polis*, we cannot appeal to the shifting and circumstantial insights of mere *phronêsis*.

---

[104] *PS*, 92.   [105] *PS*, 92.   [106] *PS*, 93.

We must make the laborious ascent to a non-human view from above and see things (or attempt to see things) as the untroubled gods behold them.[107] And from this point of view, as Homer already saw, merely human affairs are as fleeting as the wind. The tragic and lyric poets might counsel mortal thoughts for mortal creatures, but poets often lie. As Jonathan Lear makes the Aristotelian point in his psychoanalytic reading of the *Nicomachean Ethics*: "What is best about being human is the opportunity to break out of being human. Or: to be most human is to break out of the ordinary conditions of human life."[108] And while some of Aristotle's recent defenders attempt to mitigate the swerve away from *phronêsis* toward *sophia*, Heidegger squarely confronts the tension in the Aristotelian account of the good life and the final aspiration to shake off the conditions of mortal life.[109] On Heidegger's view, even Aristotle, the great advocate of practical life, succumbs to the lure of what Nagel calls "the view from nowhere."[110] If Heidegger is prepared to take the Cartesian to task for endorsing an escapist demand for unshakable certainty, the professor at the University of Marburg is equally ready to challenge the Stagirite for refusing to stay put in the elusive world of our uncertain affairs.

Concluding Remarks

Phronetic ethics and its ontological interpretation may not provide sufficient moral and political protection against the lure of fascism. If you are suspicious of Cartesian detachment and generally binding ethical and philosophical truths, altogether beyond what a rich experiential life has to deliver, and wonder what value there might be in the enlightened idea of universal humanity and cosmopolitan citizenship, you might, in certain circumstances, flirt with political agendas that stress our differences at the expense of what we have in common and collective ideals that build upon the values embodied in a unique, *volkish* way of life. You might become intolerant, disdainful of everything public, defensive, and uncritically committed to your own untested ways. If you enter the political arena,

---

[107] As Heidegger notes, *phronêsis* would be equivalent to *sophia* if the human being were the *ariston* in the world. But "there are still other, much more divine beings ... than human Dasein" (*PS*, 94): "For Aristotle and the Greeks, as well as for the tradition, beings in the proper sense are what is always existing, what is constantly already there" (*PS*, 94).

[108] *Happiness, Death, and the Remainder of Life*, 55.

[109] See Martha Nussbaum's argument in *The Fragility of Goodness* and Ackrill's "Aristotle on *Eudaimonia*" in *Essays on Aristotle's Ethics*, ed. Amélie Rorty. Kraut, among others, argues for a coherent view of the good life throughout the *Nicomachean Ethics* in *Aristotle on the Human Good*.

[110] Nagel, *The View from Nowhere*.

you will be unlikely to embrace the public criteria and intellectual stand-ards of free and open dialogue and debate. For these reasons, it may prove desirable to weave into the phronetic account a conception of practical reason guided by more generally applicable principles of action, slightly detached from the local and particular, and aimed at a larger circle of significant others.

But the philosophical trajectory sketched in this chapter might also be integrated into a philosophical defense of the virtues we often associate with a liberal democratic way of life. For it now seems more obvious that concrete deliberation and choice, *regardless of your politics* or religious orientation or general *Lebensform,* are poorly conceived on a Cartesian model of rationality and better captured and characterized along the Aristotelian lines espoused by Heidegger in the opening pages of the lecture course on Plato's *Sophist*.[111] And it should now appear more compelling to grant that the philosophical difference between the two accounts of what it is to reason well can be fruitfully developed in the language of competing views on *truth*. Heidegger's critique of Descartes and his creative (and critical) appropriation of Aristotle *can* be taken in an unsavory political direction, as Heidegger clearly and lamentably does in the 30s, but this is a road not taken by the philosopher in Marburg.

---

[111] See Charles Taylor's appreciative remarks on Heidegger's philosophical importance in "Overcoming Epistemology" and "Lichtung or Lebensform: Parallels between Heidegger and Wittgenstein," both reprinted in *Philosophical Arguments*.

CHAPTER 3

Excursus on Being and the Good

Categories in Absentia

The charge that *Being and Time* fails to offer an account of the human good – that it either ignores the ethical or, what's worse, casts doubt upon the ontological value of moral relations – is among the weightiest objections to have been raised against Heidegger's fundamental ontology. It underwrites Levinas's attempts to replace ontology with ethics as "first philosophy,"[1] and it finds a voice in Tugendhat's claim that "the moral, and indeed the normative as such, does not appear [in *Being and Time*]."[2] If fair, the complaint is targeting something truly remarkable about Heidegger's *opus magnum*. A work devoted to our own distinctive way of being, which the philosopher himself calls *care* – a work that appears to privilege the practical life of engagement and finding things to be significant or "letting them be relevant"[3] over the theoretical life of contemplation and the detached seeing of mere things and the relations, causal or otherwise, that hold between them – has nothing to say about what is arguably among the most important facts about us *as agents*. We do all things *sub specie boni*, and this doing is tied to an image, concept, or idea of what we ought to do or, perhaps more profoundly, to be. (The language of *Sollen* is, I think, even rarer in the early work than the language of *das Gute*, *agathon*, and *bonum*, except in cases that are idiomatic ["It should

---

[1] I have in mind *Totality and Infinity*, of course, although Levinas's worries about Heidegger's ontology find expression in so many places that it is probably fair to say that Heidegger is his chief interlocutor throughout.

[2] Tugendhat, "Wir sind nicht fest gedrahtet. Heidegger's 'Man' und die Tiefdimension der Gründe," quoted by Crowell in "Conscience and Reason: Heidegger and the Grounds of Intentionality" (*Transcendental Heidegger*, 47).

[3] For a perceptive discussion of the language of *sein lassen* in Heidegger's early period, see John Haugeland's essay "Letting Be," the seventh chapter in *Transcendental Heidegger*.

rain tomorrow" where we mean "It is possible that tomorrow rain will come"] and so have little to do with moral or ethical responsibility.[4])

As we have been arguing throughout, it will not suffice to say that the philosopher's interest lies in *being* and its meaning (*Sinn*) rather than the good, or that he is only trying to account for the possibility of intentionality in Husserl's sense (the bare consciousness *of* something): for it surely calls for argument and evidence that our own being can be determined without reference to the evaluative concepts we employ to interpret and justify what we take ourselves to be *about*, and the sense we discover upon deliberation that our projects are worthwhile, or failing somehow to live up to something we take to be important. An account of intentionality or comportment (*Verhalten*) that ignores the *importance* of what we care about and intend is surely no account of *human* intentionality.

As Heidegger frequently reminds us, in opposition to what he takes to be Husserl's value-free phenomenology of perception, I see the blackboard *as* a blackboard because I interpret it in relation to a project I take to be important.[5] Even our bare perceptual hold on things is normally charged with what we might call, in a traditional register, aesthetic values: to see the sun-drenched rocky mountain landscape in early morning is to find the spectacle beautiful or sublime, and so to pronounce it good in some respect, if only in the sense of being *worth seeing*. An omission of this sort, leaving aside the good under any description, would not be a case of casual and innocuous neglect of something one might take up on another occasion. It would be more like the failure of a treatise on human nature to mention our capacity to think, or a revised edition of *Grey's Anatomy* neglecting to include a chapter on the brain or the heart.

It is true that the language of the good is conspicuously absent from *Sein und Zeit* and the early lecture courses, with one important exception (SS 1924). As far as I can tell, there is only one occurrence of *agathon* in *Sein und Zeit*, in the discussion of the phenomenological method of the work, but it is casual and non-committal and meant only to illustrate a point about the possibility of being deceived (*Schein*).[6] Most of the uses of "good" reveal no deep and abiding interest in *the good*, with the important

---

[4] For more on the statistics of Heidegger's employment of the language of the good, see my entry on "Good" in *The Heidegger Lexicon*, forthcoming with Cambridge University Press, edited by Mark Wrathall.
[5] Heidegger presents an especially lucid and convincing version of this argument in WS 1925/6, *Logic: The Question of Truth*, section 12a.
[6] *SZ*, 29.

exceptions of the account of the vulgar interpretation of conscience in the second division (*vide* section 59), which seems dismissive, and a pregnant remark on the "good" as a matter of heritage (*Erbe*) in the chapter on *Geschichtlichkeit*, to which I turn below. There is, as we remarked in the Introduction, a pervasive interest throughout the work in being authentic as a necessary "ontic" condition of discerning certain ontological structures, but, as critics of the "existential analytic" are likely to point out, Heidegger seems eager to dismiss any moralizing interpretation of the phenomenon of authenticity.[7]

Yet, even a casual survey of the landscape of Heidegger's ontology reveals strong evaluative language throughout, and often in contexts where he appears eager to dissociate himself from the preoccupations of traditional moral theory or ethics, in a broad sense that includes reflection upon what sort of life it would be admirable or desirable to live, and the various ways in which certain approaches to coping with the human condition fail to live up to something like an ideal of human existence. And in several early lecture courses, Heidegger grapples with his predecessors in a way that shows an abiding interest, despite certain reservations, in what passes for the good within the philosophical tradition. A central stretch of a course on Augustine (SS 1921), for instance, places the search for God in *Confessions* X, as a quest for the *beata vita* and the *summum bonum*, at the very center of his phenomenological interpretation. And in an important course of lectures on Aristotle, Husserl, and Descartes (WS 1923/4), discussed in the last chapter, Heidegger traces the Cartesian determination of *verum* as *certum* squarely within the Scholastic tradition of transcendental inquiry into the nature of the true (*verum*) and the good (*bonum*), with reference to the often-overlooked discussion of the two concepts of freedom deployed in the Fourth Meditation's account of the possibility of error. In what follows, I hope to begin making the case, in an admittedly abstract way (meant to indicate a necessary structural relation, not to fill in the details), that while Heidegger avoids speaking in *Sein und Zeit* directly about the good, the topic forms the background theme of what he undertakes to illumine throughout his early ontology: Our standing toward the good in a variety of shapes (the worthwhile, the conducive, the noble, the authentic) is, on the view I hope to motivate

---

[7] Prefacing an account of Dasein *verging* toward inauthenticity, Heidegger observes: "it may not be superfluous to remark that the interpretation [to follow] has a purely ontological intention and is far removed [*weit entfernt*] from any moralizing critique of everyday Dasein and from the aspirations of a 'philosophy of culture'" (*SZ*, 167).

in what follows, what the early work is meant partly to illuminate, in the admittedly abstract language of "being."

The Teleological Implications of Heidegger's "Pragmatism": Moving Toward the Good

Let's begin with a few claims about Heidegger's project in *Sein und Zeit*, and see where, at least formally, they lead. Heidegger's early ontology was directed against a certain picture of human life, common enough among his contemporaries but traceable back to the Greeks, in which theoretical detachment takes the lead, and ostensibly distorts the (engaged, practical) phenomena of our daily being-in-the-world.[8] The target of the early years, and to some degree in *Being and Time* itself, is (as we argued in the first chapter) an early twentieth century conception of epistemology,[9] according to which what shows is, for instance, a mountain as something merely, or initially, to be known, and not as something to be climbed or admired or worshipped, as something the reality of which has to be demonstrated, or clarified, before its "value" can be properly considered. Heidegger's well-known experiential starting point in *Sein und Zeit* is the fact that we find ourselves surrounded by things that fascinate and repel, serve and fail to be of use, that matter and leave us indifferent. The objects we encounter at first are things we take to be significant in our practices, not things we take merely to be or not to be (present, without worth or utility), or things answerable to a concept of substance qualified by way of predicates.[10]

This alone is enough to justify something like a teleological construal of the first division's detailed descriptions of a distinctively human way of inhabiting the world: Heidegger's account of the "background conditions" of what Dreyfus calls our "everyday coping skills" brings into relief the way our use of equipment tends always toward some *point*, in a normatively structured encounter.[11] To be a person (Dasein), as opposed to being a thing, is to be about something, to take an interest in the success of a particular enterprise. Even in the local setting of a particular *Umwelt*, in moving around in the workshop, say, Dasein is trying to accomplish something; and where something (meaningful, purposive) is being made

---

[8] See, for instance, the chapter on the genesis of σοφία in *Platon: Sophistes* (*GA*19, 64–131).
[9] This comes out clearly in 1927 in Heidegger's efforts to overcome the problem of the reality of the external world, in section 43a of *Sein und Zeit*.
[10] "The Greeks had an appropriate term for 'things': πραγματα, that is, that with which one has to do in [one's] concernful dealings (*pragmata*)" (*SZ*, 68).
[11] Hubert L. Dreyfus, *Being-in-the-World: A Commentary on Heidegger's "Being and Time," Division I.*

or done, norms that decide between success and failure, between coping well and faring ill, play an essential role. The references (*Verweisungen*) embedded in our coping, however automatic the coping often is and un-thematic the references usually are, cannot be made out fully without highlighting the good under some description, if only in the shape of what "conduces"[12]: The shoes to be produced, for instance, refer essentially to "possible wearers for whom they should be [sein soll] 'made to measure.' Similarly, the producer or supplier is encountered in the material used as one who 'serves' well or badly [gut oder schlecht]."[13] It is constitutive of tool-being ("in itself," as Heidegger playfully suggests[14]) to be good *for* this or that. Even nature, Heidegger observes, shows up in our practices as "the *power of nature*. The forest is a forest of timber [good for building], the mountain a quarry of rock [good, perhaps, for sculpting], the river is water power, the wind is wind 'in the sails.'"[15]

What is being denied in Division One, then, is not that things are good (for), but that their being good (for) is something we normally take notice of in an explicitly performed act of consciousness, that we have first to perceive the presence of an object with certain properties in order to go on to attribute value or utility to the thing in question, in a higher, founded act of consciousness. (The target here includes Husserl, although the analyses of active and passive synthesis in Husserl's lecture courses, which place being moved and taking an interest in what appears at the center, raise some doubt about the justice of Heidegger's frequent complaints about his mentor's phenomenology.[16]) The being-good-for of equipment is *there* for us, as the basis of what we go on in motivated judgments to say about what originally shows in our pragmatically structured dealings with things. When something (we know not quite what to make of) shows, the question is not (usually) "What is this?" – posed in a sense that asks for a list of properties or necessary attributes to be attributed to a subject – but "For what does it call?" (We shall see shortly that the same holds, roughly, for Heidegger's quest for a definition of human life.) Our asking *what* something is, at least in everyday situations of encounter, displays a practical incompetence; if we are (knowingly) in an unfamiliar workshop,

---

[12] An earlier version of the first division's account of being-in-the-world, in a course of lectures devoted to the "autochthony" of Aristotle's basic ontological concepts, makes this structure explicit in the language of the *agathon*, in the instrumental sense of the *sumpheron*. See *GA* 18, 55–62.

[13] *SZ*, 117.   [14] Ibid., 69.   [15] *SZ*, 70.

[16] The charge against Husserl does seem to fit the stratification offered in the second book of the *Ideen*, which Heidegger read in manuscript [see *SZ*, 47, footnote 1], but see, for example, the discussion of "The Phenomenon of Affection" in *Analyses Concerning Passive and Active Synthesis*, 196–221.

we know at the very least that the item in question is something that could be put meaningfully to use, if we had the skill or know-how (*Sich-Auskennen*) to take it up in the appropriate way.[17] It is only within the arguments of some philosophers that we face (mere) manifolds of sensible intuition waiting to be brought under the unity of concepts of utility, value, significance, and the like in order to become (for us) things of use. Things (*pragmata*) announce themselves "*immer schon*" as to be used, enjoyed, taken up (into a practice), or to be ignored as irrelevant, in light of the point of what I take myself to be doing (*prattein*).

On the basis of this commonplace, everyday ability to take things up in the surrounding world (*Umwelt*) with purpose and insight (*Einsicht, Umsicht*), to see things under the aspect of utility, before we take an interest in the enterprise of theory, *Sein und Zeit* sketches out an ontology of human life centered on the fact that human beings are creatures for whom things matter, or, in Heidegger's own terms, "Dasein is a being that does not only occur among other beings. Rather is it … distinguished by the fact that, in its being, this being is concerned *about* its very being [*um dieses Sein selbst geht*]."[18] Again, "Dasein is never to be understood as a case and instance of a genus of beings objectively present. To something objectively present, its being is a matter of "indifference," more precisely, it "is" in such a way that its being can be neither indifferent nor non-indifferent to it."[19] This "being concerned about …." is the datum, if you will, that much of the work means to clarify. What *Sein und Zeit* has to offer along the way are what I have elsewhere called "care-categories" (Heidegger calls them "existentials"), meant to articulate the fact that "we understand ourselves and our existence by way of the activities we pursue and the things we take care of."[20]

Now, it seems reasonable enough to claim that an entity that moves about in the world in the way of care, an entity defined pragmatically in terms of its "for-the-sake-of-which," is a being defined by its ends or aims. "To be a person," as Okrent notes (with Kant and Heidegger on Kant in mind), "is to be an end or a purpose."[21] If ends, or basic possibilities, turn

---

[17] For a discussion of know-how and its ontological implications, see, for instance, the discussion in *GA* 19, 40–7.

[18] *SZ*, 12.   [19] Ibid., 42.

[20] *Basic Problems of Phenomenology*, 159. For a helpful short discussion of Heidegger's pragmatism, worked out in relation to Kant's conception of transcendental apperception, see Mark Okrent's "The 'I Think' and the For-the-Sake-of-Which' in *Transcendental Heidegger*. See also Okrent's *Heidegger's Pragmatism*. Dahlstrom criticizes pragmatic interpretations of truth, including Okrent's and Rorty's, in *Heidegger's Concept of Truth*, 423–33.

[21] *Heidegger's Pragmatism*, 29.

out to be the sorts of things we can *choose*, and not the sorts of things we simply have (like hair, height, lungs, and the like), a claim Heidegger defends in the discussion of conscience,[22] this can only be because we find some aims, ways, and means to be *better than* their alternatives. Which is to say: Dasein is a being for whom the good under some description, or at least its own good, matters.

In line with the ontological intentions of the work, Heidegger refuses to discuss "what Dasein [in fact] resolves upon," although he does, in a rare use of "good," suggest that we inherit our sense of what is (possibly) good.[23] But the existential analytic does provide us with reasons to take the normative dimension of our projects seriously; and the account of being-in-the-world reinforces the idea that when we do find significance in things and projects, it is not because we project values and other subjective entities onto a world that includes nothing of the kind. Any conception of the world that leaves the good altogether out of account will fail to be a conception of the world as the abode of a creature for whom things matter. In this way, *Sein und Zeit* could be said to make substantial contributions to "meta-ethical" reflection on the source of our sense of why, on what basis, we take ourselves to be bound by one thing rather than another; or, more simply, how it is possible for us to have something like a hold on the good in the first place. (Again: this is not incompatible with our sometimes failing to discover something worth doing. The account of *Angst* in section 40 shows, among other things, that our hold on significance is a slippery one.[24]) But the instrumental account of how what is good for x shows, on the basis of a pragmatic experience of the world as the space of significance, is not self-standing. It needs support in an account of what it would be good to pursue, or to (aspire to) be. As Aristotle argues, in a move Heidegger considers in an earlier course of lectures, our local and provisional or instrumental ends run the risk of running into the indefinite (and so being "empty and vain") without the delimiting support of an end taken

---

[22] *SZ*, 268. As Heidegger notes in section 58: "nothingness [*Nichtigkeit*] belongs to the being-free [*Freisein*] of Dasein for its . . . possibilities. But freedom *is* only in the choice of one [possibility], that is, in bearing responsibility for not-having-chosen and not-being-able-to-choose another" (*SZ*, 285).

[23] *SZ*, 343.

[24] We should also note here that Heidegger denies that our being (someone in particular) and the "good" we seek to embody are in any way matters that can be settled: "'Being at stake' [or the mattering of something] entails that *what* I am concerned about is *not a solid possession*. In fact, the 'at stake' belongs to existence as such as long as existence is. Therefore, the 'what is at stake' is *never* a solid possession" (*Logic: The Question of Truth*, 195; *GA* 21, 234–5).

up for itself. This suggests, contrary to some remarks on Dreyfus's part,[25] that we cannot ignore the second division's account of *Eigentlichkeit*, where Dasein's being toward itself and its "finalizing" "for-the-sake-of-which" (*Umwillen*) come more clearly into view.

Authenticity and the Good

In the passage in *Sein und Zeit* from section 74 noted above, Heidegger makes the surprising (and pregnant) claim, often overlooked, that "the character of 'goodness' lies in making authentic existence possible."[26] It is, to be sure, pitched in the form of a conditional statement ("If everything 'good' is a matter of heritage and if the character of 'goodness' lies in making authentic existence possible, then handing down a heritage is always constituted in resoluteness."). And Heidegger does little in *Sein und Zeit* to spell out what it means. But it highlights a connection between the idea of the good and the idea of *Eigentlichkeit* that, as far as I know, has not been fully appreciated. In order to bring this connection more fully and plausibly to light, let us begin with a brief rehearsal of the very idea of authenticity (or ownership) and the role it plays in *Sein und Zeit*.

The idea itself includes at least two strands, or registers, which we would do well to distinguish. In a number of well-known passages scattered throughout the work, "being authentic" appears to mean something like "being (true to) yourself," in what Heidegger stages as a necessary struggle against the dominance of the public sphere, or the "dictatorship" of *das Man* ("the One," "the Anyone," or "the They"), and the norms and standards that apply indifferently to anyone and no one. In this rather traditional register, which is not unique to Heidegger, authenticity amounts to something like making choices of one's own (perhaps even choosing for the first time to choose, as Heidegger sometimes remarks), and assuming the responsibility for having taken one's stand, despite the social cost. (Think of Nora in Ibsen's well-known play.) Or, in a more metaphysical, and more obviously (German) romantic cast (I'm thinking here of Schleiermacher and his colleagues in Jena in the late 1790s): unfolding the unique kernel or core of your being along a path unchecked by the inhibitions, mostly social, standing in your way. Call this "authenticity in an ontic key" or a concept that orients us toward the personal

---

[25] Dreyfus defends the exclusion of Division II from his commentary on *Sein und Zeit* in the opening pages of the Preface, pp. vii–viii.

[26] *SZ*, 383.

sphere, at the expense of things common, in the sense of being widely and easily shared, and more or less taken for granted. Unfortunately, this strand can misleadingly suggest that Dasein becomes most authentic when it detaches itself from the world and comes to it*self.*

But there is another concept, equally evaluative but also more obviously consistent with the general ontological import of the work, that grips something like *being the very thing itself,* or – in keeping with the normative direction embedded in our sense of having possibly failed or succeeded in something – owning up to, or acknowledging in our thoughts and practices (or in our "being," in Heidegger's preferred way of speaking), the ontological status of being human (Dasein). In this register, *Eigentlichkeit* is more like displaying adequately and transparently the structure of beings like us – embracing, acknowledging, or owning up to death, guilt, nothingness, finitude, and the like, as "categories" woven into the being of Dasein itself, and from which it is, paradoxically, possible to flee). Or "becoming who you are"[27] in a way that embodies something you share with others, in a sense of "sharing" that cuts deeper than those wide-spread opinions and norms of "good behavior" that may well conceal something more essential about ourselves. Authenticity in this deeper, more structural sense may very well challenge certain self-conceptions that seem convincing to someone who takes herself to be authentic in the first sense.[28]

These two conceptions are not necessarily at odds. One might argue that the second conception makes possible a plausible defense of the first. If an appeal to what is my own is to carry any weight, even if only at first ostensibly for me, it has to issue in something someone else can, at least in principle, understand, and this in light of what we both take ourselves commonly to be, at various levels of "ontological generality" – at some level we will reach a shared being-in-the-world and being-human. But the second view keeps more with the *philosophical* dimension of Heidegger's project; and the first has the palpable disadvantage of leaving some readers with the misleading impression that the author of *Sein und Zeit* is committed to defending some variety of subjectivism. Despite the subjective bent of Heidegger's many formulations – that "*Angst* individualizes and thus discloses Dasein as 'solus ipse,'"[29] for instance, and the frequently repeated claim that death is altogether "non-relational," and the many

---

[27] "The command, 'Become what you are!' – understood ontically – is possible only if, taken ontologically, *I am* what I am becoming" (*Logic: The Question of Truth,* 341; *GA* 21, 413).

[28] The second conception of authenticity is central to the culminating chapter of Sacha Golob's *Heidegger on Concepts, Freedom and Normativity.*

[29] *SZ,* 188.

diatribes against *Öffentlichkeit* (publicness) – I take it for granted here, having argued for it above, that *Sein und Zeit* offers a more or less sustained assault on the subjective orientation in the modern philosophical tradition toward internal and merely subjective experience that made the more romantic conceptions of "ownership" in the German tradition possible. As Heidegger notes, almost in passing, in that part of *Sein und Zeit* where the traditional concept is most in evidence, "Authentic being a self is not based on an exceptional state of the subject, detached from the they, but is an existentiell modification of the they as an essential existential."[30] To take another passage from a later part of the work, "As authentic being a self, resoluteness does not detach Dasein from its world, nor does it isolate it as a free-floating ego."[31] This does not exclude someone's doing something comparatively unprecedented or unusual, but it does place constraints on whether or not what has been said or done can be said to mean. I can take something to heart, in opposition to what others take to be worthwhile, and come to think myself mistaken, or just *be* mistaken, regardless of what I come to think. Nowhere in *Sein und Zeit* does Heidegger suggest that my feeling and conviction, however strong, are sufficient to determine the worth of what I have to offer. The good is not to be sought in the sentiments, beliefs, and convictions, however sincere, of what Hegel, cribbing from Goethe, calls "the beautiful soul." This is not to say that our moods are necessarily misleading, or merely subjective, but the topic of what dispositions and moods "disclose" would call for another discussion altogether.

The second strand in the conception of *Eigentlichkeit* (being the very thing itself, construed actively as owning up to the human condition) has the added advantages of being more obviously consistent with the ontological role played by the concept of authenticity in *Sein und Zeit* – to prepare for the work of grounding Division One's analysis of Dasein's being in terms of care in the more fundamental phenomenon of temporality, by bringing out the proper senses of "wholeness" and "being-limited" for creatures like us – and helping to explain Heidegger's obscure claim, with which we began, that authentic life is somehow empowered by the good. For it is the burden of the account of authenticity to tell us at once (1) what sorts of beings we fundamentally *are*, (2) what it would be *good* to be, and (3) (this is more controversial) why both "being" and "the good" are *Wechselbegriffe*, reciprocal concepts.

---

[30] Ibid., 130.   [31] Ibid., 298.

Let us begin with the first issue, and see how it necessarily folds into the second. The project of *Sein und Zeit*, inherited from the early lecture courses, is largely *definitional.* Despite Heidegger's larger ontological ambitions to characterize *Sein* itself, what the published "torso" actually accomplishes can, I think, be accurately described as the protracted elaboration of a definition of human existence – first in terms of care (*Sorge*), eventually, and more originally, in light of what Heidegger calls "primordial time" (*ursprüngliche Zeit*) or "temporality" (*Zeitlichkeit*). The details of the many-layered analyses terminating in the account of temporality in section 65 cannot concern us now; my interest lies in the definitional strategy Heidegger puts to work.

As the word itself suggests (*definitio, horismos*), definition (as a task) involves placing something within its proper *limits*: a definition of x offers the thing in question as properly *de-limited*, and so, by implication, as distinguished from other kinds of things.[32] I would like to suggest that the work of delimiting can be discharged in two distinct ways. On a model of definition Heidegger often considers in the early lecture courses but ultimately rejects as tailored to the "being" of indifferent objects, the task is to survey the range of things merely extant, to compare and contrast the various attributes they display, and to single out those necessary and sufficient characteristics that allow us to pick out objects of the type in question. On an alternative model of definition we can call "exemplary," the task is to interpret the entity in light of an ideal instantiation of what, in deference to the tradition, we can call its *species* (*eidos*) – of *how* it shows when in rare instances it measures up to a successful version of itself.[33] In this case, the work of defining is unavoidably evaluative. Heidegger's name for the value-laden embodiment of the thing in question – ourselves throughout the early period – is *Eigentlichkeit*, the "ontic ideal" that underwrites the ontological interpretation of human existence in the second division of *Sein und Zeit*.

The model for this sort of definitional practice in *Sein und Zeit* is Heidegger's own interpretation of Aristotle's definition of "Dasein" as *zôê praktikê* and *psuchês energeia* in an important course of lectures delivered in 1924, which is all the more important, for our purposes, for making explicit the relationship between the interwoven tasks of defining

---

[32] For an instructive account of the nature of definition in ancient and modern philosophy, see *GA* 18, 9–41.

[33] Dahlstrom appears to have something like what I'm calling "exemplary definition" in mind in *Heidegger's Concept of Truth*, 338–41.

human existence, clarifying its authentic possibility, and searching for an adequate concept of the human *agathon*. I do not mean to imply that the definition Heidegger attributes to Aristotle is in every respect his own, although there are, I think, important parallels between views he attributes to Aristotle, on, for instance, being in a situation, and insights he works into *Sein und Zeit*. What I mean to suggest is that Heidegger models his own practice of delimiting Dasein in *Sein und Zeit* on a version worked out three years earlier.

It is noteworthy that Heidegger approaches the Aristotelian concept of human life by way of the *ergon*, which he renders, in typical Heideggerian fashion, as "the 'authentic accomplishment' and the 'concern' in which human beings … live in their being-human."[34] The *ergon* in question in Aristotle's own search (in *EN* I.7) cannot be among Dasein's specific professions and concerns (builder, shoemaker, and so on): for the proper target of ethical inquiry is not the success of a particular class of persons, but human flourishing as such, or *Eigentlichkeit* in its general structure. So, the question is whether "there is still another *ergon* of human beings that would be *idion*, 'proper,' to human beings as [such]."[35] Is there something "for-the-sake-of-which" human existence should be, in order to become properly limited and so to come into its *own*?

In keeping with Heidegger's primary source (the *Nicomachean Ethics*), the limits in question come into focus as matters of action (*praxis*): the work of coming to exist within human limits involves something like reaching out for the properly human end (*telos*), which Heidegger consistently construes as *peras* (not end, in the sense of aim, but limit). But this leads directly into a consideration of the *agathon*: for the limit that *matters* to creatures like us is no mere boundary that stakes something off from something else, but one that shows up in a concern (*Besorgen*). As Heidegger notes, "As knowing-one's-way-around, concern about something has an *agathon* within itself, explicitly there. Concern is not something different than, and so only accidentally, a being-after [the good]."[36] In a move that anticipates his own subsequent account of *Eigentlichkeit*, Heidegger observes: "*Agathon* is not an objective thing buzzing around, but is a *how of being-there itself*."[37]

Clearly not every way of being-limited counts as good: in a way, anything that can be said to be must possess boundary and shape. A poorly shaped hammer is as clearly bounded, visually speaking, as its

---

[34] *Basic Concepts of Aristotelian Philosophy*, 31.   [35] Ibid., 68, *GA* 18, 98.   [36] Ibid., 47.
[37] Ibid., 49.

well-crafted counterpart. Even the seeker after mere pleasure has her final end. (*Vide* Aristotle's *Nicomachean Ethics* I.5.) In keeping with the brief remarks about exemplary definition offered above, the concept of *peras* that comes forward in SS 1924 is decidedly "normative" – a concept of what has come into its limits *well*. The good is what makes for being-limited in the right way.

*

If we had more space, we would give the abstract idea of being properly limited flesh and blood, taking up Heidegger's subsequent discussion, a bit later in the course, of the notion of αρετη (virtue), drawn from the second book of the *Nicomachean Ethics*.[38] The parallels between the concept that shows there and the features of authentic existence in *Sein und Zeit* are remarkable, and go even further along the path blazed here of overcoming the suspicion that *Eigentlichkeit* has no discernible ethical content.[39] The point of this interlude has been merely to show that the ontological analysis of Dasein cannot be cleanly divorced from evaluative judgments concerning what sort of life it would be worthwhile to live.

What is surprising in Heidegger's early trajectory is not that he came upon the idea of the "good," compelled, perhaps, by the pressure of the things themselves, but that it plays no conspicuous role in *Sein und Zeit*. It does, however, make another important appearance in SS 1928, in the context of an extended discussion of the principle of sufficient reason. What has logic to do with the good? On the surface of our ordinary way of thinking about logic, as one discipline among others, distinct from ethics, the answer is clearly – nothing. But then one might well ask: What does logic have to do with being-in-the-world, or being affected, or the structure of reality?

In the second major part of the course, Heidegger takes Schopenhauer to task for failing to grasp the root of the principle of sufficient reason, and for ignoring the *potius quam* (the "rather than") is his translation of Leibniz's formulation: for this "rather than," Heidegger argues, is the chief problem in the principle. As Heidegger notes, "The *principium rationis* is *the principle of the 'rather than,'* the principle of the primacy of something

---

[38] *GA*18, section 17c.

[39] Heidegger's account includes, *inter alia*, the phenomena of "being-in-a-situation," acquiring a lasting disposition to behave well, being-resolved, and deliberating within "the moment" (*kairos*, *Augenblick*) about the best course of action.

over nothing, of this thing over that, of this way over another way."[40] Without stretching things too far, we might say that what is at issue is the basis of preference and choice, which hangs upon a conception of what is best. This clearly cannot be divorced from serious engagement with the idea of the good. In a move that should no longer surprise us, Heidegger affirms that what he means by "transcendence" and "being-in-the-world" is nothing less than what Plato's Socrates meant in the *Republic* by the *idea tou agathou*, beyond the "visibility" of *ousia* itself.[41]

---

[40] *Metaphysical Foundations of Logic*, 114.

[41] "What we must ... learn to see in the [idea of the good] is the characteristic described by Plato and Aristotle as ... the *for-the-sake-of-which*, that on account of which something is or is not, is in this way or that. The [idea of the good], which is even beyond beings and the realm of ideas, is the for-the-sake-of-which. This means that it is the genuine determination that transcends the entirety of the ideas and at the same time thus organizes them in their totality" (Ibid., 184–5).

CHAPTER 4

Things and Persons
A Kantian Exercise in Moral Ontology

So impure is our concern for . . . others: it is mostly no more than a
selfish joke; while it is, on the other hand, a deadly serious matter to
keep our relations with the living constantly alert and alive.

Goethe, *Elective Affinities*

"When was Heidegger not a Kantian? It is almost like asking, 'When was
Heidegger not a German?'"[1] Although the precise nature and extent of
Kant's influence on the project of *Sein und Zeit* are open to debate, and
while some have questioned the value of Heidegger's sudden rediscovery of
Kant during the winter semester of 1925/6 (an encounter, reported
enthusiastically to Jaspers in December, that clearly helped shape "the
final draft of [*Being and Time*]"[2]), Kisiel's observation is beyond dispute:
Heidegger's early efforts to motivate and clarify the *Seinsfrage* by way of an
analysis of human existence (Dasein) are closely tied to sustained critical
engagement, sometimes muted in the published text, with the transcendental philosophy of the first *Critique*, and various misunderstandings and
distortions of Kant's thought Heidegger attributes to the neo-Kantians.
As a matter of philological reckoning alone, it is worth noting that
Kant and his successors, from Fichte to Husserl, make important appearances in nearly every course of lectures Heidegger delivered between
1919 and 1927.[3]

---

[1] Theodore Kisiel, *The Genesis of Heidegger's "Being and Time,"* 408.   [2] Ibid., 409.
[3] Already in KNS 1919 (the first extant course), in the context of Heidegger's attempt to define and
defend an idea of philosophy as the "pre-theoretical" science of human life, Heidegger draws from
Kant's analysis of the idea in the Transcendental Dialectic of the *Critique of Pure Reason*. (According
to the Editor's Afterword, Heidegger had originally announced a two-hour course on Kant [*GA* 56/7,
221].) The next semester (SS 1919) is devoted to the transcendental philosophies of value developed
by Windelband and Rickert. Kant makes important appearances in courses devoted to ancient
philosophy as well. See, for instance, the discussion of definition in Kant's *Logic* in section 3 of
SS 1924 (*Basic Concepts of Aristotelian Philosophy*) and the provocative suggestion in the same course
that Aristotle's conception of the human good "is echoed in the *Kantian* definition of the human
being: the rational being exists as an *end in itself*" (*GA* 18, 95).

III

It should come as no surprise, then, that Kant occupies a central place in the literature on early Heidegger. Two topics tend to dominate the discussion, and for good reasons: (1) the (apparent) transcendental structure of Heidegger's analysis of Dasein in *Sein und Zeit* and the surrounding lectures,[4] and (2) the temporal structure of experience, judgment, understanding, care, and being itself.[5] Both (interconnected) themes – really a method (call it transcendental) and a topic (time or temporality) – come clearly into view in WS 1925/6 (*Logic: The Question of Truth*), which provides the first of many detailed interpretations of central themes in Kant's *Critique of Pure Reason*, and offers what appears to be a regressive, transcendental argument from the capacity to make true or false propositional assertions to its *a priori*, temporal conditions in an act or comportment (*Verhalten*) of "making-present" (*Gegenwärtigen*).

There is nothing to complain about in this scholarly focus, which has generated some of the better accounts of Heidegger's project, as it took shape in the crucial months leading up to the publication of *Sein und Zeit* in 1927. That Kant's theoretical philosophy played a crucial role in Heidegger's temporal interpretation of human life is beyond question. But obsessive attention to Kant's first *Critique* does leave out a pregnant Kantian resonance in Heidegger's own conception of Dasein, as ontologically distinct from every other sort of entity, call it the distinction between persons and things; for in the same course of lectures, Heidegger associates his own conception of human life as *care* (*Sorge*) with Kant's idea of the human being as an end in itself, having absolute value in itself, in his contributions to *moral* philosophy.[6] What's more: this discussion of a central doctrine in Kant's moral philosophy was taken over, without reference to Kant, in the discussion of authentic and inauthentic *Fürsorge* – the care-for that leaps ahead of the other and liberates her, on the one hand, and the care-for that leaps in and dominates her, on the other – in the first division of *Sein und Zeit*. As Heidegger observes in a pregnant remark not included in the corresponding section in 1927: "This kind of

---

[4] See, for instance, *Transcendental Heidegger*. Taylor Carman situates Heidegger's project in light of Kant's conception of epistemic conditions in *Heidegger's Analytic*. Mark Okrent interprets Heidegger's project in terms of a pragmatic version of transcendental argumentation in *Heidegger's Pragmatism*.

[5] Representative works include Charles Sherover's *Heidegger, Kant, and Time* and William Blattner's *Heidegger's Temporal Idealism*.

[6] *GA* 21, 220. I don't mean to suggest that Heidegger's concept of care was developed in confrontation with Kant. The idea finds a place in the religion lectures of 1920/1 (*curare* in Augustine, *Bekümmerung*). In SS 1923, as well as WS 1921/2, Heidegger is already prepared to claim that the proper being of human life is *Sorgen*.

[inauthentic, dominating] being concerned-for treats the other like a nothing [*ein Nichts*], as if he had nothing of Dasein about him."[7] On this view, the failure to treat the other as *another Dasein* appears to be anchored in an ontological failure to distinguish between human existence and the being of "something merely present in the world [*etwas weltliches Vorhandenes*]."[8] The moral potential of Heidegger's meta-categorical distinction between Dasein, on the one hand, and things of nature and of use, on the other, could hardly be clearer, although the moral import of his insight gets buried in the existential analysis of *Sein und Zeit*.[9]

The importance of this apparently marginal Kantian influence, or echo, in the early period cannot be overstated. At the very least, the reference to Kant shows, against the influential criticisms of Levinas and Tugendhat, among others, that Heidegger's project includes additional resources for the development of a strand in what I've been defending as a Heideggerian *moral* ontology of human life. The moral potential latent in the very idea of fundamental ontology is most obvious, I intend to argue, in the second division of *Sein und Zeit*, where phenomena like conscience, choice, and responsibility play a crucial role in the articulation of the "ontic ideal" that underwrites the ontological account of Dasein in terms of temporality.

I hope in what follows to flesh out the implications, at once moral and ontological, of Heidegger's affiliation of the care-structure of human existence with Kant's distinction between things and persons in the second section of the *Grundlegung*[10] (which all but disappears in 1927), and to motivate Heidegger's growing interest in Kant's concept of freedom in the aftermath of *Sein und Zeit*.[11] My approach will be for the most part indirect, and will advance by way of what I hope will be a fresh interpretation of the Kantian dimension of Heidegger's "practical philosophy" in *Being and Time*.

[7] Ibid., 224.   [8] Ibid., 224.
[9] Anticipations of the argument I intend to develop here can be found in the sixth and seventh chapters of Irene McMullin's *Time and the Shared World*, Sonia Sikka's "Kantian Ethics in *Being and Time*," and Charles Sherover's "Founding an Existentialist Ethic."
[10] See *Groundwork of the Metaphysics of Morals* in *Practical Philosophy*, p. 79 (Volume 4 in Kant's *Gesammelte Schriften* [*GS*], p. 428). In referring to Kant's work, I follow the usual practice of supplying the relevant volume in the *GS* followed by the page number (4:428, for instance), with the exception of the *Critique of Pure Reason*, which I cite using the familiar A/B format, where "A" stands for the first edition of 1781 and "B" the second edition of 1787.
[11] I'm thinking of the course of lectures on the metaphysical foundations of logic (SS 1928) and the lecture courses delivered in the early 1930s on freedom and truth.

Metaphysics of Morals, Ontology of Dasein

Heidegger's attitude toward Kant in *Being and Time* is ambivalent. Although he appropriates Kant's claim that the work of clarifying "the covert judgments of common reason" is the very "business of philosophers,"[12] praises the *Critique of Pure Reason* as a "productive logic" that spells out "what belongs to any nature whatsoever,"[13] against what he considers epistemological distortions of the work,[14] and singles out Kant's achievement in the obscure chapter on the schematism of the pure concepts of the understanding as the first serious attempt to investigate "the dimension of temporality"[15] (a theme taken up and developed in some detail in the Kant-book of 1929), Heidegger just as often accuses Kant of a number of serious ontological shortcomings – in his conception of the mind (under the uncritical influence of Descartes),[16] in his views on time (under the unacknowledged influence of Aristotle),[17] in his conception of orientation in space,[18] and in his account of the "I" as absolute logical subject in the act of judgment.[19] In connection with the last complaint, Heidegger notes in passing that Kant failed to catch sight of "the phenomenon of the world," and so "the 'I' was once again driven back [in Kant's analysis of transcendental apperception] into an *isolated* [sphere of subjectivity] that accompanies representations in a way that is ontologically indefinite."[20] Hence Kant's misguided attempt, in the Refutation of Idealism added to the second edition of the first *Critique* (B274–9), to demonstrate the reality of the external world, to which Heidegger devotes several sharply critical pages in the final chapter of the first division of *Being and Time*, dismissing the project as an egregious misunderstanding of human existence as "always already" in the very world Kant means to demonstrate.

Now what is striking about the items on this list of complaints is their textual and thematic target: they are, without exception, limited to Kant's offerings in theoretical philosophy. And they amount to the now familiar and overworked charge that Kant, too, fails to appreciate the distinction between Dasein and other (non-human) entities, a failure that Heidegger

---

[12] *SZ*, 4.   [13] *SZ*, 10–11.
[14] This claim is developed in considerable detail in WS 1935/6 (*Die Frage nach dem Ding*), which is unique in Heidegger's interpretations of Kant for centering on the principles of pure understanding in the first *Critique*. A new translation of this important course of lectures (as *The Question Concerning the Thing*) by James D. Reid and Benjamin D. Crowe is forthcoming with Rowman & Littlefield's New Heidegger Research Series.
[15] *SZ*, 23.   [16] *SZ*, 24.   [17] *SZ*, 26.   [18] *SZ*, 109.   [19] *SZ*, 318–320.   [20] *SZ*, 321.

consistently associates with the metaphysical tradition *tout court*, beginning with the ancient Greeks and including every major philosophy, ancient and modern, that Heidegger sees fit to include in his interpretations of traditional figures, early and late, with the possible exception of Dilthey and Count Yorck. Heidegger notably ignores, at least in 1927, the bearing of Kant's practical and moral philosophy on the issues *Being and Time* means to clarify.

This is astonishing, in light of at least three facts about Kant's thought, as it bears on central conceptions developed carefully in *Being and Time*: (1) Kant's philosophy *as a whole* lends support to the primacy of practical reason,[21] in the loose sense that practical matters are more important to human beings than merely theoretic concerns (the latter are themselves interests, and so have practical significance), but also on some readings (notably Fichte's) in the sense that the very conditions of theoretical inquiry are themselves of a practical nature or bearing. On the latter view, theoretical reason is itself an instance of practical reason. There is some reason to think that Heidegger's early work defends some version of the "primacy of practice" thesis in both senses. (2) Kant appears to hold that metaphysics or ontology stands some chance of succeeding, where the traditional discipline has failed, provided it begins with the practical or moral point of view we necessarily take upon ourselves, whenever we act, but also often overlook when we're pursuing merely theoretical problems.[22] This is at least minimally consistent with Heidegger's claim that ontology as such finds, or ought to seek out, its proper roots in a faithful account of our practices and reflection upon their necessary conditions. And (3) it is *only* in the sphere of practical/moral philosophy that we discover compelling reasons to draw the *morally* charged distinction between things (*Sachen*) and persons.

---

[21] Kant himself employs the phrase in a section heading of the Dialectic of the *Critique of Practical Reason* (5:119). In a frequently cited passage from the Preface to the second edition of the first *Critique*, Kant informs his reader that he found it necessary "to deny knowledge in order to make room for [practical, moral] faith" (Bxxx). In the Preface to the second *Critique* Kant claims that the concept of freedom, which has no direct use in theoretical philosophy, although it does participate in the generation of an antinomy, when combined with the causal necessitation that rules in nature, "constitutes the *keystone* of the whole structure of a system of pure reason, even of speculative reason" (5:3–4).

[22] Again, this idea finds some support in the Preface to the second *Critique*: "all other concepts (those of God and immortality), which as mere ideas remain without support in [speculative reason], now attach themselves to [the practical] concept [of freedom] and with it and by means of it get stability and objective reality, that is, their *possibility* is *proved* by this: that freedom is real, for this idea reveals itself through the moral law" (5:4).

This last claim touches on what is arguably Heidegger's central thesis in *Being and Time*; for the work as a whole means to offer a novel account of the difference between creatures like us – who *exist*, in Heidegger's special sense of *Existenz* – and all other, non-human entities, merely extant, present-at-hand, or available for use and ready-to-hand, like tools and other similar sorts of entity that play some instrumental role in our ongoing practices. As Heidegger puts the point early on in *Being and Time*, "any being is either a *who* . . . or a *what*," and the first ontological task is to clarify as fully as possible the basis or the reasons for making this distinction, and why we often fail to draw it.[23] I suggest that Heidegger's way of drawing the distinction, and his way of motivating our recurring failure to draw it, owe more to Kant's practical philosophy than readers have noticed. (Later I'll say weigh in more directly on the moral implications of Heidegger's Kantian analysis.)

The sheer fact that Heidegger makes such a distinction does not, by itself, distinguish his philosophy from most traditional accounts of the uniqueness of human life; nor does it give us reason to think that moral considerations play any role in his account of human existence. (Some philosophers today, working within the shadow cast by Darwin, and in light of the findings of neuroscience and animal biology, might argue that Heidegger's failure is precisely to have drawn an all-too-sharp distinction between Dasein and other animals, or, more reductively still, between human beings and complex material systems; and that this alone is reason enough to think that Heidegger's ontology is *too much* under the influence of a tradition we would do well to reject, or at least to rethink.) It is hard to think of a traditional philosopher who does not in some way single us out as a distinctive sort of animal – for possessing reason, among any other faculties we might be said to share with other entities (desires, emotions, and instincts, say), for being self-conscious beings, with the capacity for self-ascription and a possible sense of responsibility for what we do, for making reflective, normative use of tools, including language, for being political, in some robust sense, or, more controversially, by virtue of living with an awareness of the sacred, and having what Tillich called an "ultimate concern," or, in keeping with Heidegger's own Kantian leanings, or for being, in Schopenhauer's description, a *metaphysical animal*, capable of asking questions that transcend the bounds of sense or possible experience. (Montaigne stands out as a notable exception, but the author of the *Essais* is not widely viewed as a philosopher in the traditional sense.)

[23] *SZ*, 45.

I would like to begin with the less controversial notion that the concept of understanding (*Verstehen*) plays a crucial role in Heidegger's account of what distinguishes creatures like us from other beings, including non-human animals, and then to argue, against the grain of some readers of *Being and Time*, that the Heideggerian conception bears some striking resemblances to Kant's account of practical agency; then I'll go on to say something about why Heidegger thinks we often fail to draw the distinction between Dasein and other entities, in a motivated flight and impoverished understanding (in what I take to be a sort of Kantian account of our failure to take responsibility), before turning to those texts in which Heidegger comes closest to working out the moral implications of his own way of drawing the Kantian distinction between things and persons.

The first point calls, I hope, for no detailed defense. Understanding, along with interpretation and assertion, "runs like a thread throughout the fabric" of *Being and Time* (Carman); and Heidegger's views on these three closely related themes underlie his critique of the tradition's infatuation with theory and the theoretical point of view, which (as Dreyfus insists in his commentary on the first division) forms one of the Heidegger's central and most original endeavors. Nearly every phenomenon the book addresses – including the use of tools and the distinction between *Zuhandenheit* and *Vorhandenheit*, inhabiting an *Umwelt*, being disposed, affected, or attuned (*Befindlichkeit*), entanglement, falling, or lapsing (*Verfallen*), death, conscience, and history – is shown to be a mode or instance of *Verstehen* in action; and the very project itself, as the development of a "fundamental ontology, from which alone all other ontologies can originate," is said to be possible, perhaps even necessary, because Dasein, uniquely, understands something like being.[24]

What Heidegger says about understanding, if not precisely what he means, is fairly straightforward. By "understanding," Heidegger does not mean to single out one species of cognition (*Erkenntnisart*) among others (explanation, for instance), but to capture the most basic way in which we move about in the space of significance he calls *world*: we *are* by way of understanding in the primary sense, "the basic kind of disclosing characteristic of Dasein,"[25] whether engaged explicitly in scholarly projects of understanding and interpreting (texts, e.g.), explaining physical occurrences, getting informed about something, and, more often, just going about some business (building a shed, balancing a checkbook, strolling through the park). As others have noted, drawing from Heidegger's initial

[24] *SZ*, 13.   [25] *SZ*, 170.

approach to the phenomenon in the third paragraph of § 31, understanding is more like practical ability, knowing *how* rather than knowing *that*,
being up to something, competent or skilled, "*getting it* where the 'it' in
question can be anything from a bodily technique to an esoteric joke."[26]
In short, understanding just is our ability to make sense of things, the
remarkable capacity of our activities to gear into what is intelligible, at least
for us. (I'm leaving out of focus for a moment how we move forward when
things do not appear to make sense, in situations where intelligibility in
some sense breaks down, when we find ourselves in doubt about the
significance of our projects, for instance, or face another culture the
defining practices of which strike us as absurd. But the possibility of
breakdown needs keeping in mind, as experiences of this sort will play
an important role in motivating a Kantian reading of *Verstehen*.)

In order to complete this rough sketch, we need to add three more
features to the emerging picture, which deserve to be called focal: the form
of understanding Heidegger has in mind is not merely displayed in
knowing how to use, say, a hammer, but involves, crucially, grasping
(Heidegger calls it *projecting* ourselves toward) the very point of
hammering, the primary "toward which" that Heidegger names the *Worumwillen* (the "for-the-sake-of-which"). This amounts, secondly, to
moving about in a peculiar space of *possibility*, which "as an existential
[structure of *human* life, as opposed to one of three modal categories, along
with actuality and necessity] is the most primordial and the ultimate
positive ontological determination of Dasein."[27] And finally, every
instance of local understanding and coping makes sense because it is tied
to something like a sense of its relevance to the (purposively structured)
significance of my life *as a whole*: "As disclosing, understanding always
concerns the whole ... of being-in-the-world."[28] Again, understanding
reveals to me "*what [my] very being is about*," what in the end concerns me,
the global stance I take upon myself as an entity for whom its very being is
an issue.[29]

Now all of this strikes a rather obvious Kantian chord. We have, on the
one hand, what resembles the primacy of the practical thesis, in an
admittedly broad sense of the "practical" and "practice" – every comportment (*Verhalten*) involves the teleological organization of our activities
around some point, end, or aim (human beings become what they are by

[26] *Heidegger's Analytic*, 19.   [27] *SZ*, 143–4.   [28] *SZ*, 144.
[29] "Dasein is a being that does not simply occur among other beings. Rather it is ... distinguished by
the fact that in its being this being is concerned *about* its very being" (*SZ*, 12).

setting ends for themselves) – and, on the other hand, a practical version of Kant's well-known claim in the first *Critique* that every form of consciousness is rooted in an underlying (possible) *self*-consciousness, which we can formulate in a more Heideggerian vein by saying: every form of understanding (significance, involvement or relevance) just is an instance of *self*-understanding, where this amounts to projecting upon or pressing into self-defining possibilities or possible ways to be. But Heidegger has one or two more things to say about how to understand and interpret understanding that create a serious stumbling block to any straightforward assimilation of his views on practical life to Kant's, the most influential of which run: in coping successfully (understanding at its best, on some readings) Dasein is fully absorbed in what it's about (not conscious, not reflective); and in projecting itself (which clearly underlies every case of local coping) Dasein "has nothing to do with being related to a plan thought out [in advance], according to which Dasein arranges its being," and does not grasp its possibility "thematically," which would "degrade it to the level of a given, intended content."[30] In a dark remark Heidegger observes, "project throws possibility before itself, and as such lets it *be*."[31] Passages like these appear to support the contention that the author of *Being and Time* is not targeting only the hegemony of theory in the philosophical tradition's self-understanding, but has something like self-reflective rational evaluation of practical and social life in mind as well; and if this interpretation can be sustained, the claims I'm trying to defend here will not be supportable.

Unfortunately, many of *Being and Time*'s most careful readers in the Anglo-American universe of Heidegger scholarship offer interpretations of understanding that lend (unwitting?) support to the sorts of anti-intellectualist (and anti-Kantian) worries I'm trying to forestall. Blattner, for instance, following in the footsteps of Dreyfus, whose views he fruitfully modifies and occasionally, if gently, criticizes, has made a forceful case that Heideggerian understanding is a precognitive, pre-conceptual, and pre-propositional practice that, as he puts it, "lacks the structure of the *as*."[32] As his case rests upon Heidegger's distinction between understanding and interpretation, we would do well to explore what *Being and Time* has to say about this, and to pinpoint where, textually and substantively, I think Blattner goes astray.

[30] *SZ*, 145.   [31] *SZ*, 145.
[32] "Ontology, the *A Priori*, and the Primacy of Practice" in *Transcendental Heidegger*. The claim that understanding lacks the as-structure falls on p. 16.

Heidegger is pretty clear about a few things: interpretation is a derivative phenomenon that depends upon understanding; and interpretation is the development or cultivation (*Ausbildung*) of understanding, or understanding made explicit. Blattner is probably right to insist, further, that in many cases of explicit understanding, we are moved to interpret, on Heidegger's view, "when we are not equal to the task, when we cannot manage what we are doing."³³ This leaves out cases of interpretation motivated by a desire to understand better, out of sheer curiosity, without any straightforwardly practical interest, but we'll leave that aside; and Blattner could easily single out passages in *Being and Time* that appear to target curiosity as an inauthentic mode of understanding and interpreting. But Blattner goes on to develop a reading of Heideggerian understanding and interpretation that holds, more questionably, that we are doing something really distinct from what we're up to when we understand things straightforwardly, and that the structure of interpretation introduces something altogether novel in our relation to what was once merely understood. And while I do not think Blattner means to say that understanding is *better* in every way than its explicit counterpart, his account does leave Heidegger open to the charge that "mindless coping" is superior to its reflective counterpart. (This keeps well with Blattner's attempt in *Heidegger's Temporal Idealism* to minimize the role played by the analysis of authenticity in the account of the deep temporal structure of human existence in Division Two of *Being and Time*.) Blattner's position boils down to an assimilation of the "as-structure" and the "fore-structure" of what Heidegger, I think, locates in the understanding itself, to *explicit* acts of understanding or interpretation, in a way that both mystifies the transition from *Verstehen* to *Auslegung* and occludes the moral potential of Heidegger's interpretation of *authentic* understanding and self-interpretation.

The textual evidence speaks strongly and pretty clearly against Blatter's reading. Heidegger tells us, in the section devoted to understanding and interpretation, that in the act of interpreting "understanding [itself] appropriates what it has understood understandingly. In interpretation [or interpreting something] understanding *does not become something different* [my emphasis], but rather [comes more fully to be] itself."³⁴ In the very next paragraph Heidegger notes that what is explicitly experienced *as* something, in an act of interpretation, belongs originally to the understanding itself: "What has been [interpreted] has the structure of *something as something*. The circumspectly interpretive answer to the circumspect

³³ Ibid., 12.   ³⁴ *SZ*, 148.

question of what this particular thing at hand is runs: it is for [something, in order to do something]. Saying what it is for is not simply naming something, but what is named is *understood* [my emphasis] *as* [Heidegger's emphasis] that for which the thing in question is to be taken."[35] As far as the *Vorstruktur*, which Blattner treats as, by and large, something that arises only in an act of interpretation, Heidegger explicitly assigns it to the understanding.[36] I bring these passages forward not to collapse interpretation into understanding – some difference needs maintaining, as Blattner rightly stresses – but to suggest, at the very least, that the difference is not as sharp as Blattner thinks. If understanding lacked the joints and the distinctions we go on to make thematic in interpretive gestures, however motivated, there would be no reason to think that some interpretations of what is going on (understandingly) are better than others. Blattner may be right to say that understanding calls for no cognition of what it understands, but we need an account of understanding that makes cognition possible, and not (as his account, I think, unintentionally implies) one that runs the risk of making explicit understanding a projection onto something altogether estranged from what we have to say about it, or worse – a distortion of what understanding catches sight of, before it makes any explicit claims about what it sees. We may decide, interpretively, that some varieties of interpretation are misleading, and that their alternatives will need grounding in what someone has somewhere managed (inexplicitly) to understand; but if the project of understanding and interpreting *better* is to make any sense, the structural relation between the two activities needs maintaining.

More to the point, I think that Blattner, and Dreyfus, fail to distinguish sufficientlty between the sort of understanding deployed in using a hammer, and the more important (and often far more troubled, if less easily unsettled) understanding of *ourselves*, as the basis of our capacity to take hammers and other entities and their contexts seriously. It is in just those cases of breakdown in our capacity to understand *ourselves*, or when we find ourselves facing a situation that calls for fresh thought, and not because anything's broken (consider trying to decide whom to vote for, or whether to pursue a degree in philosophy, medicine, or some other profession – there's uncertainty here, but no obvious breakdown), that a

---

[35] *SZ*, 149.

[36] "How are we to conceive the character of this 'fore'? Have we done this when we formally say 'a priori'? Why is this structure *appropriate to understanding* [my emphasis], which we have characterized as a fundamental existential of Dasein?" (*SZ*, 151).

Kantian model of human agency becomes relevant in the interpretation of Heidegger's thoughts on understanding and interpretation. (Those who think that Heidegger's account of understanding cannot possibly be squared with Kant's account of setting ends, for reasons having to do with the tacit nature of understanding in Heidegger's rendering and the self-conscious nature of end-setting in Kant's, might consider Kant's disturbing reflections, in the opening pages of *Groundwork* II, on our inability to know what we really will [the sources of the self's initiative being largely unfathomable and the sincerity of our moral commitments consequently unknowable], and the related account of the inscrutability of human agency in the treatise on *Religion*.)

In order to get clear about where the Kantian accent falls in Heidegger's account of understanding, or where it might be fittingly placed, we need to take up briefly Heidegger's controversial phenomenology of interrupted, everyday coping, or what Pippin calls *failed meaning*, which he interprets as the extreme possibility *"that [meaning] could fail, utterly, and in a way absolutely."*[37] What I'd like to suggest is that what fails (in *Angst*, for instance, and the experience of conscience) is not meaning in every sense, but significance (Pippin does not distinguish between *Sinn* and *Bedeutsamkeit*) or meaning *in a strictly functional sense*, and in a way that reveals the bare possibility of *taking responsibility*, holding oneself accountable, even "choosing to make [explicit] choices" or, as Kant would say, setting an end *for oneself*. (There are two distinct accounts of breakdown in *Being and Time* that play distinct methodological roles: the first [the failure of a piece of equipment to serve its pre-thematic role] is supposed to bring into focus the world [or the *Umwelt*] as the context of [instrumental] significance within which everyday coping moves, while the second [the collapse of significance itself] reveals something of myself in relation to what shows in the first. Only the second case of breakdown is relevant here.)

The phrase "one *is* what one does" captures what is at issue in the sort of collapse of significance I have in mind, and recurs like a leitmotif throughout *Being and Time*, as an expression of one way of construing the capacity for self-understanding that much of the work means to clarify. It has a clear and obvious everyday sense: one *is* a tailor, a father and son, a student or a teacher, an epistemologist or a fundamental ontologist, *because* one carries on precisely those activities that bestow whatever robust identity one can be said to have. Its meaning in everyday settings is so obvious, and so

---

[37] Robert Pippin, "Necessary Conditions for the Possibility of What Isn't: Heidegger on Failed Meaning" in *Transcendental Heidegger*, p. 206.

clearly uncontroversial most of the time (as a first approach to someone unknown to us it makes good sense to ask her what she does), that many readers of the work take it for granted that this is how Dasein ought fundamentally to be viewed. In addition to its characterizing, naturally, the way we tend to understand and interpret ourselves, in what Heidegger calls (and means to take more seriously than he thinks the philosophical tradition has) Dasein's "average everydayness," it has the advantage of offering a compelling way out of the essentialism *Being and Time* is supposed to have rejected. ("Thus Dasein is what, in its social activity, it interprets itself to be. Human beings do not have some specific nature."[38]) What else *could* I be, after all, beyond the various roles I assume and enact in the public sphere? To ask, for instance, what the philosopher *really* is, in addition to reading, teaching, giving talks, writing books, is like asking what hammers and benches *really* are, beyond being the embodiments of the instrumental roles they have been assigned, and reducing, perhaps, the significance of their involvement or relevance (*Bewandtnis*) to the neutral properties and accidental characteristics of something merely extant. Any meaningful answer to the question is going to involve specifying just *another role*, perhaps one with which she identifies more strongly (being a mother, say, or a Muslim). Surely there is nothing that comes before or lies beneath her being this or that in the public sphere (even her private self-interpretations embody some shareable sense of *what one does* in private), nothing like a true and proper self that her social status and stances obscure, or prevent from showing. If these somehow manage to collapse, and so to reveal themselves as being (deeply) "without importance [*ohne Belang*]," what else could be said to remain as a sustaining source of (the meaning of) her ongoing self-understanding? The answer appears to be precisely – *nothing*. (And so we have the infamous Heideggerian phenomenology of the *Nichtigkeit* of Dasein, its being "permeated with nullity through and through," and all the related interpretive difficulties of how to understand our ability to press on, to move forward in our projects in the absence of solid ground, beyond the contingent tasks and functions we take up from the social sphere.)

Now, I think this manages to get something right about how we ought to think about our identities; and it captures accurately the tenor of what Heidegger has to say about how we "initially and usually" embody a defining sense of the importance of what we care about. It would be odd, or perhaps the beginning of some jest, to tell a stranger at a cocktail

[38] Dreyfus, *Being-in-the-World*, 23.

party that I see myself as "the thrown ground of a nullity," permeated by nothingness. But this view on identity, or the *Worumwillen* upon which each of us projects herself, occludes something important that Heidegger's account of failed *significance* is meant to address; and it overlooks passages in *Being and Time* that cast the expression in an unflattering light. So what do these functional self-definitions occlude?

The failure, I suggest, lies not in their being (the self-conceptions of a self-interpreting animal), but in their being (taken to be) *just so*, by which I mean: *not* possibilities for which I take myself to be called upon to assume responsibility, but given and fixed functional roles and self-assessments one can safely and conveniently take for granted as defining characteristics. *Just so* and so not possibly otherwise. The mistake they embody is what I'll call "irresponsible *social essentialism*." They embody a failure to distinguish between *persons* – which are never (fully) *what* they are – and those *things* (instruments and things of nature) that can be said, within certain limits, to possess clearly defined roles and fixed essential characteristics. What becomes impossible in the collapse of significance, then, is not meaning as such, but a certain way of thinking about what meaning is, and how we ought to sustain it. And what Heidegger's analysis shows is our tendency, including Pippin's, to confuse meaning and its sources with instrumental significance, and the importance of drawing a distinction between Dasein and, to place the accent elsewhere, "*what* one is or does."

This failure to distinguish adequately between Dasein and other entities (persons and things, in the traditional [Kantian] way of speaking) is no mere cognitive error, like mistaking a person for a tree in the forest at night (how could it be?) but a *motivated* cover-up, something more like a failure to assume *responsibility*. Heidegger hints at this in the first division's account of *Verfallen*, but it comes more fully into focus, I think, in the second division's discussion of conscience, which is arguably the most Kantian chapter in *Being and Time*, despite Heidegger's effort to distance his account of *Gewissen* and the guilt (*Schuld*) it reveals from Kant's conceptions of conscience and "the relationship to an ought and a law."[39] What, then, does conscience show?

Conscience, like broken or missing tools, reveals, at first, a certain kind of failure – the failure, or breakdown, of Dasein's everyday way of understanding itself, in untroubled coping with the tasks and "responsibilities" the day has to offer. Heidegger locates a similar collapse of

---

[39] *SZ*, 283.

significance (I won't say meaning, for reasons that should already be clear) in the experience of anxiety. But unlike *Angst*, with which *Gewissen* is often interpretively confused, conscience does not merely disclose the necessary possibility that significance can fail, leave me empty and without resources for pressing ahead. (This would merely repeat, at least functionally, what the account of anxiety already accomplished in the first division.) Nor does it merely display the *Nichtigkeit*, or finitude, of my projects, although this is, I think, one of the more prominent morals of Heidegger's admittedly obscure ontology of conscience. This would merely repeat, again functionally, what the account of death is meant to show. We need to accentuate a strand in Heidegger's discussion of conscience, then, that distinguishes its lesson from the tuitions of both anxiety and death; and, just as importantly, we need an account of conscience that makes clear how, or on what basis, Dasein *can* press ahead, given that *Angst* presents something of an impasse in our "everyday absorbed coping," with no clear outlet (and some reason to think there could be none, as long as it represents a complete failure of meaning in every conceivable sense), and death gives us nothing to do.

If we search the chapter on conscience for something in particular we ought to do or to avoid doing, we are bound to be disappointed; in this respect, the account makes no real advance upon the phenomenology of authentic being-toward-death or the analysis of *Angst* that precedes it. In the chapter on history, Heidegger says explicitly that it is not for the existential analytic to tells us "what Dasein *factically* [in particular] resolves upon."[40] (Although he does, in the very same section, remark, as observed in the previous chapter, that "the character of 'goodness' lies in making authentic existence possible."[41] And this at least implies that his account of "anticipatory resoluteness" has some normative [possibly moral] weight; that some conception of what it would be good to be, if not specifically to do, underwrites his account of authenticity; and that there are some ways of being we *ought* to consider better than others, regardless of any ontological pronouncements such ways of being make possible.) Conscience provides no direct and specific information on how to be a more conscientious student, teacher, parent or citizen, and reveals no violation of some particular obligation, however egregious, no specific lack that needs redressing, and no clearly defined action for which I ought to hold myself responsible. As Heidegger observes in § 57, the self reached in the call of conscience "remains indifferent and empty in its what. The call passes over

---

[40] *SZ*, 383.   [41] *SZ*, 383.

what Dasein ... understands itself *as* in its [self-] interpretation in terms of taking care [of its everyday affairs]."[42] All that appears to remain in the Heideggerian analysis of conscience is the now familiar experience of *Unheimlichkeit*, feeling unsettled, not fully at home in the pragmatically interpreted world, and so (once again) finding myself stranded among the wreckage of so many empty possibilities of finding meaning *here* rather than somewhere else; or perhaps, in keeping with a cliché, barring further interpretive work, the equally empty possibility of becoming and remaining true to myself.

Now: I think the cliché actually manages to capture what's at issue here in what Heidegger thinks conscience gives us (or, more precisely, gives me, or each of us) to understand. But if that is true, then it becomes all the more urgent to single out what could possibly remain of my*self* once I've been deprived of all the usual ways of singling myself out, and of talking meaningfully about myself – my specific cares and concerns, and the preoccupations of those with whom I share a life, my accomplishments, what has moved me and perhaps moves me still, what I've pledged myself to, feel guilty about not having realized, in short: all those "characteristics" that give a life, any life, some material content, and so appear to individuate each Dasein more robustly and meaningfully than "being ready for *Angst*" and "authentically being-toward-death." Recall that conscience calls silently, and what it gives us to understand refuses to be talked about.

The only thing that could, I think, be said to remain, provided we wish to remain faithful to what Heidegger actually says, is just the capacity to sustain a certain way of life (or to begin the work of going about things differently), in a way that displays something like self-initiative, agency, and *explicit* choice, against the inveterate tendency (mindlessly) to conform *for the sake of conformity* or (better) as part of a larger pattern of behavior that seems designed to obscure the responsibility that comes with having (explicitly) to choose. (Hence all those remarks in the first division's discussion of *Verfallen* that, departing from neutral structural analysis of the social conditions of any meaningful activity on our part, strongly imply that what is going on in "lapsing" is, among other things, a self-imposed abandonment to something [tempting], even a *self*-tempting [*sich selbst versuchend*] surrender to what makes things easy and tranquilizes.[43] And in a way that makes it hard to pinpoint "who is 'really' [*eigentlich*] choosing."[44]) The evidence for this comes forward fairly clearly in the opening pages of the chapter on conscience, where Heidegger notes that authentic

---

[42] *SZ*, 274.   [43] *SZ*, 177.   [44] *SZ*, 268.

Dasein *makes up for not choosing* by "choosing choice – deciding for an ability-to-be, and making this decision from its own self."[45] As Steve Crowell has recently pointed out, in a convincing analysis of the chapter on conscience, what *Being and Time* means by "being the ground" and "taking over the ground" can be usefully interpreted, in light of the ambiguity of *Grund* (which can mean "reason" as well as "ground"), as Heideggerian ways of speaking about being *responsible* or taking responsibility, and entering the space of reasons, which is to say: being willing to give an account of what *one* does and is about to do or, in opposition to prevailing practice, what *I* propose to do, in light of what I (actively) take to be worth doing.[46] (This arguably resonates with the very practice of *Being and Time* itself, which clearly presumes to be cutting against the grain, but not without rendering an account of the various moves it makes, and in a way that invites others to consider whether the descriptions and arguments carry any weight.)

From this point of view, what is at issue in the analysis of conscience is what Kant calls *autonomy* and the capacity to set ends for ourselves (call it Dasein's ability to understand authentically, or to begin something "from its own self as such"[47]); and the failure being diagnosed, beginning with the ostensibly (morally) neutral account of *Verfallen* in Division One, is comparable to succumbing to the tendency, or the temptation, to treat ourselves as mere things (social roles, instrumental functions, and anything else with a clearly specified *Wasgehalt*), in the sort of *just-so* reasoning about ourselves and our identities I singled out above as one of Heidegger's principal targets in *Being and Time*. If the experience facing ourselves as end-setters goes traditionally by the name of "respect," then the Heideggerian account of conscience, as the revelation of personality in *this* sense, displays some resemblance to the Kantian account of *Achtung*. Although Heidegger admittedly denies that his conception of conscience collapses into the moral experience of being guilty (of some concrete omission), he *is* prepared to grant that *being* guilty, in the sense of being explicitly *responsible* for, and at our best responsive to, the sorts of beings we *are*, "is ... the ... condition of the possibility of the 'morally' good and evil, that is, for morality in general and its possible factical forms."[48] Before I can see myself as someone who has failed to live up to some standard, moral or

---

[45] *SZ*, 268.
[46] See Steven Crowell, "Conscience and Reason: Heidegger and the Grounds of Intentionality" in *Transcendental Heidegger*.
[47] *SZ*, 146.   [48] *SZ*, 286.

otherwise, *authentically* (from my very own self), I need to hold myself responsible for living up to moral norms, and norms more generally, *as such*. I need, in short, to consider myself *free for* normative claims, and so capable of responding, without (external, social) compulsion, to the space of practical reasons. (This is one reason to think, with Mark Wrathall, that Heidegger is not a straightforward social externalist.) This is the surplus that outstrips, or undergirds, whatever "factual characteristics" I can be said to have (what Blattner calls my "ability-characteristics"), and occasionally overwhelms my ordinary sense of being *this* or *that*, not because I'm *not* this or that (in any sense, factual, factical, or in terms of what I take myself to be), but because my being *just so* is mine to be acknowledged or disavowed. As Heidegger himself suggests, "an ontology of Dasein" which clears the way for the value, or the dignity, that I experience in certain privileged moments, should be able to fulfill the same demands as the Kantian "metaphysics of morals."[49]

Authentic Concern for (Others): A Missed Opportunity in "Being and Time"

It might seem odd that we have come so far in our analysis without mentioning others, and in a chapter meant to argue for a moral ontology of social life, or "being-with," in early *Heidegger*. This, it seems, is even consistent with the failure of *Being and Time* to offer a sustained account of concrete ethical relations, beyond the culpably brief discussion of authentic and inauthentic *Fürsorge* in § 26, the care for (or about) others that leaps ahead and "frees the other for himself in his freedom," and the care for others that leaps in, disburdens, and dominates the other.[50] As Taylor Carman notes, with a hint of irritation, "*Being and Time* seems to offer no account of [the] other-oriented dimension of selfhood," and suggests further: "learning to see ourselves as others do, and perhaps coming to see others as they see themselves, is a necessary condition of empathy and the most basic form of moral awareness, and Heidegger's failure to account for it is, I suspect, bound up with his more general failure to understand ethics as a proper branch of philosophy."[51] If we look to other parts of the book for help – for instance, to the chapter on history (or historicity) in the second division – our efforts might appear altogether misguided; for as some have suggested, going back at least to Löwith, Heidegger's views on authentic community appear to strike an uncomfortably collectivistic note.

[49] *SZ*, 293.   [50] *SZ*, 122.   [51] *Heidegger's Analytic*, 268, 269.

At the very least, we seem compelled to conclude that Heidegger missed a crucial opportunity to address a topic that any work presuming to illuminate being-in-the-world cannot afford to marginalize, with or without a moral agenda.

This widely circulating complaint seems to me fair. In its light, as I suggested above, the charge of Levinas, that Heidegger privileges being (and being myself) over *facing others* appears justified. But there is, I think, a mystifying quality in Levinas's account of the face-to-face encounter, and an unhelpful abstractness in his discussion of the Face, that leaves certain phenomena out of focus. I do, for instance, encounter others in an (often shared) experience of what they are trying to do. Dreyfus is right to accentuate this aspect of our involvement with others, as a strand (officially) neglected by some members of the tradition. As I was writing the present paragraph on the porch I saw a neighbor walking her dog along the front of a house owned by another neighbor. She was, for an instant, for me, some*one* who walks her dog, typically, in the early part of the afternoon, and neither a combination of sensible qualities calling for explicit interpretation *nor*, in this setting, a person with an inner life I feel moved to enter into and to get to know better. I'm not even sure she would want me to see her, for now, in any other way. I see the homeless person *as* someone trying to find something to eat, picking plums off the overburdened tree in my side yard. (What else would he have me see him *as*, at the very moment when he asks permission to eat? He may wish to tell me his story, but that's another story, and one that carries me away from *what* one in certain circumstances feels strongly, and rightly, moved to do.) I see my students *as* co-inquirers into the meaning and importance of Heidegger's ontology; or (more troubling still) I see, at least in photographs, the victim of the Holocaust *as* someone degraded in the death-camp, *as*, among many other things, malnourished, withered in body and mind by work in the quarry, fearful or, after enduring so much, perhaps indifferent. I may be mistaken, or prone to read the outward signs meanly, but that will only come out in further encounters and, if possible, in the course of conversation. The concrete situation of the encounter, and the common characteristics or traits that show in the public sphere of our *Besorgen* and *Fürsorge*, cannot be dissolved into an abstract experience of the Face, not, that is, without leaving me helpless to know *what* the encounter *calls for* now, in the flesh, or what was called for *then*, in a massive (collective?) failure to respond to others with moral sensitivity. Or so it appears to me. The problem is not that others show up for us in what they do, or that we sometimes feel moved to attend and respond to those more obvious visible characteristics they share with others in comparable circumstances; the moral failure appears when that is all I manage to see.

What I hope to have shown so far is nothing less than the (Kantian) structure of human agency that, in Heidegger's account, Dasein *as such* displays, beyond the (inauthentic) reduction of Dasein to *what* one does; and in this sense, the interpretation lays out what *I* would have to acknowledge to be true of others, if something like a moral orientation is to be possible on Heideggerian grounds. Something has to show *beyond* my trying to get something done that makes genuine moral relations possible, something about the other's status in our being mutually impli-cated or involved in a task that does not reduce her to being a helper along my way; something about her*self* needs showing that cannot be reduced to what she has done or can do – for me, or even for *us*, perhaps in some sort of "we-intentionality." If I see her merely as the embodiment of "what one does," I miss something essential about her – that she is the subject of a life, say, beyond or beneath her various accomplishments (that she, too, "has her being to be," as a "thrown project" and a possibility [to be herself], to speak as Heidegger does in *Being and Time*). The other, in short, needs showing *as an other* (Dasein), with her own stake in what is being done, beyond what I'd like to see come into being between us and because of us. This will involve something like an overcoming, in our very practices and perceptions, of the "category mistake" *Being and Time* as a whole was partly meant to overcome, at least in the space of philosophical theory, or fundamental ontology.

But pointing this out is still not enough to show that *Heidegger* realized the (possible) moral bearing of his account of Dasein and other entities in *Being and Time*, and what I take to be its Kantian provenance. So, to complete the account, I'd like to turn briefly to Heidegger's earlier discus-sion of care and care-for (others) in a course of lectures on logic held in 1925/6, which shows, if nothing else, that I'm not simply reading pious wishes into a position that will not support them.

The opening claims of § 17, on care as the being of human existence, concern-for (others), and concern-about (things and affairs), will strike a familiar chord to those conversant with *Being and Time*: Dasein is in the world as the space of significance in the way of involvement (with things of use), concerned about its own being, related somehow to others, and fundamentally constituted by *care*. What is surprising, and often over-looked, is Heidegger's unprecedented reference to Kant: "Clearly Kant had this state of affairs in view when he said, using traditional ontological categories: The human being belongs to those 'things whose existence is an end in itself.' Or as he once formulated it: 'The human being exists as an end in itself.' Or again: [human beings are those beings] 'whose existence has an absolute value in itself.'"[52] Heidegger goes on to note, with apparent sympathy, that this concept of being human makes (ontologically, metaphysically) possible the categorical imperative of morality. As one might expect, Heidegger complains that Kant's use of *Zweck*-language, along with the language of value (*Wert*), betrays a traditional orientation; but Heidegger shows no signs of rejecting the experiences he takes Kant to be struggling to clarify. This alone, I think, vindicates much of the work I've been doing throughout the bulk of the present chapter.

But what is even more interesting, in light of the concern that has driven us all along, is Heidegger's Kantian application of the care-structure of my own being to being-with-others. Not only, Heidegger suggests, is my (i.e., Heidegger's) own being as an "end in itself" at stake in the use of chalk (Heidegger's own example in the classroom), but "the current Dasein of those who are listening and understanding is likewise at stake. One might think that the care of the Dasein communicating is "concerned-for" and has to deal with listening others [*hörenden Anderen*], that they are in each case merely present [*vorhanden*] in the surrounding world and hence fall into the circle of the surrounding world about which one is concerned. [But] you, the listener, are not an object-concerned-about [*ein Be-sorgtes*]."[53] We have here, in other words, an instance of shared care (*Mitsorge*) and concern-for (*Fürsorge*). And it is in just this context, inflected by Kantian concepts and concerns, that Heidegger offers the first (extant) version of what entered into § 26 in *Being and Time*, namely, the distinction between authentic and inauthentic "solicitude." In the former case, "I certainly do not understand the other existence primarily in terms of the world I'm concerned about. Rather, *I understand the other's existence only in terms of himself* [my emphasis]."[54] In the latter case, by implication, I understand the other in terms of something I take him to be trying to do, and in a sense that fails to respect his own agency in the event. And in a remarkable passage, which one can only wish had found its way into *Being and Time* itself, Heidegger suggests that inauthentic concern-for "treats the other like a nothing [*ein Nichts*], as if he had nothing of Dasein about him," as though he were "something merely present [like a thing] in the world [*als etwas weltliches Vorhandenes*]."[55] It took a work like *Being and Time*, in the wake of Kant, to spell out more fully the nature (and at least to indicate, without explicit argument, the deep historical roots) of this

[52] *Logic: The Question of Truth*, GA 21, 220.   [53] Ibid., 222.   [54] Ibid., 223.   [55] Ibid., 224.

ontological mistake; but it did so (sadly) in a way that left the moral
implications of the failure, clearly in evidence here (if not exactly overworked), too much in the dark.

The Persistent Problem of Moral Motivation

This still leaves open a pressing problem, both for Kant and for Heidegger.
We can grant the importance, at once ontological and moral, of the
distinction between things and persons and still wonder what, if anything,
provides the motive for acknowledging the distinction in everyday life and
living up to what it demands in our concrete relations with others. That we
know the difference between plants and stones, animals and human beings
is not sufficient to guarantee that we will treat our fellow human beings
with the respect this fundamental ontological difference requires. What, if
anything, guarantees that we will "use humanity . . . always at the same
time as an end, never merely as a means"?[56] Abstract conceptions of such
differences are notoriously ineffective in governing concrete moral relations
between persons. As Stanley Cavell observes, it will not suffice to say of the
slaveholder that he treats certain human beings as things: "What he really
believes is not that slaves are not human beings, but that some human
beings are slaves."[57] Further: "Everything in his relation to his slaves shows
that he treats them as more or less human – his humiliations of them, his
disappointments, his jealousies, his fears, his punishments, his attachments," etc.[58] The sorts of indignities to which we subject are fellows
are, in fact, structurally anchored in a recognition of their humanity. The
slaveholder sleeps with the very slave he earlier whipped, and would never
think of eroticizing his plow. It is a commonplace to note that some Nazis
were "good Kantians."

If it is possible to ask "Why be authentic?" – why not live life as
pleasantly as possible? – it is equally sensible to ask "Why be moral?"
The cynic, perhaps in the spirit of Thrasymachus in Plato's *Republic*, is
likely to answer: We shouldn't, provided we can get away with behaving
badly, as the weak are likely to describe our conduct. We can acknowledge
that some things are persons, other things not, and still maintain that our
relations to others are only subject to moral obligations by convention or
force. Our social lives become matters of *pleonexia*, striving to get as much
as possible at the expense of others, unfairly, as moralists are likely to say.

[56] *Groundwork*, 4:429.   [57] *The Claim of Reason*, 375.   [58] Ibid., 376.

The answer appears to be that no good *reason* is sufficient to motivate the moral point of view. We are always at liberty to say "no."

A full account of Heidegger on moral motivation, or the incentives to aspire after the ideal of authenticity, would require a book-length study in its own right. Heidegger speaks often in the early lecture courses of "motives" and "tendencies" in "factical life," but questions concerning motivation, however central in the early period, only come forward up to a point in the period leading up to the publication of *Sein und Zeit*. For the most part, motives come into play as a way of incentivizing the philosophical quest – what speaks for it in everyday life, what stands in the way. This is almost certainly tied to Heidegger's reluctance to traffic in what he sees as the psychology of philosophy. But for reasons more intrinsic to Heidegger's philosophy of *care*, the answer is difficult to come by, and for reasons we began to spell out above and return to in the final chapter. There are no philosophical arguments or neutral appeals to reason that can be said to move someone (necessarily, by virtue of logical implication, say, or by the sheer power of moral reason) to take a moral interest in the distinction between persons and things, if she is not already moved to take the distinction to heart *in a morally inflected way*. One might appeal to a principle of enlightened self-interest; but the noun gives voice to a tautology (every interest belongs to a self whose being is at issue for itself), and the adjective only matters to someone who antecedently cares about being or becoming enlightened. Kant himself seems to come close to this view in his defense of our imperfect duties to others (helping those in need, e.g.), as if to say: we should be convinced, or can be led by the voice of reason to believe, that the world is just better when organized around a principle of coming to the assistance of the less fortunate. We are, after all, subject to the vicissitudes of chance. But for someone like Thrasymachus, being enlightened reduces to pursuing one's own advantage and securing power; the rest is for the impotent to care about, masquerading as virtue. And every principle is, on Heidegger's Aristotelian view, beyond the scope of proof. No amount of mathematical ingenuity can convince someone indifferent to mathematics that calculus ought to matter. Similarly, no amount of moral eloquence and ethical preaching is likely to reach someone for whom the claims of moral life are out of bounds.

I think we can say, at this point, that (for Heidegger) being authentic amounts to acknowledging the agency of others. At the very least, this is a claim Heidegger is officially prepared to make in WS 1925/6. But it isn't clear why we should care to own up in the first place. As Golob notes, "the demand postulated by Heidegger [to be authentic, or moral, under some description] is radically different from requirements such as the categorical imperative."[59] Heidegger himself has a fairly complicated story to tell about how easily we fall into existential (and moral and philosophical) apathy. What he calls "average everydayness" carries tremendous weight in the course of human existence by default. The struggle is ongoing and, it seems, the majority of us will succumb to the *tentatio*. Reason alone is powerless to dictate how we ought to live, in part because reason, in the Heideggerian account, is subject to certain conditions (historical, social, etc.), in part because reason in the broad Kantian sense (the discursive power of judgment, syllogism, moral deliberation, and the like) is not the most fundamental fact about us. There is, in short, "no unconditional obligation to be authentic."[60] This contrasts sharply with Kant's insistence that we have unconditional obligations to act in such a way that our maxims are consistent with the giving of universal law, or to treat others always as ends and never merely as means, or to help realize a kingdom of ends, governed by the principle of autonomy. (This will, in the eyes of some, place Heidegger at a distinctive moral disadvantage.)

There is a short, if philosophically unhelpful, response according to which the problem of motivation simply falls outside of the tasks of moral philosophy proper. It is, after all, up to the individual to decide between good and evil, just as one can take or leave the hard demands of the philosophical life. (The unexamined life may not be worth living for a human being, as Socrates insists in Plato's *Apology*, but the insistence is motivated by the widespread tendency to shirk the labor of self-examination.) One might even be suspicious of rhetorical strategies meant to cajole the morally indifferent into taking an interest in the life of virtue. If morality is a matter of what the human being makes of herself, the choice between virtue and vice is always the individual's private concern; the event occurs in a realm untouched by external forces and ostensible moral authorities. As Kant often insists, we carry the paradigm of moral excellence within ourselves. Any attempt to root moral deliberation in examples of virtue risks clouding over the true sources of moral normativity. "Even the Holy One of the Gospels," in the Kantian account, must be compared with the true paradigm of moral reason, lodged in the common human understanding, in order to be judged a fitting example of

---

[59] *Heidegger on Concepts, Freedom and Normativity*, 239.
[60] Steven Crowell, "Sorge or Selbstbewußtsein? Heidegger and Korsgaard on the Sources of Normativity" (*European Journal of Philosophy*, 326).

the moral life.[61] The choice is always ours to assent to moral law or to subordinate the categorical imperative of morality to a principle of mere self-interest. Anything else reduces to what Kant calls "heteronomy." The task of the metaphysician of morals, or the fundamental ontologist, is simply to make explicit the principle of morality and to articulate its metaphysical foundations, or to elucidate certain structures of human existence that stake some claim, without coercion, upon our thoughts and actions. The rest is up to each of us.

Despite appearances to the contrary, Kant himself was deeply troubled by the problem of moral motivation. The account of morality in the *Groundwork* leaves one with the initial impression that we have everything we need to make the right choice (a moral law, freedom of the will) in every circumstance, but abuse our freedom (or our *Willkühr*, to employ an important term in Kant's *Religion*) for our own selfish ends. Kant's distinction between pathological and practical love trades upon precisely this capacity: we may not be able to love someone (as a matter of affection) upon command,[62] but we can always love someone (as a matter of action) in a way consistent with the requirements of pure practical reason.[63] But Kant was also deeply interested in the tasks of moral education, and in a way that takes seriously the task of helping agents-in-the-making become responsible moral agents.[64] And his account of respect (*Achtung*) in the second *Critique* and elsewhere draws attention to the affective dimension of our moral commitments.[65] In the end, there may be no definitive rational argument available to convince the reprobate to treat others as ends in themselves, but both Heidegger and Kant have a story to tell about the *affective* dimension of our capacity for moral conduct that sheds light on what it would be like to be responsive to the claims of others.

This is not the place to develop a detailed account of Heidegger's longstanding interest in the affective life.[66] But it is worth noting that,

---

[61] *Groundwork*, 4:408.   [62] *Critique of Practical Reason*, 5:83.

[63] For the distinction between practical and pathological love, see, for instance, *Groundwork*, 4:399.

[64] Kant's interest in moral education comes forward in the "Doctrine of the Method of Pure Practical Reason," which brings the second *Critique* to a close. But see also the section on "Teaching Ethics" in the *Metaphysics of Morals*.

[65] Kant's most sustained discussion of respect is located in the *Critique of Practical Reason*, Part One, Book One, chapter 3, which bears the relevant title, "On the Motives [or Incentives, *Triebfeder*] of Pure Practical Reason" (my emphasis).

[66] The literature on Heidegger on affectivity is extensive. I've learned a great deal from the second chapter of Matthew Ratcliffe's *Feelings of Being: Phenomenology, Psychiatry, and the Sense of Reality* and, more recently, by Katherine Withy's short but illuminating "Owned Emotions: Affective Excellence in Heidegger and Aristotle" in *Heidegger, Authenticity and the Self*. See also Rick Anthony Furtak's *Knowing Emotions: Truthfulness and Recognition in Affective Experience*, which draws

in addition to powerful arguments in favor of the grounding role played by attunement (*Stimmung*) and disposition (*Befindlichkeit*) in opening up a world of care and concern, Heidegger singles out the Kantian phenomenon of respect in a course of lectures held in the summer semester of 1927, shortly after the appearance of *Sein und Zeit*. In a way that supports our earlier insistence on the primacy of the practical point of view, Heidegger grants that "the true and central characterization of the ego, of subjectivity, in Kant ... lies in the concept of *personalitas moralis*."[67] And he centers his account of moral personality (or *responsibility*) on the phenomenon of *respect*, according to which the moral agent has herself (as a rational being) in the form of a distinctive moral *feeling*. In a revisionary move, meant to distance Kant's ethics from rational principle alone, Heidegger observes, in opposition to Scheler's critique of Kant's so-called "formalism": "Kant's interpretation of the phenomenon of respect is probably the most brilliant phenomenological analysis of the phenomenon of morality that we have from him."[68] To be sure, Heidegger goes on to criticize the Kantian analysis of moral personality. The criticism, however, does not amount to the charge that personality is nothing moral, but that Kant has failed to provide an adequate ontological foundation for the moral existence of the person.

How we come to experience respect remains an open question. But one point is clear: We discover an interest in the moral life by way of being affected in a certain way. We come to acknowledge our own humanity, or personhood, by way of "a disposition to become moved to act, to become affected by what" our nature or being enables us to do.[69] And affectivity is not (entirely) within the individual's control. To gain mastery over emotion and mood is not to be without either, but to replace one emotion or mood with another. Heidegger cites Spinoza in this context. But the position finds expression in the discussion of attunement in *Sein und Zeit*: "we never master a mood by being free of a mood, but always through a counter mood."[70] If Heidegger is right, then, we are never without mood. Mood is no fleeting, subjective phenomenon, but a grounding condition of our having world and taking an interest in what world has to give, including those moral responsibilities that, in the Kantian view, cannot be forced but need somehow to show. Respect is a peculiar way of having

---

selectively from Heidegger to make the case that our affective experience plays a grounding role in our capacity to have a world (of truth and meaning) at all.
[67] *The Basic Problems of Phenomenology*, 131.   [68] Ibid., 133.
[69] Frank Schalow, *The Renewal of the Heidegger-Kant Dialogue*, 273.   [70] *SZ*, 136.

myself, of *feeling* myself, not as a sensible being but as a moral being, capable of assuming *responsibility*. Respect is "a revealing of [myself] as an acting being."[71] The phenomenon of respect does not, however, narrow the scope of my concern to my own being, but opens me, in Schalow's words, "to the more expansive concern that speaks the demands of *one's relations* to others."[72] The moral law, announced in the feeling of respect, "strikes down self-conceit."[73]

We opened this chapter with a quotation from Goethe's *Wahlverwandtschaften*, the "moral" lesson of which appears to be that we are not at liberty to decide what our decisions will bring about ("No one can foresee what will come of them"[74]). More troublingly still, we are not even at liberty to decide freely in the first instance ("if it is not our own will . . . that drives us . . ., chance, necessity, passion, circumstances and I don't know what else drives us . . . instead"[75]). The best-laid plans of its protagonists come to grief, and the moral intentions of its characters are nothing secure, but held hostage to ungovernable sentiment and passion. One of Heidegger's terms for affectivity is *Befindlichkeit*, a matter of *finding* ourselves disposed to think and behave in certain ways, beyond and beneath what we explicitly choose. While he almost certainly did not have Goethe in view, his views on the affective dimension of our experiential lives resembles, at certain points, the tragic depiction of human character and its fate in Goethe's novel, ending in death.

This may just be another way of saying that the problem of moral motivation is insoluble, that nothing in the nature of human reason or the structure of human existence is sufficient to motivate a lasting commitment to a certain (moral) form of life. But if the problem of moral motivation is insoluble in early Heidegger, it should come as no surprise that it is a problem that persists throughout the philosophical tradition that both Kant and Heidegger inherit and one that remains with us today. It falls to education (a topic of interest to Heidegger as well as Plato and Aristotle), but with no guarantee of success. The best the moral ontologist, or the metaphysician of morals, can do is to conceptualize a vision of a better way of life, leaving the concrete pedagogical task to others, and to each of us, provided we are properly attuned.

When the task concerns morality, this might seem like hard wisdom. We'd like our moral commitments to be more stable, our intentions more clearly discernible, ourselves and our pupils tractable. But Heidegger, like

---

[71] *Basic Problems*, 133.   [72] *The Renewal of the Heidegger-Kant Dialogue*, 275.
[73] *Basic Problems*, 134.   [74] Goethe, *Elective Affinities*, 35.   [75] Ibid., 233.

Kant, is willing to acknowledge that human existence cannot be manufactured, that our motives and incentives remain elusive, and that moral despair cannot be overcome by the force of argument or pure reason alone. And, unlike Plato's Socrates in the *Republic*, that the autonomy of human existence is a *conditio sine qua non* of any worthwhile way of life. The sheer fact that the problem of motivation remains a problem is perhaps an index of the dignity of being human.

CHAPTER 5

Owning Up to Life and Death

Essentialism and Its Discontents

Heidegger's early lecture courses and manuscripts often argue against the philosophical and moral tendency to generalize in favor of commitments to the concrete and particular. If the being of the human being is *Sorgen* (*curare*), if we are creatures for whom things matter and the world is a space of meaning, the proper object of our cares and concerns is the particular life, and world, each of us is called upon to live.[1] "Factical Dasein is what it is always only as one's own Dasein and never as the Dasein in general of some universal humanity. Expending care on the latter could only ever be an illusory task."[2] What I take myself to be, and what I ought to do, depends on where I happen to be, and how I end up construing my own life in relation to this irreducibly singular location, a meaningful place, a meaningful time, and a particular community of like-minded individuals. Any suggestion that certain constraints, belonging to something like human nature, might place limits on what I can meaningfully think or do or aspire to be should be dismissed as inauthentic. In a more aphoristic vein, we might say that it is the nature of the human being to have nothing like a fixed and abiding nature: the first step toward owning up to the human condition is to acknowledge that there is none, beyond what history has made of us.

As attractive and as liberating as this view can be, it is difficult to square fully with what early Heidegger has to say about the (general) ontological constitution of human life and the price of failing to live up to the sort of being we (human beings *überhaupt*) have and are. As we argued in the previous chapter, Heidegger recovers a Kantian strain that opens onto general reflections concerning human agency and dignity as such; and we argued briefly in the third chapter that Heideggerian authenticity is

---

[1] See, for example, *GA* 62, 352.   [2] *Supplements*, 114.

tethered to a definition of the very being of human existence *as such*. On the view I think early Heidegger is struggling to defend, it is not enough to be concerned about my own particular life and the life of my community. It is equally important to clarify and conceptualize what it generally *is* to have a particular life to live and to be a member of a particular community, or to inhabit particular spaces of significance. The historicist's claims in early Heidegger often give way to, or stand in tension with, the claims of an essentialist of sorts, centered on the essential *finitude* of Dasein.

One might still wonder whether Heidegger was mistaken, or just confused about what he was trying to do. Therefore, we ought to ask whether it is plausible to say that we have something that looks like a nature (and if so, how we come to know it, where it has to be sought, and why the apparent diversity of self-conceptions across time and social space) or whether the human being is just the fleeting embodiment of a contingent language game. Why not speak with the late Richard Rorty of a "temptation [to be resisted] to think of the world, or the human self, as possessing an intrinsic nature, an essence"?[3] Would it not be better, less oppressive and confining, to embrace the timely suggestion that "most of reality is indifferent to our descriptions of it, and that the human self is created by the use of a vocabulary"?[4] And should we not prefer the strand in early Heidegger that encourages us to disavow essentialism of every sort, despite other strands that seem more philosophically conventional?

Expressed as an ethical issue: Is there something for which we are called upon to assume more general responsibility, something about us humans that demands something like acknowledgment? Or are we, at our best, the inventive authors of our own lives and being and failures insofar as we will not or cannot create ourselves as a work of art? If we are not drawn to the ideal of unconstrained self-creation, do we commit ourselves to a conception of ethical truth as correspondence to or imitation of a transcendent criterion of human flourishing? What alternative(s) might there be to the idea of getting in touch with a timeless standard of human perfection, woven, so to speak, into the fabric of the cosmos?

These are no merely theoretical questions. How we answer them, if the answers are taken to heart, will give shape to a distinctive sort of life. It makes a difference *in practice* whether I think that I am in touch with a

³ Rorty, *Contingency, Irony, and Solidarity*, 6.   ⁴ Ibid., 7.

general ideal of human life or believe that shared standards are nowhere to be found. It matters whether my ideal is the philosopher, here the discoverer of the truth about the world and human life, or the poet who, on the Rortian view, in some sense fabricates the things we take to be or, more minimally, causes things to mean what they do or, in Rorty's ambiguous phrase, "makes things new."[5] Where the task is no longer to fit a conception to the world or to discover the true contours of the self, but to word the world and ourselves freshly out of the contingent stuff of a particular life, where I am no longer concerned to get matters right but to do or say something unfamiliar or unique, I will try to live more spontaneously and originally, more artistically and less conventionally than my more serious, moralizing counterpart.

What we can, for the sake of convenience, call "the Rortian stance" is easy enough to dismiss; it has been capably criticized by Putnam, among others, and despite Rorty's own acknowledged historicism, the historical work that underwrites it is probably tendentious. We might be tempted to leave the stance alone, perhaps in the same spirit that governs the Rortian's own relation to the tradition she aspires to shake off. But while it has its philosophical shortcomings, as I hope to show below, the stance does seem to capture several salient features of our intellectual landscape, and addresses concerns an essentialist of sorts should, I think, attempt to make her own.

It captures, first, the sense we have of ourselves as historical beings, located in contingent social landscapes, and surrounded by people who say and do things differently. This is what early Heidegger is largely trying to understand and to defend; and much of his criticism of extant philosophy is tied to the view that the philosophical tradition has tended to ignore the historical dimension of human life, in the name of timeless ideas and ideals.[6] As Edie aptly remarks, commenting on Husserl's phenomenology, "there is no truth that does not have its 'date' ... and its determinate historical situation."[7] Some ways of life may be like our own in some respects, and it may turn out that two or more apparently heterogeneous ways of construing life are not incommensurable, but nothing guarantees that different worldviews and modes of life can always be reduced to a common measure of value or that disputes between conflicting parties can

---

[5] Ibid., 13.
[6] See, for instance, the engagement with Descartes and Husserl in WS 1923/4, discussed in the second chapter.
[7] *Phenomenology and Skepticism*, 28.

be situated on a shared, neutral terrain where they can, in principle, be resolved.[8] We seem more willing to accept the need to choose between, say, the life of a liberal democrat and the life of an Islamic fundamentalist, and (perhaps slightly more reluctantly) to resign ourselves to the impossibility of reasoning with certain adversaries and, in urgent situations, to resort to force when the gentler voice of what we call reason falls on unreceptive ears. Values are often tied to the particular, historical shape of the lives that embody them.

This is one reason why it requires so much imaginative effort to comprehend an alien form of life. It also helps to explain why many of the best defenses of our own liberal democratic institutions and the ways of life they promote and preserve are guided by the history of democratic life and thought. We (North Americans) never simply perceive *the* essence of democratic politics, whatever that might be, but tell ourselves some story about the success of democratic ideals in the early history of the Republic and sketch out concrete, historical reasons why certain alternatives did not suffice in the colonies. We draw upon the biographical details of the founding representatives of our ideals, cite and analyze crucial historical documents, and consider the testimony of Franklin, Jefferson, Hamilton, and other, less conspicuous figures against our own present experiences and concerns. We examine possible or actual alternative histories and ask ourselves whether *we* would still be able to flourish if they were somehow our own; and we alter our tentatively settled convictions in the light of novel ethical situations and evolving social and political circumstances. We do not (or at least not usually) appeal to neutral facts or deep inner longings that others without comparable histories can be expected to acknowledge immediately as their own. We might continue to hold certain truths to be in the abstract self-evident, but most of us are willing to grant that what we no longer seriously question was once hotly contested, that our own self-evident truths have a history, and were not always considered self-evident and are not currently self-evident to others living in different social, political, and historical circumstances. In the end, we expect others to understand and to appreciate what we value most fully only when liberal democratic values have become a (historical) way of life for them.

---

[8] For a short account of commensurability and the stigma of relativism that attaches to the denial of it, see *Philosophy and the Mirror of Nature*, 316ff. The notion of incommensurability is developed in relation to Kuhn on pp. 322–33. On Rorty's view, the acknowledgement of incommensurability is compatible with what he calls "*simply* hope for agreement" in the absence of the traditional conviction that such hope is "a token of common ground which, perhaps unbeknown to the speakers, unites them in a common rationality" (318).

The stance resonates, further, with our heightened sense of the value of the particular and the unique and the elevated worth we attribute to the products of so-called genius, which promises the freshness of novel vocabularies and unfamiliar, untried paradigms. In Walter Pater's words, "To burn always with this hard, gem-like flame, to maintain this ecstasy, is success in life. In a sense, it might even be said that our failure is to form habits: for, after all, habit is relative to a stereotyped world, and meantime it is only the roughness of the eye that makes any two persons, things, and situations seem alike."[9] Value is not located in a heavenly space divorced from the concrete objects and affairs that pervade everyday life, but in *these things here and now*.

Both sets of closely related convictions are often combined with the further belief that essentialism is morally oppressive and socially and politically dubious, that essences too frequently figure in questionable efforts to make others over in an image of what *we* consider true and good, whether justified or not, and in willful neglect of the considered judgment, capacities, and experiences of those whose lives must at all cost resemble our own.

Finally, there is a justified fear of dogmatism, a refined epistemological awareness that human life is too messy, too diverse, and too malleable to be traced back to something unequivocally fundamental, absolutely certain, epistemically guaranteed, an intuition that the specter of relativism is less threatening and pernicious than an overly ripe confidence in the stances we take, hostility to the refusal to consider human life otherwise and a love of experimental attitudes. As Heidegger observes in SS 1924, commenting on the Aristotelian doctrine of the mean, *"For our being, characterized by particularity, no unique and absolute norm can be given."*[10] From this point of view, essentialism appears driven by a longing for *terra firma*, fixed frameworks that provide assurance, objects to which we can cling in the midst of an otherwise unstable world, and reliable precepts that place constraints on the unruly and uncertain world of human affairs. To struggle against essentialism is to work toward the realization of a flexible, more spontaneous, and more openly dialogical culture in which the demand for constraint and the quest for certainty no longer find a central place.

Together, these convictions seem to amount to a coherent view of life, centered on the idea that we are *self-interpreting*, historical animals. There is no nature that stands outside our various interpretations and active

---

[9] Pater, "Conclusion" to *The Renaissance*, 152.   [10] *Basic Concepts of Aristotelian Philosophy*, 126.

embodiments of it. Our nature as nourishment-seeking animals always displays or realizes itself in particular culinary practices and construals. We are unlike other animals in this: we are to some extent free to decide what it means to have to eat, to incorporate necessity in a contingent shape that bears the impress of collective or individual efforts to assign a meaning to this particular biological imperative.

But it is one thing to point out that a certain group of people eats human flesh, another eats no meat, while some enjoy fish, and still others attempt for various reasons to eat as little as possible, something else to deny that human beings as such have to eat in order to survive. It is one thing to say that death for some means the shedding of our mortal coil, another thing to deny that human beings are mortal. Why not say that the diverse expressions or embodiments of what we are, are just so many ways of responding to the very thing itself? We can think away a diverse body of practices and establish their contingency. But can we always think away the exigencies to which they respond and still discover a meaningful *human* way of life?

These questions and the controversy they rehearse clearly open onto a topic as large as the contested human condition itself. We can, however, at least *begin* to think about what speaks in favor of a (chastened) version of essentialism if we narrow our field of vision to one allegedly essential structure of human life, and consider in depth and detail what speaks for its having, or playing, the essential role it might play in shaping (for good) a human way of life. In what follows I argue along lines sketched, if not fully fleshed out, by early Heidegger that death is one salient feature of the human condition that we can either acknowledge or disavow;[11] and I argue, further, that it makes no small practical difference whether we own up to the human condition of mortality or fail to cope with it and to care properly about it.[12] As Heidegger observes in an early essay on Aristotle, death "as an object of care" and properly acknowledged somehow "makes the present and past of one's own life visible."[13]

As we shall, I hope, come to see, owning up to the condition of mortality is neither unacceptably confining nor inconsistent with a vigilant concern for the particular, but an essential aspect of what it means to come

[11] The *locus classicus* of this view is, of course, *Sein und Zeit*, Division II, Chapter. It is also suggested in WS 1921/2 and developed in the "Natorp Essay" (1922).
[12] This way of putting it may give the impression that death is just one category among many; but it is central to Heidegger's account of human existence in the early period, and central because it discloses the wholeness of Dasein.
[13] "Phenomenological Interpretations in Connection with Aristotle" in *Supplements*, 118, 119.

to terms with the concrete situations and tasks that define our concernful, historical lives.[14] There is something to be said for the liberating power of mortality and the *finite* shape of life that the acknowledgment of death makes possible.[15] But before we get clear about the ways in which death grants sense and shape to human life, we ought to ask (with Heidegger) how death itself is revealed or discovered and where.[16] In the first part of what follows, I follow up Heidegger's suggestion that death is neither an object, out there in the world, nor something merely subjective (like a thought or an opinion or a mere feeling) but a *way to be*, woven (structurally) into our various comportments and stances. Getting clear about this, we will then be better placed to defend at greater length in Part Two (and somewhat independently of the arguments Heidegger himself deploys in *Sein und Zeit*) the claim that death helps constitute the *intelligibility* of practical life; and we will finally be in a position to appreciate more fully the normative claims that shape Heidegger's ontic ideal of *Eigentlichkeit*.[17]

Death in the Heart of Practical Life: A Questionable Suggestion

Infants and toddlers do not seem to be plagued by an awareness of death. They appear to live, as Nietzsche suggests, "in blissful blindness between the hedges of past and future."[18] But while they lack the adult's unsettling perception of time and live "fettered to the moment," their cries seem to

---

[14] Although I won't argue the point here, I think we have to distinguish between three planes of analysis: there is (1) the empty and impoverished consideration of a characteristic or structure of human life at an extreme level of abstraction (where, e.g., we are content merely to say that human life is mortal); (2) a richer perspective, like the one being offered here, of the structure in relation to other structures of human life and with an eye on some of the particular situations in which the characteristic becomes relevant; and (3) a perspective so thoroughly trained upon particulars that we lose sight of the structure or characteristic altogether. I grant that the first plane is, if not useless, not altogether helpful or informative. But I am also resistant to the idea that contextualized particulars are all we've got. We don't have to choose between getting lost among abstract universals and getting stranded among particulars. Not every account of the general structure of human life is culpably detached or abstract; and not every grasp of something particular has to ignore what sort of thing in general the particular in question is.

[15] This, I think, is *in nuce* what Heidegger intends to say about the "ontic" consequences of acknowledging *Sein zum Tode*; but his account is slightly marred by the awkward suggestion that death is my *ownmost* possibility. Philipse, among others, justly observes that there are other possibilities, bound up with our embodiment, that each of us alone must actualize: no one can eat or defecate for me.

[16] Death, as Heidegger observes already in 1922, "is always in one way or another there for [human life], i.e., there as seen in one way or another, even if this takes the form of pushing away and suppressing the 'thought of death'" (*Supplements*, 118).

[17] It bears noting, in light of some controversy about what death means in early Heidegger, that I take death to be what we usually mean by *death*, and not, say, the loss of certain possibilities.

[18] *Untimely Meditations*, 61.

speak of pain, hunger, and other deprivations. Their movements suggest the dawning awareness of a world of things that come and go and more reliable objects that stay put. And, knowing these things, they are already acquainted with what the normal adult associates with the tokens of mortal life. They seem to sense the presence of powerful agencies that tend to their bodily needs and offer comfort, assurance, and the shelter of a "facilitating environment," and seem to know, or to sense, something of the absence that stings. When the mother or the surrogate parent is away, perhaps they experience something like the absence of the dead. The apparently insatiable longing to be held speaks against a certain comforting picture of early life: contrary to idyllic fantasies, the infant lives in an aleatory world composed of strange forces held temporarily at bay by familiar figures. The world might be interesting and enticing, an endless source of wonder and awe, but it is also a perilous theater where income and outcome are nothing assured.[19] Unless we picture an automaton in place of the developing child, it seems safe to assume the presence in early childhood of an inchoate sense of the risk, uncertainty, and danger of merely being alive. But knowledge of what we call death comes belatedly on the scene and ripens rather slowly. Full acceptance of its implications comes much later, if at all.

Death, then, appears to be something out there in the world, like parents, cribs, and food, discovered in the child's lengthy apprenticeship in the school of the real, alongside the qualities and behavings of bananas and honey bees, tables and chairs. Death, we suspect, "would have to be understood in the sense of an imminent event to be encountered in the surrounding world."[20] Coming to know something about it is like getting acquainted with an initially strange custom or becoming familiar with the use of a novel tool or learning the details of human anatomy. It is a fact about us, an ascertainable item that helps to complete the child's gradually emerging picture of the world. Death is woven into the fabric of things, merely waiting for each of us to make the discovery and the appropriate adjustments occasioned by the finding. Our first encounters make us aware of empirical cases of death.[21] For a time we could not see it, then suddenly death was there: unfocused vision finally yields to more mature insight.

---

[19] On this point, see Rousseau's *Emile*, especially Book One.   [20] *SZ*, 250.
[21] Heidegger acknowledges that cases of death provide the "occasion for the fact that Dasein initially notices death at all" (*Sein und Zeit*, 257).

But death is a peculiar fact. Awareness of it seems to behave differently, as Heidegger frequently reminds us. Unlike the familiar things that come and go, impressing me lightly, carving out more lasting marks, or leaving me indifferent, death enters and gets to me (*geht mich an*) as few things can, with matchless intensity and persistence. Knowledge of death concerns and penetrates more deeply and unsettles more forcefully than knowledge of mere objects usually does: no one who is not insane or already otherwise disturbed is profoundly troubled by the awareness of rotting fruit. We do not flee the gentle rain as swiftly as we run from a menacing mountain lion in hungry pursuit of a meal. The sight of a decaying tree is not as revolting and unsettling as the glimpse of a bloated corpse pulled out of a local river.

When death does come more sharply into focus, it alters the very contours of the world we thought we knew. It is not something that merely adds to the picture of a world otherwise finished, as just another item in the interminable inventory of what belongs to this immense cosmos. The sequestered offspring of some well-meaning Crusoe, reared on an island knowing nothing of death and dying, aging but unable to read the signs of her mortality, would not be merely deficient in factual knowledge of the world. We would sooner say that he does not belong to the same world we do, as though coming to be at home in the world and becoming acquainted with death were two sides of the same proverbial coin. What we come to know is neither a thing nor a property but something that *happens* to certain privileged things, depriving us of what was once reassuringly there, embedded in our habits and accompanying our uncertain strivings.[22] C. S. Lewis conveys the sense and scope of this incomparable loss, facing the death of a loved one, movingly in *A Grief Observed*: "So many roads lead through to H. I set out on one of them. But now there's an impassable frontier post across it. So many roads once; now so many culs-de-sac."[23] Death takes away more than it adds to what belongs to our world. It finds itself at home in a piercing sense of the vulnerability of what we find significant, sometimes threatening the sense of significance itself.[24] Here at least, the loss is irreversible and complete. And strangely intangible: hammers and nails, Heidegger's early favored

---

[22] Again, in Heidegger's terms, death usually appears as an *Ereignis* that overtakes in the public realm. See *SZ*, 252–3.

[23] *A Grief Observed*, 59. See also Shakespeare's 64th Sonnet.

[24] As Heidegger says of *Angst*, the world comes to have the pervasive character of "complete insignificance" (*SZ*, 186).

examples of coping with the world, are useless implements in the struggle to come to grips with death.

We might be tempted to look for death in the intangible spaces of the mind itself. If empirical instances of death occasion the general awareness of mortality, death itself enters human consciousness and lives on in newly acquired shapes inside the life of the mortal subject, coloring its perception of the world and the various pictures it paints of itself. To say that death alters the contours of our world and shapes our sense of life is just to claim that death takes up residence in us. The moment we become aware of the thing itself, death is no longer "out there" but somehow "in here," where it lives a life of its own, regardless, sometimes, of what is merely present or at hand.[25] This justifies our saying that death *impresses* us, makes its mark, and leaves its indelible traces behind. This is why our fictional islander cannot be said truly to inhabit our world. Death has found no place in the stream of his blissful mental life. Mortal truth is missing from the beliefs and desires that form the furniture of his mind.

As long as death remains on the outside, a mere *Todesfall* (a case of death) and a public event (*Ereignis*), there is something almost unreal about it. As soon as we become more acutely aware of death (as soon as it implants itself more firmly in the mind), it begins its proper work and acquires its true dimensions in the mortal life of the thinking subject, shaping its thoughts and attitudes, and giving body to its concrete perceptions. This is the only place where death appears to make a difference: it is not the public event itself that unsettles – if that were the case, we would always be troubled, for someone somewhere is always dying – but the painful or unsettling thoughts we attach to it. On this view, death is a disturbance of the soul, like anxiety, love, and hate. What Tennyson records in a famous poem is not the objective event that snatched away his beloved, and certainly not the anatomical features of the deceased, but the shifting state of his own mind in response to the death of a close companion. Or when Hamlet tells us that death is "the undiscovered country from whose borne no traveler returns," this tells us less about what death itself is, and more about what Shakespeare happened to be thinking when he gave these lines to the play's protagonist.

If we can come to grips with death, it is because our minds belong to us and we are always free to work upon our thoughts and dispositions: death

---

[25] See Freud's account of the incorporation of lost objects into the texture of the mind in "Mourning and Melancholia" in *General Psychological Theory*, and the discussion of melancholy and the inner world in Jonathan Lear's *Love and Its Place in Nature*, 158–68.

is neither good nor bad but *thinking* makes it so. The therapeutic strategies of a Stoic or an Epicurean would be powerless and the ideal of *ataraxia* empty if death were not chiefly a mental disposition or a belief of some kind. What death might be *in itself* is far less important than what it is *for us* and *in us.*[26]

*

These are compelling claims. It does seem plausible to look within, to scrutinize our own web of perceptions and beliefs, if we hope to discover what death *means*, and how it governs our diverse stances toward life, perhaps, as some Hellenistic thinkers recommend, ultimately in order to get a grip on mortal life for the sake of unsullied enjoyment of what it has to offer. Unless we are hostile to the very idea of the subjective life, in the spirit of behaviorism or positivism, what we think and perceive, and how our thoughts and perceptions come diversely to expression, will continue to matter.

But there are also compelling Heideggerian reasons to be skeptical of both sorts of attempts, objective and subjective. For we suspect that death is not truly in the mind, any more than death is merely an object we stumble across in the world. Thoughts trained upon the inward landscape capture perceptions, beliefs, desires, memories, images, and other thoughts; and some of these inner items are importantly *about* death. But death itself is nothing mental. If we are reluctant to place death in the world of mere objects and objective events we simply record, we should be equally unwilling to locate it solely in the mind. Death is no more mental than trees are. And if the claim is that death is nothing but what a mind happens to think it is, we are certainly mistaken: our imagined islander and the unknowing infant are not immortal but out of touch with something that somehow belongs to our world. Death does not come and go with the passing of fugitive thought.[27]

Neither are we likely to place much confidence in what most of us (knowing adults) most of the time *say* we think about mortal life. As Freud obsessively reminds us, our passing utterances and the occasional thoughts they voice often fail to reach the thing itself. What we normally think and

---

[26] In the letter to Menoeceus, Epicurus insists that death *itself* is "nothing to us." It lives only in our anxieties and fears, and truly becomes what it is in the life of the sage, where death has lost its sting.

[27] "Being-toward-the-end does not first arise through some attitude which occasionally turns up, rather it belongs essentially to the thrownness of Dasein which reveals itself in attunement (mood) in various ways" (*SZ*, 251).

say about death in typical circumstances, on the margins of our routines and habits, is superficial and sentimental enough. And not by accident, as Heidegger reminds us: Our public way of behaving toward and speaking about death *"does not permit the courage to be anxious about death."*[28] Our thoughts can fail to register the extent to which our lives are held captive by their endings, despite every sign of good faith in the telling. It is not sufficient to think that death has lost its sting or to stop brooding over it. We can be mistaken about ourselves in countless ways. Our explicit views can be shown to conflict with other, more compelling testimony. And Mind is less sovereign here than elsewhere: Although we construct images, frame judgments, perform mathematical operations, and contemplate possibilities more or less at will, we are not always free to adopt a stance as we please. The detached surveyor of the mortal scene is no credible witness. If death is somehow internal to life, we are still at a loss to say what precisely this means. We need to look elsewhere (beyond the scope of our explicit thoughts but not out there in the world of mere things), and to consider ourselves (and our minds) otherwise.

It is difficult to locate important things: we easily misplace our thoughts about the more crucial features of the human landscape. At times, we draw them too near and mistake an easy familiarity for more painful and difficult truth; sometimes we pretend to discover them at a safe distance, where they no longer make contact with our sense of life as a whole. The attempt to locate death in the world of mere things fails in one way, the effort to discover death in the mind aware of itself fails in another. In both cases, the place where death resides (and *how* it takes up residence in human life) has been overlooked.[29]

In the second division of *Sein und Zeit*, Heidegger offers a compelling account of death (or dying) as "a way to be" (*eine Weise zu sein*), essentially *owned*, woven into our concrete understanding of life and its possibilities (and, in fact, a distinctive possibility in its own right, that somehow reveals what the possible is *for me*[30]), and grounded in *care*. To say that death is my own way to be is not to deny the incontestable fact that I come to learn

---

[28] *SZ*, 254 (Heidegger's emphasis). As Heidegger notes, we prefer to think of death as something temporally remote: "One dies at the end, but for now one is not involved" (*SZ*, 253).

[29] This isn't to say that death is never an object. Nor is it to deny that we have thoughts about death. Death is at times a public event, accompanied by ceremonies and rituals. And death is something about which we have many explicit thoughts. But death is also internal to life in ways that escape the two paths outlined above.

[30] "Death is the possibility of the absolute impossibility of Dasein. Thus *death* reveals itself as the *ownmost, non-relational possibility not to be bypassed*" (*SZ*, 250–1, Heidegger's emphasis).

about death empirically. The infant and the sheltered progeny of island solitude know nothing of death because they have not heard anything about it or observed any interpretable cases of it. When they do, they enter a new phase of life with an indefinite but certain end that somehow "*enters into*" their concrete lives.[31] Nor does it imply that death is never an object of thought. We can always detach ourselves from our involvements and muse over the meaning of death, wonder when and how it might strike, and make plans for its inescapable arrival. It does, however, mean that death resides most deeply in what we *do* and how we *are*, in our actions and behaviors and the dimly acknowledged stances they reveal. (This fact helps to explain why some readers of Heidegger take death to be something other than what Heidegger often calls *demise*.)

According to this view, death is not only something that matters when I happen to think about it; it would be more truthful to say that death obscurely *shapes* what matters and how things are allowed to matter, regardless of what we permit ourselves explicitly to think. Taking to heart the apparently obvious facts, that our future is terminal and our close friends mortal, makes no small difference in the concrete shape of practical life. A project without temporal limits is not the same as a task bounded by the sense of an unchosen ending. An immortal beloved is not cared for with the same intensity and vigilance as a fragile one. And it adds to this observation the further point that what we think about death – our own as well as the possible death of others – is more faithfully displayed in our comportments and concerns than in our conventional precepts and detached pronouncements. Death might be internal to our thoughts (and in some sense subjective), but our thoughts are not always our own; and those that really belong to us and impact our understanding and evaluation of life most strongly often go unacknowledged. Whether death is something unspeakably terrifying or the soothing promise of endless sleep is for the "eternal spectator" something that cannot be decided.[32] Of course we are free to say anything we like. But our behavings often betray the vanity of our public avowals and solitary confessions: within the confines of action, not all things are equally possible. If we really care about what we truly think, we should be willing to give weight to the significance our behavings bear and to attend more carefully to the settled dispositions they disturbingly illuminate. "Death," as Heidegger observes, "is a way to be that Dasein takes over as soon as it is."[33]

---

[31] *SZ*, 248. Death's certainty and indefiniteness come into focus in section 52. See *SZ*, 258–9.
[32] The expression is Heidegger's. See *SZ*, 106.   [33] *SZ*, 245.

But have we made any real advance with the suggestion that death (or dying) inhabits our actions and finds some sort of expression in our stances and behaviors? Do our comportments (*Verhalten*) reveal death any more surely and certainly than our thoughts? It is one thing to argue that our genuine convictions about death are more reliably displayed in what Jaspers calls *Grenzsituationen*, in those moments of crisis that force us to contemplate something we usually suppress or fail to notice: the concrete cares of life normally and rightfully overshadow and overtake every morbid preoccupation with death, but every now and then we are granted an opportunity to take stock of what we think about the disquieting end of our lives. It is something else to maintain that death is a constant companion that takes up permanent lodging in the less reflective and world-oriented life of action, where thoughts of death easily (and usefully) give way to forgetful participation in the urgent affairs and more pressing demands of an active way of life. Death may be recognized as a certain fact of life, as something we sometimes think about and take conscious action against in dire circumstances, but the suggestion that death is woven into our conduct and dispositions is even less obvious and more questionable than the initially plausible suggestion that death is nothing but what we think it is, on those occasions when we are *driven* to think about it. We can, it seems, *do* what we have to do without having to reckon with the mortality of our own active lives. Death gives us nothing to accomplish, unless it be to someone suicidal or to those of us who labor to delay what will eventually come. If there are forms of human action genuinely pervaded by a sense of mortality, it belongs most conspicuously to doctors and their patients or to soldiers in the heat of battle. Those for whom death is really an issue in everything they do are morbidly preoccupied and unreliable witnesses. For the rest of us healthy and active adults, death is truly as Spinoza thought it ought to be for the sage – nothing. This is not a moral prescription but a mere description of the essential structure of purposive action: we are either thinking about death, and so no longer acting, or we are acting and death is no longer an issue. Death shows up for us in the inactive spaces between our more active comportments, in those pauses and extended periods of leisure that separate one moment of involvement from the next.

Our actions and passions run their course without any clear relation to the sense of an ending as unwelcome as death. Death is an unchosen end that cuts blindly into life, depriving the agent of every unrealized possibility and every further opportunity to find fulfillment. Death is simply "no-longer-being-there" – no longer being able to perceive, to walk, or to think, and no longer having to act.[34] To modify an Epicurean tag: As long as I am acting, I am not yet dead. When I am dead, I will no longer be acting. And we might add: in order to act well, it is best to leave death alone. Not only is action not intrinsically death-bound, but the sanity of an active life is upset by morbid preoccupations with the final end of life. In principle and as a matter of spiritual health, acting and dying are separate affairs.

If we confine our attention to episodic instances of action, it is hard to locate anything like death in our routine comportments and daily concerns. Death seems to have little to do with a trip to the grocery store or an evening spent with close friends. Some isolated episodes of action may be driven by the *fear* of death, and motivated by the desire to escape from danger, but their end is simply the continuation of life. On the other side of danger, when the threat is no longer imminent, the normal ends of life will come once more into view and life will resume its course. An end inhabits action as the goal that gives it a meaning and an aim. The ends of action genuinely *shape* the movements that realize the agent's intention. But with the exception of pathological cases, death is hardly the aim of life. It is a mere boundary: on this side, a diversity of intentions and goals, and shifting construals of the sense and significance of my life; on the other side, nothing but what others choose to make of my successes and failures and unfinished projects. And as a boundary, death is less significant than the real obstacles we encounter in the concrete world of human action: the mountain I cannot climb limits my activity meaningfully and, if I refuse to be defeated, fuels the desire to exceed myself in endurance, strength, and facility. But death, as Sartre observes, is not meaningful but mute, not an integral aspect of my projects or a limit to be surpassed, but simply absurd: "In this sense every attempt to consider it as a resolved chord at the end of a melody must be sternly rejected."[35] For the chord that completes the melody grows out of the notes that come before, while death is an arbitrary *cursus interruptus*, a brute *given*.[36] What at first blush resembles a compelling claim about the location of death at the heart of an active life turns out to be a questionable artifice devised by the mind of a moralist.[37]

---

[34] *SZ*, 236.   [35] *Being and Nothingness*, 533.   [36] Ibid., 547.
[37] This is the conclusion drawn by Philipse in *Heidegger's Philosophy of Being*: Heidegger's account of death, devoid in the author's view of any real philosophical insights, is said to form part of a grand Pascalian strategy designed to prepare certain individuals for the religious life and to make some of us ready for "an afterlife in which we can be really ourselves" (351).

Death and the Intelligibility of Practical Life: A Fuller Defense

These Sartrean suspicions flow from a conception of action defended in *Being and Nothingness*. On this view, ours is "an existence which perpetually makes itself," sustaining and altering itself in a series of choices that endow an otherwise featureless world with human sense and significance.[38] The former gambler is always free to pick up the dice again and to resume the way of life she has temporarily repudiated. The author of *Being and Nothingness* is always free to continue his work, despite periods of dryness and in opposition to whatever obstacles the writer happens to encounter, or to take up sewing instead.

To continue gambling or writing is undoubtedly to live for now within certain limits, and to acknowledge their significance as features that give shape to the situation in which the chooser now finds herself cast. The world of dice and poker chips is not the world of the former gambler reciting prayers at a solemn Sunday mass. Conduct appropriate in a casino would be out of place in the quiet atmosphere of a cathedral. A freedom truly unlimited is incoherent, worldless: "There can be a free for-itself only as engaged in a resisting world."[39] The unimagined presence of resistance is what makes the difference between the earnestness of action and the playfulness of wishful fancy. But the limits that allow us to distinguish between doing and dreaming are forever only *for us* self-chosen makers, established in the "nihilating rupture with the world" that makes every genuine commitment possible and gives body to the world of action. If the mountain I intend to climb is perceived as an obstacle, it is only because I freely choose to take the mountain seriously, because it just happens to play a role in one of my freely adopted projects. In the life of another, the mountain might be a beautiful feature of the landscape or little more than an object that blends indifferently into the background of more pressing (because freely chosen) concerns. It lies always within our power to see the mountain otherwise and to place the limits in which we supposedly find ourselves elsewhere: there is no limit in heaven or on earth but freedom makes it so.[40] Death, like any other allegedly necessary limit, is just one more brute fact in a world of facts, the significance of which is largely up to us. We are always free to make of it what we will or to ignore it altogether. To say that we *are* mortal, to insist that death gives bounds to the sense of human life and constrains our awareness of what is possible and desirable,

---

[38] *Being and Nothingness*, 438.   [39] Ibid., 483.
[40] "... no limits can be found to my freedom except itself ..." (Ibid., 439).

is to subscribe in bad faith to the myth of the given; while in truth, there is only unfettered doing rooted in a freely adopted "fundamental project." The grounding condition of authentic action embodies itself fully in an interminable "escape from the given."[41] If I maintain that death inhabits our comportments and helps to shape our sense of life as a whole, I am simply recording a contingent fact about my own self-styled relation to the world of active life: death is this sort of limit *for me*.

We can begin to think about what might be wrong with the Sartrean view (or, if not wrong, where its limits might be shown to lie) if we shift the terrain from the episodic causes of action, the beliefs, desires, motives, and freely adopted intentions that usually figure in the analysis of an isolated instance of behavior, to the meaning and value of what we do and the sort of person we hope to become by doing certain things and avoiding others. This shift requires the adoption of a long view on the life of action. Some features of the moral landscape only become visible when we consider the larger temporal extension of human action, when we aspire to see life more steadily and to view it whole.[42] This does not have to involve the questionable ascent to an ethereal view from nowhere: as Nagel convincingly argues, and as we had occasion to note earlier, in connection with Heidegger's appropriation of Aristotle's account of practical truth in the *Nicomachean Ethics*, there are some points of view that do not make room for *human* significance at all. If we look too far beyond our particular concerns and perceive everything from above, we lose sight of ourselves and our concerns and the point of our actions altogether. But it does imply that the salient features of some of our activities do not come into view when we restrict ourselves to the playful dance of a waiter in a Parisian café.

Some of our concerns do not extend much further than the episodic activities that realize them. The significance of a trivial amusement or a fleeting sexual encounter is more or less complete as it happens; its location in a larger temporal context is irrelevant. (Although, even here, I think, a longer view can reveal unsuspected connections. An episode of heavy drinking might be a mindless night out or part of a larger pattern of habitual avoidance, depending on its location in the developing history of a life.) But those activities that take on a weightier value are rarely episodic. They belong rather to what Dilthey called the temporally extended and

---

[41] Ibid., 485.

[42] On this point, see MacIntyre, *After Virtue*, 204–5. Heidegger himself introduces the topic of death in a chapter on the *Ganzsein* of Dasein.

developing *Zusammenhang des Lebens*, which informs early Heidegger's conception of *Geschichtlichkeit*.[43] And those actions that truly exhaust their import in an isolated instant are usually trivial: a significance that can be confined to a passing instant probably deserves to stay there. We may be at liberty to detach ourselves from our most valuable projects, to revise our concerns, and to alter our plans, perhaps drastically; but turning away from a significant project is not like deciding no longer to drink apricot cocktails, except from an impoverished point of view that considers in abstraction the mere act of renunciation.

There is an obvious difference that only shows up in the long run between drug-induced contentment and the pleasures of completing a book long in the making. Although both can be enjoyed in the moment, the pleasures of the latter are tied to the historical conditions that made the work possible, and the meaningful history of writing itself, with all the promises and disappointments and obstacles somehow overcome in the life of the dedicated writer. The short view of action does not allow us to discriminate between an entertaining stroll through an art gallery and more meaningful encounters with significant artistic influences in the life of a practicing artist. Human excellence and significance are not the work of an hour: like experience and *aretê* in Aristotle's account of the human good, they accrue to life over time and require vigilant practice and patience.[44]

But so does our *knowledge* of what is more lastingly significant, beyond what we self-servingly tell ourselves and report to others about what matters to us. As Merleau-Ponty reminds us, "Besides true love, there is false ... love."[45] While the difference between the two can flare up in an instant of intensely focused awareness, the moment of revelation is made possible by gradually accumulating insights, and is itself a fresh configuration of more ancient if ambiguous truths. If the insight is not to be dismissed as spurious, it must be questioned in relation to a complex history of involvement with this particular object of concern. Otherwise it is not possible to distinguish between a compelling realization and a momentary lapse of energy or an unrelated episode of boredom or depression. Epiphanies too have their histories.

---

[43] See the seventh volume of Dilthey's *Gesammelte Schriften*, and Heidegger's account of *Geschichtlichkeit* in *Sein und Zeit*, Division II, chapter 5. Heidegger takes up Dilthey's concept in section 72 (*SZ*, 373).

[44] See Heidegger's account of Aristotelian *phronêsis* in *Platon: Sophistes* (*GA* 19) and the discussion in Chapter 2.

[45] Merleau-Ponty, *Phenomenology of Perception*, 378.

We are not asking why these particular things are granted weight or discovered to be significant rather than others, why some find value in formal philosophical activity while others prefer to write novels and still others choose to fight against the spread of injustice in underdeveloped countries. Questions concerning motive are, as we saw in the previous chapter, notoriously elusive. MacIntyre is probably right to search for answers in the concept of tradition. And different traditions undeniably promote different values and conceptions of human excellence, as Nietzsche reminds us in *Zarathustra*. Some pursuits will be more vital (more living options in James's sense) than others: it is absurd *for me* to live a life more suitable to Achilles or to show up at a faculty meeting sporting a Roman toga. The bare fact that some things are promoted rather than others is not altogether of our making. Sartre's literary obsessions are inconceivable before the dawn of writing.

We are, however, asking about the temporal conditions that make possible the growth and deepening of whatever significance we happen to find in those things we happen to pursue: and these conditions, if not the pursuits themselves, are not up to us. We are free to deny significance altogether and to live comically or tragically with the absurd.[46] But some of the conditions that make the global value of what we do possible are not arbitrary constraints we are free to ignore, *if* we choose to remain *in time*.

But to remain in time in the fullest and most active sense is not merely to puzzle over or to contemplate the significance already embodied or still underway in an unfinished life. The retrospective point of view can help to clarify what we've become and what has been meaningful *so far*, but life is lived forward. Living, concernful life belongs to the future: the primary temporal feature of *Sorgen* is *Sich-vorweg-sein*.[47] From the vantage point of a life still in the making, every established meaning and value can be revised or undone, every plan refashioned, every concern brought to a halt and replaced by something else. A failed poet can still become a good father; and the good father is somewhat free to minimize the significance of the former poet's efforts. It is precisely the open-endedness of the future that validates our hesitation and uncertainty and justifies talk of *Auslegung* rather than simple *Anschauung* when the significance of a life is at stake. It

---

[46] For now, I leave it open whether an even longer (historical) view would reveal further connections between what the individual experiences and what the culture at large makes possible and, if not impossible, at least unlikely, the sorts of questions pursued by later Heidegger, Habermas, Blumenberg, MacIntyre, Pippin, and others about the questionable (and risky) break with the ancient regime at the dawn of the modern era and the self-justification of modernity.

[47] See *SZ*, 192 and the account of the temporality of care in section 65.

is just this indefinite horizon of things to come that makes it possible for us to do things differently and to construe what we've already done and become otherwise. For what we want to know when certain facts about former perceptions and embodiments of significance assail us, when we acknowledge that a dream has died or see a project brought to completion or just pause to take stock of what we've done, is not usually something about what has already taken place and now lies finished behind us. What we more urgently hope to clarify, when we are not simply basking in the light of previous accomplishments or brooding over painful catastrophe, is an answer to such questions as: What comes next? How should I go on? Where should I place those concerns that shape a vital sense of who I am because they tell me what I might become? The real import of what we discover depends upon what we take ourselves to be doing; and what we are doing is trying to move ahead. Living significance is tied to the future by countless invisible threads woven in freedom. Even someone who has "settled his accounts" and, having lost a vital sense of the possible, earnestly believes that nothing significant remains to be done, except perhaps to die, is still somehow ahead of himself, if only in the form of awaiting the inevitable.

But the train of thought just sketched (on what only begins to show up from the long view of human action) is still not enough to justify the radical thesis Heidegger is trying to defend. From the standpoint developed over the last few pages, death matters only if and when I find myself or feel myself to be approaching the end. And the mattering or the indifference might be nothing more than a contingent psychological fact about me. As long as I remain alive or live with an active *Lebensgefühl*, death is possibly a matter of indifference. The fact that my projects and experiences must end pales in significance alongside the urgency of what I am now striving to accomplish. *That* I must die has nothing to do with the passion of the writer struggling to meet a publisher's deadline. What gives body to a life of action is just a certain configuration of the social world, the complex weave of norms and standards that enables each of us to make some provisional sense of our lives and the social interactions that strengthen or weaken the threads of concern that tie us here to these projects and significant others.

An explicitly formulated reason for caring shows up against this shared, contingent background of the *Mitwelt*, and is just the development of a shared understanding of what it makes sense to do. It is because I occupy this particular social space of reasons that writing a book matters more to me than the number of hairs on my legs. (I can imagine a culture in which being-hairy is far more important than being a writer.) The urgency of getting it published has little to do with the sense of an Ending: I probably want to be admired or to win a coveted spot on the faculty because I enjoy the feelings success normally brings and the financial security that comes with a tenured professorship. Perhaps more nobly, because I want to express a sense of life and to share my thoughts about the human condition with others, or to see how my ideas fare in the public sphere.

If death comes prematurely or unexpectedly, it cuts short my life like an unwelcome intrusion in the ongoing conversation I carry on with myself and significant others and brings to an arbitrary end whatever I was working to complete: "Even 'unfulfilled' Dasein ends."[48] What I might have left undone will of course remain undone, its significance dependent on the good will or enmity of those who were somehow involved in my projects, or find themselves moved to weigh in. Others might carry on my plans and help complete my work, but that is their affair. My historical significance as a writer might have been augmented had I had time to complete the work cut short by my death. That may be sad to those I leave behind, who know, as I no longer can, what might have been had I had more time to act. But until it comes to this, the significance of the actions that compose my life will remain open, and my future will remain, for me, unbounded. What matters is always only what I happen to be doing, whether I take responsibility for my deeds or refuse to acknowledge the import of what I've done, and how I stand toward my own uncertain future. None of this is bounded in any way by vague intimations of mortality. The prospect of the gallows might, in the words of Doctor Johnson, wonderfully concentrate the mind, but coffee and cigarettes can be just as effective. There seems to be no intrinsic connection between what and how things matter in the concrete life of action and the arbitrary fact that the future of each individual is finite. The long view has revealed important features of the geography, but death is still nowhere to be found. And what we did discover was not what we initially thought or hoped it would turn out to be – a meaning always dependent on what we just happen to take ourselves to be pursuing in our sense-making practices, oriented forward, uncertain and adrift, a more compelling case for anti-essentialism and the contingency of what we care about and how and with whom.

So how can we make a case for the mortal shape of human *praxis*? How defend the related claim that something like acknowledgment and

[48] *SZ*, 244.

disavowal are possible here? Does death grant to life a meaning it would not have without it? Is it in Heidegger's sense a condition of the *intelligibility* of life and action?

If we descend from the heights of abstraction and renounce the tedious mechanism of a *pour-soi* always fleeing from the *en-soi*, we find ourselves better placed to acknowledge the mortal intelligibility of our own active lives. Death is more tightly woven into the fabric of what we do and how we care than the Sartrean is able to see. This is not to say that we are always thinking about these connections, any more than we can be said to be always pondering our freedom or contemplating what it means to occupy a situation, to be indebted to the past, and to move always toward an indefinite future. They may not seem relevant to the agent simply absorbed in the ongoing activity of coping with her world. In her more reflective moments, she might rightly insist that if she pondered them too deeply she would be deprived of the partial ignorance that makes it possible to care, that it would be better somehow if they were left in the background. But they can be lifted out of obscurity as the targets of our *reflective* sense-making practices, when we ask ourselves whether human life as we understand it and normally live it would survive in the absence of mortal limits. It is the responsibility of the philosophical interpreter of life and death to do this, when we strive, like Kermode's literary critic, "to attempt the lesser feat of making sense of the ways we try to make sense of our lives."[49]

This seems like a most promising suggestion. There are many activities that lose their point in the absence of death. We cannot imagine all the care that goes into the preparation of the body, the funeral service, burial rites, expressions of grief, and the tending of graves in the (unfortunate) lives of the Struldbrugs portrayed by Swift in *Gulliver's Travels*.[50] These activities are out of place in the immortal human comedy. But it is also impossible for us to imagine these fascinating creatures facing death on the field of battle, where the stakes are high because the risk to life is great. We can picture them doing anything – playfully jousting, perhaps, or taunting one another or admiring one another's swords and shields – but nothing like flouting death or fleeing from real danger in mortal terror. (Taking flight could only provoke laughter or dumb amazement.) And we can scarcely conceive anything comparable to the bravery we sometimes

[49] Kermode, *The Sense of an Ending*, 3.
[50] See Heidegger's remarks on caring for the dead (*SZ*, 238), which build upon the concept of *Fürsorge* introduced in the fourth chapter of the first division.

admire and occasionally strive to emulate in the vulnerable individuals who belong to our world. For this is what it means to show this sort of courage: to be willing to die for the sake of one's country or to brave death in order to win a reputation for valor in the contest of war.[51] The movements of the soldiers might be just as graceful, the wounds just as painful, and the rewards equally alluring, but the threat that allows us to pick out genuine acts of bravery would be more imagined than real, and the activity itself would be something else.[52]

They would probably continue to care for their immortal bodies and to shield themselves from the gentle forces of nature. But these activities, too, would no longer be what they are for us mortals. For the care of the body loses its seriousness along with its vulnerability, becoming a merely aesthetic affair. We can imagine vain Struldbrugs in our time seeking out the best plastic surgeons, working out obsessively, and eating well, but only because Swift has them age. (That they grow old but will not die is partly why their lot is unenviable, as an initially envious Gulliver soon realizes.) And the perception of nature as a real threat is tied to our sense of mortal fragility. As Heidegger observes in *Sein und Zeit*, "The forest is a forest of timber, the mountain a quarry of rock, the river is water power, the wind is wind 'in the sails.'"[53] We might add: the sky is the threat of fire, the sea a deadly hurricane, the waterfall a dangerous abyss. In the life of the deathless, the unleashing of terrible natural forces would be a thing of beauty, a mere spectacle to be enjoyed: nature as "what overcomes us"[54] would no longer be an object of possible experience, and the activities that reach their end in the protection of the mortal body would be almost inconceivable. The awareness of the natural landscape that frames the active life of thoughtful mortals and partly drives the breathless development of technology is tied to the sense of an inevitable Ending, possible at any moment.

But there are also some contingent but (for most of us) central concerns that would be deprived of their depth, seriousness, and intensity in a life without mortal end. We might be able to imagine them going on in some way. But something would be missing: the activity itself would be significantly impoverished, a mere simulacrum of its fuller realization in the mortal life we have to live.

[51] See Aristotle's account of *andreia* in the *Nicomachean Ethics*, Book Three, Chapters 6–9.
[52] I owe this and a few other examples to Martha Nussbaum's insightful essay on Lucretius in *The Therapy of Desire*.
[53] *SZ*, 70.   [54] *SZ*, 70.

A large part of what goes into the rearing of children and the cultivation of lasting friendships is hard to locate in an imagined life without temporal limit. It isn't necessary to give unqualified assent to Rousseau's idealized education of the young Emile in order to agree that *for us* a decent upbringing has to nurture those capacities and abilities that enable the developing child to cope with real adversity and to come to grips with the condition of mortality. For ours is "an estate ... exposed to assaults on all hands; and therefore it is very advisable to get children into this armor as early as we can."[55] A childhood world without some perception of danger – the world of the overprotective caretaker, inhumanely shielding the child from the slightest risk of bodily harm or psychological discomfort – is in the long run a world more detrimental than good. The child must come eventually to know not only that there is an aggressive world beyond the life of fantasy (where merely thinking something magically makes it so), but that this same world that offers resistance to her unimagined efforts is as well the place where she can (and eventually will) die: in this world, death *"is possible in every moment."*[56] Becoming able to live well and coming to be uneasily at home in the world is, among other things, learning to perceive peril accurately and getting to know how and when to avoid it. It is as easy to go wrong here, and it is difficult to succeed; but we know failure, at least, when we see it. And the criteria of success and failure that guide human effort cannot be applied to the very different (and almost inconceivable) work of bringing up an immortal. Here, too, mortality makes a crucial difference, adding as much as it takes from us in the concrete shape it grants to our otherwise unformed or dimly shaped pursuits.

Friendship, too, and love (and the humbler care for a devoted pet) borrow some of their seriousness from the sense of an encroaching limit to their duration and an acknowledgment of the vulnerability of our mortal companions. How much of what we prize in companionship would survive the alchemical transmutation into undying solidarity? What we *lose* in being deprived is easier to say, and is a constant theme in some of our best literature and poetry, all of which would be scarcely intelligible, if not laughable, to the immortal lover and her immortal beloved. It is hard for us mortal lovers not to be stirred by Hölderlin's complaint in "Menons Klagen um Diotima": "Aber das Haus ist öde mir nun, und sie haben mein Auge/Mir genommen, auch mich hab' ich verloren mit ihr." [But the house is empty to me now, and my eyes have been taken along with the

---

[55] Locke, *Some Thoughts Concerning Education*, 86.   [56] *SZ*, 258.

loss of her.][57] The poet who has lost his eyes in losing his beloved knows well enough what it means to have loved a mortal companion. The depth of the potential loss might give us pause as we consider the vulnerable targets of our own uncertain affections.[58] Something of the deprivation in less intimate cases is captured as well in Heidegger's moving philosophical tribute to a distant philosophical interlocutor in the *In memoriam Max Scheler* that finds its way into a lecture course on the metaphysical foundations of logic: "Max Scheler is dead. We bow before his fate. Once again a path of philosophy falls back into darkness."[59]

Companionship rooted in an undiscriminating pursuit of shared pleas-ures – the *philia* that aims at mere *hêdonê*, the lowest and least reliable form of friendship in the Aristotelian account – would probably survive more or less intact, although what is found pleasurable and why would probably differ in the life of the undying. All those relatively stable friendships based on expediency and utility might find a home in a deathless world in other respects like our own, where the pursuit of economic ends and means occupies a central place in the pursuit of the good. Some of the nobler instances of *philia* might be possible as well: we can imagine a shared interest in whatever excellence is available to creatures who cannot die, but are able to care about some things and to shun others and to recognize the difference between what they consider worthwhile and what they consider trivial.

But much of what we value in our human relations and the intensity of our commitments to others would find an awkward and unstable place in a deathless world. The sense of generational solidarity – the sense that we are united by concerns that set us apart from those who came before and those yet to come, the sense that *these things* are possible *for us* but not *for them* – would be diminished. As Heidegger observes, "*Authentic being-toward-death . . . is the concealed ground of the historicity of Dasein.*[60] What could possibly unite deathless friends in heaven? Thoreau's complaint about the stupidity of "Old deeds for old people" and whatever solidarity he found in the life and work (and land) of Emerson would be nearly incomprehensible.[61] The *sumphilosophein* of the early German romantics, acutely aware of their own mortality and conscious of their departure from the classical tradition, would be an unwritten chapter in the history of

[57] Friedrich Hölderlin, *Poems and Fragments*, tr. by Michael Hamburger, 238–9. My translation.
[58] See Rick Furtak's fine account of the potential suffering of the finite lover in the tenth chapter of *Wisdom in Love*.
[59] *The Metaphysical Foundations of Logic*, 52. [60] *SZ*, 386, Heidegger's emphasis.
[61] *Walden*, Economy, 5.

literary and philosophical companionship, not because there would be no interest in it but because there would be nothing to recount. What bound Sartre and Merleau-Ponty or Sartre and Aron together for a season would seem less weighty for immortal friends, with time enough to decide what is possible and desirable and what not, feeling no urgent longing to find solidarity here rather than there. The inconstant friend would be more of a fleeting nuisance than a real threat to our troubled search for a meaningful life in the company we keep.

It would be just as difficult to imagine the urgent need to choose our companionships carefully in a life without end, where every friendship dissolved is just another opportunity to fashion new links to hitherto unknown others, and every divorce signals the freedom to find a better, more companionable mate elsewhere. Where there is no threat of death there is always all the time in the world to come together and depart, and to come together again (or not): the urgency of the meeting, like the pain of departing, loses much of its intensity. It is difficult to imagine a deathless creature clinging so doggedly, so anxiously and uncertainly, to the particular attachments she happens to have formed with just these immortal others.

*

One might point out that much of what we do *would* go on, that all we've really shown is that some things matter to some people, and that these things would be inconceivable or less important in a life without the sort of end in question here. But what would become of choice itself? And the freedom that underlies it?

The Sartrean account of freedom and choice is likely to seem naïve, at best, and possibly inhumane: it is one thing to say that we are responsible for our stances and choices and the meaning and value we pretend to discover out there in the world or in some Platonic heaven of immutable forms, something else to dismiss the very idea of an innocent victim because, even in times of war or in cases of rape, "it is a matter of choice" and I am always free to acquiesce or to resist.[62] It is one thing to insist that the world as we know it is nothing beyond what we have collectively brought into being (this reduces to the truism that there is no human world where there are no human beings), something else (and something confused, I think) to claim that *I* am responsible for *everything*, including

---

[62] *Being and Nothingness*, 554.

my own birth, because I spontaneously extend myself beyond every established fact toward my own freely adopted values and ends.[63]

This may be an eccentric and implausible way of construing whatever sort of freedom we can be said to possess; and yet the claims of freedom and responsibility under some description are not so easily abjured. As Robert Pippin puts it in an illuminating study of Henry James and the unrivaled complexities of modern moral life: "There might be several reasons for the great interest taken by so many Jamesean characters in their own freedom, reasons for the supposition that what makes a life most worth living is my genuinely being able to lead it."[64] The ability to detach myself from the accidents of birth and upbringing and the tacit norms, codes, and conventions that inevitably shape me before I begin to shape myself is the capacity to live a life that belongs meaningfully to me. Freedom in this sense is the promise of a life of my own, beyond what others would have me be, and owned in some way because more deliberately and lucidly decided, not imposed upon a passive and obedient recipient, mindlessly performing a role staged, however conscientiously or carelessly, by others. It is the power to put *no* to work in the life of action, to resist the apparent naturalness of questionable conventions and the ease of carrying them on, and to search for value and significance (somewhat) beyond the contingent attitudes and practices that define the initial backdrop of my comportment: it is, in short, the incontestable power to criticize, evaluate, and modify what appears natural because it has become familiar to the point of self-evidence. In this sense, freedom is a necessary condition of philosophy itself, if Heidegger is right that the business of philosophy is to question and contest the self-evident. A way of life is not valuable simply because of its durability, prevalence, and uncontested power in a particular community: "A life plan cannot ... have the point, implications, and claims on one that it does, just by being the kind of life it is, by playing a role within a fixed social order."[65] Or, in Heidegger's way of speaking, what *one* does is not legitimate just because it's done – "it's how we do things" is not a justification but a statement of fact. As Heidegger notes in WS 1924/5, commenting on the achievement of the ancients, in opposition to common sense, "Opinions rigidify themselves in concepts and propositions; they become truisms which are repeated over and over, with the consequence that what was originally disclosed comes to be covered up again."[66]

---

[63] *Being and Nothingness*, 555.   [64] Pippin, *Henry James and Modern Moral Life*, 171.
[65] Ibid., 172.   [66] *Plato's "Sophist,"* 11.

A form of life that makes no room for questions about the sort of life one is socially encouraged to live, however socially acceptable, is in an important sense unfree. A life that does not freely question and contest, evaluate and criticize is in a crucial respect not (or not yet) owned, however else it might be weighed and found successful: "He who lets the world, or his own portion of it, choose his plan of life for him, has no need of any other faculty than the ape-like one of imitation."[67] A life of endless imitation and conformity might in every other respect be perfectly suited to me; it may embody noble ideals and human aspirations, be harmonious and good, and still be counted too mindless and servile, too dependent on what others expect of me and too simply a matter of role-playing, to count as *mine*.[68] To be free and to have a life of my own is at the very least to make an effort to make sense of what I'm already doing and will probably continue to do. The truth of a life is truly *living* only where it is freely, fully, frequently, and fearlessly discussed.[69] And when it is openly debated and a particle of truth has found itself at home in the life of a living mind, mere authority, including the authority of the sacred, loses its grip. Where significance has not been probed and discussed and *made* more freely our own, where meaning has degenerated into mere habit and dead routine, we are in no position to say what is more truly worthwhile and what is trivial. We may be right in our tacit commitments and the evaluations they involve; but we want more assurance than unchallenged authority and the untested awareness of significance and worth are able to give.[70]

In the eyes of someone else, perhaps in the collective fantasies of a group or a nation, I may be loathsome, unhandsome, crippled or simply eccentric; and it goes almost without saying that I am powerless to alter directly the pale images and stereotypes that stand between the sense I have of myself and the perceptions others project around me. But for myself and at my best, I am a freely chosen pattern of conduct; and this pattern can always deviate from the expectations woven into the rigid construals I did not choose and usually cannot change. Whether my conduct does or does

---

[67] Mill, *On Liberty* in *The Basic Writings of John Stuart Mill*, 60.

[68] "There is no reason that all human existence should be constructed on some one, or some small number of patterns. If a person possesses any tolerable amount of common sense and experience, his own mode of laying out his existence is best, not because it is the best in itself, but because it is his own mode. Human beings are not like sheep; and even sheep are not undistinguishably alike" (Ibid., 69).

[69] Ibid., 36.

[70] "Thus if . . . life relinquishes the originality of interpretation, it relinquishes the possibility of ever coming into possession of itself in a radical sense, i.e., the possibility of radically *being* itself" (Heidegger, "Phenomenological Interpretations of Aristotle," in *Supplements*, 124).

not depart, whether I allow others to decide how I will be or chart a path of my own, is often largely up to me.[71] The difficulty of deviation and the ease of conformity are no arguments against the possibility of devising and enacting a plan of my own. Cowardice and impotence are freedom's moral holidays or the complacent's convenient, ready-made excuses. For "there is no non-human situation. It is only fear, flight, and recourse to magical types of conduct that I shall decide on the non-human, but this decision is human, and I shall carry the entire responsibility for it."[72] "It is ... senseless to think of complaining since nothing foreign has decided what we feel, what we live, or what we are."[73] These are the stirring words of a moralist, calling each of us to account for the particular shape her life has assumed, to take responsibility for the way the world happens to be, and to consider the way things are in the light of how they might be. The Sartrean is inviting each of us to aspire to live freely and without excuses.

However, "what makes for a free life is not obvious."[74] Many supposed embodiments of freedom are not what their spokesmen and developing protagonists initially expected them to be. A life that begins as a bohemian quest for independence from everything merely conventional and freedom from every definite attachment or commitment can turn out to be more empty and dependent on what it scorns than a freely chosen life of convention, like "some still unattached 'nothing.'" An opinion of one's own, however sincerely maintained, can be stupid or undigested or inaccurate. What initially seems to promise risk and adventure rapidly becomes insipid, commonplace, safe and secure.

But if it is not self-evident what sort of life would measure up to the difficult demand to live freely a meaningful life of one's own – and part of what it means to be concretely free is to be able to continue searching for meaningful ways to live freely[75] – it is easier to recognize freedom's failed or less successful progeny (and almost as easy to understand why the freely detached quickly finds herself stranded). Coming to terms with the human condition as it is or happens to be is difficult: we are not like plants, rooted firmly in the soil and naturally moved by the presence of light, and unable to do anything besides what we are by nature conditioned to perform, where every hindrance is a physical force working in opposition to an equally physical force. An emotion or passion might be like a spontaneous movement toward the world of soil and light and a judgment of the value of certain things that lie outside of what we can fully control; but even

---

[71] *Being and Nothingness*, 523–4.   [72] Ibid., 554.   [73] *Being and Nothingness*, 554.
[74] *Henry James and Modern Moral Life*, 171.   [75] This is how Mill defines freedom in *On Liberty*.

here, where the heart seems most passively responsive to uncreated value, we have our passionate being *to be*. We are free to take it up and trace out its implications in the life we have to live or to deny that it has anything important to say, to cultivate the apathetic life of the stoic or to live a more passionate existence. Its meaning and importance are nothing unalterably given. Even the non-stoic may be forced to deny the importance of the most vital and stirring *pathê* because she acknowledges the dubious roots of the value their intentional objects display in what others have stupidly deemed significant and firmly implanted in her plastic and receptive mind. The value of the emotional response and the real significance of the object it intends cannot be detached from their reflective evaluation: when we consider the worth of an emotion we sever ourselves from it and ponder the thoughts we think it embodies. This situation is in no way altered when someone insists that the ultimate source of our most primitive emotional investments is something absolute – call it God or love.[76] Appeals to divinity are just ways of cutting finite evaluation and ongoing conversation short. The sheer, undeniable fact *that* we sometimes have to take a stand somewhere in order to be able to act and define ourselves in action is no reason to think that the support or principle of our self-defining comportments must be something unquestionable and absolute. In the early Platonic dialogues, Socrates is shown to be always on the way, and able to live without final knowledge of the ends and aims and sources of the good life: "The willingness to live with fallible knowledge is built into the human condition. Only a god would do without it. Only a crazy man would want to."[77] Those who, like Euthyphro in the dialogue the bears his name, profess to know what the gods want or are overly confident about what they think the good life is and where its final sources are to be found, are the ethical imposters and the unenviable targets of an unsettling Socratic *elenchos*. In the words of the *Apology*, human wisdom consists in knowing that we know nothing: every response invites a question. What it means to be moved by an eternal power is just as questionable as the trivial emotional attachments the appeal is designed to undercut. If the target of the concern is questionable, so, too, is its origin in the life of the loving agent. We always find ourselves thrown back into the world of human concerns we have uncertainly and fallibly to assess and confronting the ways of life it has to offer to the mind in search of its own significance in

---

[76] See, e.g., the opening paragraph of Kierkegaard's (or Johannes *de silentio*'s) speech in praise of the faithful Abraham.

[77] Vlastos, *Socratic Studies*, 52.

the worldly life that surrounds it. On early Heidegger's view, every appeal to eternity is essentially unearned: we always weigh and measure and critically evaluate from where we happen to be; and where I will be tomorrow, even in love, is nothing absolutely certain.[78]

But the very power to question and probe the conventions and customs that provide an initial orientation in the world of human life is also a temptation to disavow the conditions of finite life altogether, and to live destructively and fruitlessly in what Hegel calls the *freedom of the void*, "this *absolute possibility* of *abstracting* from every determination in which I find myself, the flight from every content as a limitation."[79] For it is inherent in the nature of freedom "that I am able to free myself from everything, to renounce all ends, and to abstract from everything."[80] The very power that makes it possible to live a life more fully my own – a power that enables me to decide in my own way and in conversation with receptive or fruitfully antagonistic others how to interpret the accidents of birth and education and nationality and the value of the projects I undertake – is equally the power to refuse to become anything at all and to say *no* to everything conditioned and limited. The recognition that the paths of care are to a certain extent already mapped out, that every way of life is somehow like every other, can give way to weariness or indifference. Alongside the meaningful freedom to oppose the *status quo* and to work out of a life of one's own there lies the sadly resigned freedom of someone who will not get involved, who watches the world pass her by, perhaps hoping for something to happen and waiting for some Great Event to make a difference, or peers quietly into an inner life devoid of outward resonance and effect, and for this reason shapeless and insignificant.

As Harry Frankfurt observes, "What has no boundaries has no shape."[81] The shapeless life of a scornful freedom, unwilling to get involved in the human scene, may be driven by an awareness of the flawed fabric of social life – an abstention grounded in the partially justified recognition that the social roles and customs currently available are too confining or too trivial, too unworthy of my efforts and abilities, to merit wholehearted identification. But it can also be rooted in an unacknowledged unwillingness to come to terms with the difficult burden of human finitude, and the anxiety

---

[78] The best defense of a heavily qualified version of this view, with more room for earnest skepticism, is developed by Rick Furtak in *Wisdom in Love*. The critical remarks offered above are directed at a different target.

[79] Hegel, *Elements of the Philosophy of Right*, 38.   [80] Ibid., 38.

[81] *The Importance of What We Care About*, ix. Heidegger's interest in boundaries and limits plays out in WS 1924.

of having to decide how to live and why or for what in the absence of a firmly settled and reliable view of ethical life. This is a more egregious refusal to participate: for the more justified abstention, possibilities of engagement are not ruled out *apriori*, and creative appropriation and deviation or what Rorty calls the *ironic* stance are at least conceivable; for the more extreme and uncompromising denial, nothing remains save the empty sense of an encroaching Ending and whatever just happens between now and then. The price of avoiding or attempting to skirt finitude altogether is, in a word, *Selbstverlorenheit*: freedom's *Selbstheit* is in the flesh of our involvements or nowhere.[82]

For whatever else a *self* might be – say, the uncanny power to choose itself or the bare ability to posit itself – it acquires whatever temporal shape it can be said to have in relation to a concrete world of objects of concern, and in more or less steady devotion to a self-defining project. (Where there is no constancy, there is in a sense no self, save the indefinite ability to become one, a potential self, perhaps, but a self without world. If it is possible to be too absorbed in the world, it is also possible to be too remote: absorption and detachment are equally significant losses.) For "it is by living my time that I am able to understand other times, by plunging into the present and the world, by taking on deliberately what I am fortuitously, by willing what I will and doing what I do, that I can go further. I can miss being free only if I try to bypass my natural and social situation by refusing to take it up in the first place, instead of assuming it in order to join up with the natural and human world."[83]

So what does the concretely situated self have to do with death? Is there a more reliable and essential bond between the shapeliness of a human life and the sense of an ultimate ending or are there only contingent configurations and meanings, and "final vocabularies" that bind us with whatever authority they have because they just happen to belong (historically) to us, and *we* – whoever we might be – choose to go on using them (or scornfully refuse to get involved)? Are we free to make of our mortality anything we'd like?

Freud is probably right that we quickly forget the role of chance in human life, "from our origin out of the meeting of spermatozoon and ovum onwards." It is easy to overlook that a love long in the making began

---

[82] See Merleau-Ponty's un-Sartrean phenomenology of freedom in the final chapter of the *Phenomenology of Perception*. At my best, "I am never a thing and never a bare consciousness" (453). It is therefore fitting to say that "We choose our world and the world chooses us" (454).

[83] *Phenomenology of Perception*, 456.

as an accidental encounter between two strangers who may very well never have met, as the language of accident invariably suggests, that a philosophical project would be inconceivable in other circumstances, in another place and time, with different books having been encountered, with different conversation partners, that human character itself is a *second* nature and everywhere bears the impress of *tuchê*. It is natural, too, to exaggerate the extent to which the future can be predicted and controlled. We "discount unfairly the ways in which chance future events can affect or effectively determine our sense of what was, or would have been, justified" when we adopted a stance and took a stand.[84] Unless we incline to mysticism of blood and soil, which sees more necessity in the way things take shape than reflection upon the course of our experience certifies, we should acknowledge the "network of small, interanimating contingencies" that fashion our emerging identities.[85] For there is something incoherent (and ungrateful) in the desire to be someone or somewhere else: the particular shape of the desire to be elsewhere and otherwise vanishes in another clime. The sense and significance of what we value and do, the importance of what we care about, is not so readily detached from the accidents of place and time, upbringing, experience, and education. (A Heidegger who fell in love with the French *philosophes* rather than the "Schwarzwald redneck" who took a fancy to the pre-Socratics is hard to imagine but not inconceivable. A Heideggerian commentary on Voltaire is improbable from *our* vantage point, but it cannot be ruled out in the empty space of possibility.)

Yet, brute chance alone is scarcely meaningful. We seem condemned always to discern some difference between chances that make a difference and contingencies that do not; and to mark the difference is to move beyond the merely contingent. Among those things granted importance in our lives, some salient contingencies will appear more valuable than others: for most of us there is a difference between the contingency of love's beginnings and the accidental discovery of an exotic piece of fruit at the local grocery store. A life in which all things are equally and indifferently contingent is hardly a life at all, at least not one worth celebrating or admiring. It might be true that "Anything from the sound of a word through the color of a leaf to the feel of a piece of skin can ... serve to dramatize and crystallize a human being's sense of self-identity."[86] But as the narrator of *In Search of Lost Time* shows, what matters is not only *that*

---

[84] Pippin, *Henry James and Modern Moral Life*, 8.
[85] Rorty, *Contingency, Irony, and Solidarity*, 100.   [86] Ibid., 37.

something somewhere has happened to someone or that the happening is mindlessly said to be important by just anyone; it matters also what one makes of it, how the accident is taken up in the life of the emerging literary artist, whether it comes to cohere in a certain way in the life of the dedicated poet or remains an isolated episode, without a name, without a home. There is a difference between saying "I like this madeleine soaked in lime-blossom" and caring about the place of a fleeting but significant experience in the anticipated shape of a novel and working out the difference between one contingent fact and another in the concrete life of a more stable and enduring concern. Effective and meaningful rede-scription of the persons, events, and things that captivate the serious novelist or her engaged counterpart is not the work of an hour or a day. If something encountered or thought or imagined *hic et nunc* really matters, it will show up in some shape later, if only to be repudiated or reconfigured.

Something's becoming significant depends, then, upon the place it comes to occupy in a more enduringly meaningful life-stance; and this, in turn, is anchored in a sense of what is living and what is not, in an awareness of what William James calls *live options*, what shows up, in Heidegger's way of speaking, in the space of *Entschlossenheit* and its aftermath in a history. Every vital sense of possibility may, in turn, be rooted in the contingencies of a particular historical situation: if I were not *here* and *now*, living in the United States at just this moment in the history of the world, the significance of the chance events that compose my life, and either move me or leave me indifferent, would undoubtedly be different, perhaps unrecognizable to *me*. But having to decide where to place my cares and having to mark the difference within the possible between the living and the dead are not (or at least not obviously) conditioned by where I just happen to be. I am free to place myself in thought and imagination elsewhere, to fancy what it would be like to be alive during the revolution; but these burdens – having to decide, having to place my concerns somewhere, having to assume responsibility for the boundaries of my life – cannot be thought away without losing sight of my concretely situated agency and the conditions that make choice meaningful.

It is true that death decides and settles (almost) nothing: knowing that I will die, that death is possible at every moment, imposes no task or norm. Mortal insight gives no information about how to bring a lengthy project to completion or what to do in order to parent well or where or how more generally one's energies would be best employed. No concrete ethic or moral pronouncement flows naturally or inevitably from the simple fact that each of us must die, unless we are already minded to take up this fact in a way that stands morally or ethically to reason. From the standpoint of what we already care about, death is either an empty essence or something that threatens to cut short what we hope to accomplish. To the truly apathetic, death is likely to be little more than the arbitrary end of a life surrounded by indifferent people engaged in indifferent affairs, and punctuated, if at all, by uninspiring events. For some hopeless individual who manages somehow to care about her own indifference, death might promise welcome release from an unacceptable state of apathetic estrangement.

Still, the unsettling fact that each of us is in the world only once, *"Ein Mal und nichtmehr,"* as the poet says,[87] is part of what it *means* to occupy the contingent space of significance we inhabit and to have to place our cares nowhere else but here. It is not just the sense of urgency in what we do that finds its roots in the dimly acknowledged fact of death; the very sense of occupying a unique historical situation, where not everything is possible or desirable or admirable, cannot be separated from the prospective sense of an Ending. Mortality is as limiting as what Arendt calls "natality." It is not up to me to go on waiting indefinitely for time to give birth to other historic situations and living options or to rework endlessly the dead possibilities of a bygone era, in the hope that others might eventually follow suit. If it makes sense to speak of acknowledging the contingencies that shape a particular perception of the world, there is also good reason to own up to the mortal limits of our lingering and acting in it. There is no method we can devise and no brute fact we can grasp to put an end to our uncertainty, no devious trap to capture once and for all the little mortal things we prefer to notice, and no way to fix for all eternity the significance of what we care about. From this point of view, the sense and purpose of a life is always somewhat open and fluid. But we cannot go on forever reconfiguring and reshaping; and it is death that stands in the way of our otherwise endless searchings and probings in the kingdom of the possible. Death does, after all, settle some things. If there is solid bottom somewhere, as Thoreau in *Walden* insists, it is death that makes possible

---

[87] Rilke, *Duino Elegies*, IX, 14. For a reading of Rilke in the spirit of Heidegger, but often against the grain of Heidegger's own criticisms of the poet's alleged metaphysics, see my *Being Here Is Glorious: On Rilke, Poetry, and Philosophy*, as well as my essay "On Nature, Inwardness, and Death in Rilke's *Sonnets to Orpheus*" in *Rilke's "Sonnets to Orpheus" and Philosophy*, ed. Hannah V. Eldridge and Luke Fischer (Oxford University Press, forthcoming).

the awareness of the soil in which our projects can thrive. But what Heidegger calls *Vorlaufen* and defines as the proper stance toward my own death is nothing like anxious expectation of a Great Big End that puts everything in order and makes me whole: it is only a matter of getting back into this (contingent, factical) world, where some things are bound to the living, and others found to be dead.

CHAPTER 6

The Ethics and Ontology of Formal Indication

Language and the Moral Life

In several early lecture courses, Heidegger puzzles over the Aristotelian thesis that the human being is *zôon logon echon*, in Heidegger's own way of translating the well-known expression from the *Politics*: we are "animals that have, live in, and pursue *language*."[1] This capacity to speak is no trivial fact about us. As Aristotle recognized, language or reason is deeply embedded in every recognizably human way of life.[2] Language shapes to a large extent what we are able at first to see and how, with what degree of seriousness or apathy, we respond to what there is.

As Heidegger reminds us throughout the phenomenological decade, each of us dwells in a world initially interpreted for us by others, and so already brought to expressive givenness, deposited in a language that governs what we find significant and blazes a trail through the darkness of a life devoid of *logos*. The remarkable power of the word appears to be its uncanny ability to bring into being a world of interest and desire, and to govern reflection upon what is interesting and desirable in and about the world.

According to one, now prominent way of construing our existence in speech, there is no human contact with the world that is not dependent on the enlightening power of the word: our hold on what there is in thought, but also in our various perceptions and emotions and actions, is either an embodiment of what has already been said about the world or an

---

[1] *GA* 18, 21. "The human being is an entity that speaks" (Ibid., 107). The human being, not only for Aristotle, but for the Greeks as such, is not just one being among others that happens to speak, but "a living being *has its authentic existence in conversation and discourse*. The Greeks existed in discourse" (Ibid., 108).

[2] This is apparent in Aristotle's definition of *eudaimonia* in the first book of the *Nicomachean Ethics*, where we are told that the distinctive thing human beings do is doing what they do in accordance with speech or reason, *logos*.

anticipation of what might be said about it.[3] The world of what we think, feel, and do is nothing other than what, at least in principle, can be said about that world. There is no world of any kind *in itself*, waiting to be expressed, and no meaningful world in itself we cannot express, but always only a world *for us* as the language animal. Our "intuitions," cribbing from Emerson, are brought forward in our best "tuitions." To claim inexpressible insight into the world is a naïve way of avoiding the work of finding adequate means of saying what we think we have to say. As Hegel remarks in a convincing discussion of the limits of mere sense-certainty in the *Phenomenology*, every effort to say that some things cannot be said betrays itself in the moment of utterance. What the world might have been before we were able to speak about it and what it will be after we have become eternally silent are idle questions. We gesture always toward a world that is already speaking and will go on speaking as long as it has a human witness. When we look for a world beyond speech we are looking, perhaps unwittingly, for a world of the dead.

*

If we take the line of thought just sketched seriously and see in language not an obstacle to consciousness and truth but the vehicle of our reflective awareness of truth, we will, perhaps, take more responsibility for the words we use and the forms we employ to express our ethical visions of life. A heightened awareness of the importance of language and the diversity of our linguistic construals of the world can lead to skepticism and cynicism; but it might also serve as an opportunity to speak and write about what we care about more carefully, and with greater sensitivity to the complex histories of the expressions we are prompted to use and abuse. What appears a mere theory of the role of language in giving shape to the world of human interest and insight might become a matter of cautious and conscientious expressive practice as well. In this way, speaking and writing become ethical acts. As Erich Heller cautions us, "Be careful what you say about the world. It *is* like that."[4]

---

[3] "The world," according to the "Natorp Essay," "is always being encountered in a particular manner of having-been-addressed, i.e., of an address that has made certain claims about it" (*Supplements*, 116).

[4] This is a slight paraphrase of Heller's advice "an educator can give to his pupils": "Be careful how you interpret the world; it *is* like that" (*The Disinherited Mind: Essays in Modern German Literature and Thought*, 26–7).

So how should the philosopher who cares about the moral life under some (Heideggerian) description express herself? Should she state her position clearly and directly, in unequivocal propositions that leave nothing to the reader's imagination, the sorts of statements that seem fitted to direct the mind toward some more or less obvious fact about the world? Or should she write more allusively, respecting both the darker soil of her own explicit views and her reader's own developing capacities? Is it always appropriate to aim for unrestricted universality? Or is it occasionally fitting to allow particulars to intrude? Is the best language of the moral life always the one that is most impersonal?

Transcendental Reflection and Beyond

Among those who take such questions seriously, it might appear perverse to take early Heidegger as a guide. But it is (I hope) no longer necessary to argue extensively at this point that Heidegger's ontology is responsive to some variety of moral concern, broadly construed along the lines pursued in the previous chapters; and it is even less controversial to claim that language and logic, under some perhaps peculiar description, were among Heidegger's earliest and most constant preoccupations.

In early Heidegger's view, the most significant philosophical difficulties surrounding the nature of language arise when we ask how the complex weave of our own life and experience ought to be expressed in philosophy, and how it ought to be expressed not when we already know, or think we know, what our experience can be said to mean, but when we are *seeking* something about ourselves or the world we inhabit. This amounts to asking how we ought to capture in *philosophical* prose the concerns and movements of something – Heidegger initially calls it "life" – that refuses to become an inert object, and in a way that embodies our moral interest in forms of life that satisfy our existential aspirations.

I say "philosophical prose" in part because Heidegger's own interest in the work of expression is itself philosophical, or at least tied to the tradition of philosophy as the concern of an ambivalent critic, and partly because the difficulty of finding ways of expressing the concerns of human life finds a home in our ongoing poetic, literary, ethical, and religious traditions. As we shall see, although it is true that Heidegger was sensitive to religious phenomena and attuned to poetic voices in the early lecture courses, and while he sometimes displays anti-philosophical sentiments, the work of the early 20s on the nature of language is developed in a decidedly philosophical register.

Heidegger's philosophical strategy in the early Freiburg and Marburg lectures is to employ what he calls *formal indication*. Perhaps more than anyone else, Theodore Kisiel has drawn attention to the fundamental role played by formal indications in Heidegger's intellectual beginnings, and throughout his development as a whole.[5] Any interpretation or defense of Heidegger's controversial linguistic practice will have to involve a careful interpretation of the nature of formally indicative concepts, which arguably form the methodological core of Heidegger's developing phenomenology.

But despite its central significance in Heidegger's appropriation of phenomenology, what precisely Heidegger means by and intends with the help of formal indications are questions that have spawned a great deal of controversy. A reader who comes to Heidegger by way of Husserl might be struck by the sketchiness of the former's phenomenological insights in contrast to his mentor's painstaking descriptions of the minute details of the concrete life of consciousness. *Being and Time* itself often reads like a pastiche of phenomenological insights, each calling for independent and detailed development and fuller argument, which Heidegger refuses to give. Heidegger frequently makes provocative, almost oracular pronouncements about *Stimmung* or *Verstehen*, leaving it to the reader to fill in the details and to construct the arguments for herself. Those who think that philosophical claims become plausible and fruitfully contestable only insofar as they become more fully explicit in philosophical argument, accessible in principle to anyone, are likely to accuse Heidegger of deliberate obscurity, perhaps, as Jaspers suggests, of a certain unwillingness to communicate. From this perspective, formal indications will seem culpably vague, fuzzy, and indeterminate.[6]

If we turn to Heidegger's interpreters for help, we find ourselves in an awkward situation. The most influential interpretive assessments of the concept, matter, and method of philosophy in the early lecture courses are so much at odds with one another that one might easily conclude that Heidegger was confused about what he was trying to do. According to one

---

[5] Kisiel, *The Genesis of Heidegger's "Being and Time."* The term *formale Anzeige* makes its first appearance in WS 1919/20, in a course devoted to the *Basic Problems of Phenomenology*, is developed in WS 1920/1 and, more briefly, in WS 1921/2, and continues to be used to capture the nature of philosophical concepts until WS 1929/30. But, as Kisiel points out, it is the unnamed method of conceptualizing and speaking about pre-theoretical life in KNS 1919.

[6] For early Heidegger, indeterminateness is the distinctive mark of a genuinely philosophical concept. "Philosophical concepts ... are ... vague, manifold, flowing," for reasons that will have to be spelled out below (*GA* 60, 3).

prevalent view, the method of formal indication grows out of Heidegger's early interest in the mystical tradition, and ought to be seen as a radical, post-philosophical attempt to speak about what has been traditionally considered ineffable. Heidegger's conception of philosophy, assuming we can continue to speak of it here, is something akin to mysticism. The early search for the *Ursprung* of our particular, historical lives, and the use of kinetic terms like *Ereignis* to name the motility of life, are modeled on mystical experience as the phenomenological paradigm. Despite the transcendental pretensions of *Being and Time*, Heidegger's deepest impulses and intentions are, on this view, fundamentally at odds with the transcendental tradition; and the story of the book's genesis is also the story of its demise, an account of a failed project. If Heidegger eventually comes to speak the language of transcendental reflection, this is best explained as the result of an unfortunate turn to Kant, recorded in the changed plans for the lecture course on logic in WS 1925/6: Heidegger's belated and enthusiastic discovery of the *Critique of Pure Reason* (as an anticipation of an ontology grounded obscurely in the phenomenon of time) helped shape the final draft of his major work.[7] Had he remained true to his original intentions, a very different, perhaps an even better book, would have been the result.

According to another plausible interpretation, Heidegger's project, or at least what remains philosophically viable within it, is essentially a version of the transcendental attempt to clarify and justify certain conditions necessary for the possibility of experience. On this view, *Being and Time* is no aberration, but the crystallization of transcendental tendencies operative throughout the phenomenological decade. The remarkable fact about Heidegger's breakthrough is not that it was informed by the mystical tradition, and not that it was tied to the quasi-Lutheran or Kierkegaardian ambition to recapture the vitality of primitive Christianity in opposition to ancient (Aristotelian) science, but that it evolved into a *philosophical* project, one devoted to the development of phenomenology as a rigorous science of *Leben an und für sich* (or facticity or, in the long run, Dasein). Heideggerian science might initially seem eccentric, but it is, after all, a pre-theoretical *Wissenschaft*, a science of the conditions necessary for the possibility of theoretical science, and a science trained upon the structure and sources of the space of *meaning*. Any attempt to grasp philosophically the space of meaning demands nothing less than some version of

---

[7] This is the view of Kisiel, shared by Van Buren in *The Young Heidegger*.

transcendental reflection.[8] Heidegger certainly modifies the methods of
transcendental philosophy, and includes a number of transcendental conditions not fully recognized or appreciated by Kant and his followers, but
the general form of Heidegger's most enduring arguments is a phenomenological recasting of the project of transcendental grounding and
conditioning.

A large number of passages and texts can be readily marshaled in favor of
both interpretations, neither of which can be said to be grasping at straws.
The transcendentalist can appeal to WS 1919/20, where Heidegger claims
that the *Ursprung* or original domain of phenomenology is "nothing
mystical," but something to be pursued in rigorous, scientific consideration, "and only in it."[9] The basic problem of philosophy is the problem of
method: "Every genuine philosophy is in its authentic driving force a
struggle concerning method."[10] Toward the end of KNS 1919, a lecture
course in which talk of method is abundant, Heidegger claims that the
entire course has been devoted to the problem of method.[11] Writing to
Misch a few years later on his interest in logic, "Research into the history of
logic by way of the history of problems does not take logic as a discipline of
philosophy and in the order outlined by its textbooks, but as research into
categories, in which the fundamental structures of addressing and considering objects by life are raised to the conceptual level."[12]

On the other hand, the transcendentalist overlooks a number of forceful
remarks that support the mystical or post-philosophical interpretation of
Heidegger's earliest phenomenological efforts. When Heidegger does mention the transcendental problematic explicitly in the early lecture courses, it
is usually in an effort to distance himself from it. According to WS 1919/20,
the transcendental manner of posing questions is said to lead "only to a
certain [preliminary] stage [of questioning] and no further."[13] Because
she engages chiefly in epistemological reflection, the transcendental
philosopher "fails to arrive at the center of primordial science."[14] In the
Becker manuscript of SS 1920, in the context of a discussion of the
method of phenomenological destruction and formal indication, Heidegger cautions his students that "We philosophize not in order to show that
we need a philosophy, but precisely to show that we need none."[15]

---

[8] See Crowell, *Husserl, Heidegger, and the Space of Meaning: Paths toward Transcendental
Phenomenology.*
[9] *GA* 58, 26.   [10] Ibid., 135.   [11] *GA* 57/8, 110.   [12] In *Becoming Heidegger*, 105.
[13] *GA* 58, 229.   [14] Ibid., 230.   [15] *GA* 59, 191.

A few years later, in a lecture course on the hermeneutics of facticity, the driving force of philosophical hermeneutics is said to be a desire to bring Dasein back to itself, to develop a certain wakefulness in our existence; and hermeneutics is claimed to be not really philosophy at all, but "something preliminary which runs in advance of it and has its own reason for being: what is at issue in it, what it all comes to, is not to be finished with it as quickly as possible, but rather to hold out in it as long as possible."[16] Just one year later, during the first semester at Marburg, Heidegger prefaces a lecture course intended to introduce his students to phenomenological research with the following words: "It is my conviction that philosophy has come to an end. We stand before completely new tasks, having nothing to do with traditional philosophy."[17]

It would be fairly easy to put an end to the debate if we could assign these apparently conflicting remarks to separate texts, and proceed to interpret them accordingly. We would then have a clear-cut distinction between a "scientific" Heidegger, on the one hand, and an "existential" or mystical, post-philosophical Heidegger, on the other. We could interpret each set of texts in isolation, leaving the choice between the two up to the personal taste or philosophical predilection of the reader. But the situation of the interpreter is more complicated, and more interesting, than this; and apparently conflicting stances on the nature and function of philosophy and its concepts in human life find their way into the very same texts.

In WS 1921/2, for example, Heidegger develops a critical account of two sets of misunderstandings of the very nature of philosophy and the role played by definitions in philosophical concept-formation that deserves to be taken more seriously than it has.[18] There are, Heidegger insists, two approaches to or assumptions about the problem of definition that ought to be avoided: an *underestimation* of the importance of definition, criticism of which appears to support the contentions of those who see in the early lecture courses a deepening of the general approach initiated by Kant and developed in German idealism and neo-Kantianism; and an *overestimation* of the nature and function of definition in

---

[16] *GA* 63, 20.   [17] *GA* 17, 1.

[18] Kisiel all but dismisses this course, on the (partly justified) scholarly grounds that the published (*Gesamtausgabe*) edition is "chronologically compromised" and for the (less than fully justified) reason that it covers the same territory as the "somewhat clearer draft of the *Einleitung* of October 1922" (*The Genesis*, 235). As a potential contribution to our understanding of the nature and function of formal indication in early Heidegger, it cannot, on Kisiel's view, compare with the much fuller, but interrupted discussion in WS 1920/1 (See *The Genesis*, 172.). But WS 1921/2 abounds in statements that raise serious questions about Kisiel's own interpretation of Heidegger's developing phenomenology and its religious sources.

philosophy, criticism of which lends weight to readings that stress Heidegger's departure from the philosophical tradition.

Those who claim that philosophy ought to pursue universally valid definitions that apply equally well to any and every instance of the thing in question fail to recognize that philosophy is not an object among other objects; that the ideal of definition in this sense springs from a certain "formal logic" that, however appropriate within a certain area of inquiry, has definite limits and does not apply without further ado to philosophy and its objects; and that the ways of defining should not be decided in advance and formally, but ought to grow out of deep and subtle familiarity with the things themselves to be defined.[19] This overestimation of the task of definition fails, in other words, to recognize the distinctiveness of philosophic inquiry and works with a distorted understanding of the nature of philosophical concepts and principles. The basic principle of philosophical inquiry is claimed to be nothing less than *passion*, not something that can be formulated in a manner intelligible in principle to anyone, but ultimately a matter of *decision*, something I choose to consider an important point of departure. The starting point of fruitful philosophical research cannot be fully justified or defended in light of fixed ideals or timelessly valid standards of philosophical method; it functions rather to open up and guide the further course of inquiry. A principle of philosophy is, then, no fixed proposition that, in combination with other propositions, enters into a rigorous proof that puts all matters to rest and clears up every controversy, but merely an indeterminate basis or soil out of which further exploration of the phenomena is to grow. In this sense, definition is more like a way of coming into *possession* of something: philosophy, like anything else in human life, has its own ways of coming to be properly owned in a concretely situated acquisition. Every attempt to make explicit an understanding of the being of life and world grows out of a *Vorhaben* of the thing about which we are speaking in a concrete, unique, and hence unrepeatable situation of thought and action. Ontological definition is the articulation of *a* proper way of coming into possession of something. Philosophy certainly looks, in this context, like a way of life.

But those who believe that philosophy is simply a way of life, that it would be better for the philosopher to live deeply or intensely and to

---

[19] Even this claim could, however, be taken up by the transcendental philosopher. Kant himself noted in the Discipline of the first *Critique*, possibly with Spinoza in mind, that the definition in philosophy comes, not at the beginning of the inquiry, but rather at its end. And a number of texts suggest that the categories cannot themselves be defined rigorously, but merely exposed in their relation to the experience they constitute and organize.

immerse herself in the concrete details of life, fail to acknowledge that philosophy is knowledge of *principles*: every interpretive approach to the concrete and immediate is always guided by fundamental assumptions about what and how the concrete *is* and how particulars ought to be appropriated. Philosophical opposition to the clarification of basic concepts and principles fails to see "that the defect lies not in the problematic of principles as such, but in the uncritical acceptance of a definite idea of and fixing of principles."[20] Philosophy certainly looks like transcendental reflection on the principles that shape our understanding and make possible our explicit knowledge of what there is.

We are, then, confronted with a puzzling situation: We have before us a thinker averse to transcendental philosophy in pursuit of what look like transcendental conditions; a thinker attuned to the importance of the particular who rarely speaks about particulars, and who speaks a language that seems to capture general characteristics of human life, the world, the use of tools, the nature of history, the power of death, and similarly shared phenomena. We have a thinker who seems to think that it is perfectly coherent to aspire to bring together, and systematically to unite, the interest in life *and* conceptual form, as Heidegger makes clear, once again, to Misch: "The investigations upon which the fully elaborated lectures courses are based have as their goal a systematic, phenomenological, and ontological interpretation of the basic phenomena of factic [particular, historical] life, which ... is to be brought to categorial definition in keeping with the essence of its basic comportment and coping in and with a world (environing world, communal world, self-world)."[21] But in order to clarify this puzzling situation, and to see what speaks for both sides of the interpretive divide and why both in isolation may be deficient, we have to determine more precisely what Heidegger means by "formal indication" and what roles it assumes in Heideggerian phenomenology.

A First Approach to Formal Indication: A Critical Logic Without Objects

As we had occasion to observe in Chapter 1, it is the business of the early Heidegger's philosopher to remain in close proximity to the theoretically uninhibited course of life, and to preserve in philosophical concepts the various cares and concerns that show before we become scientists and

---

[20] *GA* 61, 30; *PIA*, 24. [21] *Becoming Heidegger*, 108–9.

theoreticians. We have also seen that this involves some appeal to the *goodness*, ontologically interpreted, of what we take ourselves to be about, on the assumption that the good for us cannot be reduced to the goodness of an object (or a *pragma*) that merely serves some local purpose, and displays a structure that can be readily objectified into a thing with useful characteristics. From this point of view, formal indication is a way of speaking and writing about something that should not be treated as a mere object among objects in a world of facts (overlaid, we know not how, with values). Life itself always bears within itself a kind of *logos*, hence a meaning, sense, and worth. If objects find their conceptual home in a rigidly determined framework or order, then philosophical concepts, dealing as they do with phronetic categories (or categories of care), are not ordering concepts, but something more like *expressive* concepts: they are meant to articulate the significance of a (worldly) life in the making, in concrete situations to be exposed and interpreted.[22] From this standpoint, formal indication is a way of preserving the emerging significance of an entity that is always somehow expressing itself, in opposition to the pervasive language of theory (which, again as we saw in Chapter 1, tends to drain life of its significance). The logic of formally indicative concepts is the reflective correlate of a basic philosophical understanding of what it is for human beings to be, moving about within, and having to interpret spaces saturated with meaning and worth. Human life is always somehow meaningfully expressed and expressing. The facts of life "don't lie next to one another like stones, but they have in each case their place; and this has nothing to do with a [mere] position [or placement] within a [domain of] lawfulness [appropriate to objects among other objects in nature]."[23] Our philosophical theme, then, is not present like a table to be subsumed under

---

[22] See *GA* 58, 142–3 for the distinction between the ordering function of scientific concepts trained upon objects and the expressive function of philosophical concepts trained upon senses. In section 10 of the Becker *Nachschrift* of the concluding part of the lecture course, Heidegger notes: "*Life* is not an object and can never become an object; is it nothing objective" (*GA* 58, 236). The difference between an ordering grasp of objects and a philosophical expression of life is rooted in the difference between theoretical positing and *understanding explication*.

[23] *GA* 58, 257. In the following semester, Heidegger takes up Natorp's reconstructive psychology in an effort to deconstruct the problem of the *irrationality* of lived experience. The method of reconstruction is anchored in the assumption that lived experience does not possess a meaning to be explicated, but can only be approached indirectly, in terms of the objects constituted in an inaccessible life of consciousness. The course concludes by outlining the task of philosophy as philosophical explication of the sense of facticity. "Die Philosophie hat die Aufgabe, die Faktizität des Lebens zu erhalten und die Faktizität des Daseins zu stärken." (*GA* 59, 174) To claim that life is at bottom irrational is to overlook the "primal actuality" of the self "in the enactment of life-experience," an actuality rooted in care (Ibid., 173).

a concept and filed away, or explained in terms of natural scientific categories, but a life being lived and a meaning (often obscure) calling for expression. A philosophy that retains a healthy sense of the expressive movement of human life will be no detached scientific contemplation of an object called "life," but a distinctive conceptual articulation of the rich and diversified field of human experience.[24] Formal indication is at least a warning and a reminder that we have our meaningful being not as a finished datum, but as something we have *to be*.

But if Heidegger did no more than gesture toward the importance of remaining close to life, we could hardly speak of a *philosophical* project taking shape in the early lecture courses. This, too, was one of the more important lessons we gained from the first Freiburg period in Chapter 1. As we noted in passing earlier, literary authors and poets, often sharp and subtle critics of the philosophical tradition, recognized the value of remaining close to human experience and preserving a nuanced sense of "facticity" long before the young *Privatdozent* began lecturing on the idea of philosophy as radical phenomenological explication of the sense of life. Even if early Heidegger flirts with the post-philosophical motif, he is obviously doing something other than telling stories or writing plays and poems. One might even suspect that novelists and playwrights and poets are better poised to deal concretely with facticity than the philosopher, even one who traffics in formal indications.

Like the poets, Heidegger insists that philosophy is always about something concrete, even when it gestures toward the abstract. But like the traditional philosopher, Heidegger equally insists that philosophy traffics in concepts, albeit peculiar ones, that grasp the "being" of things, or give voice to a logic of the motility of human life, without assimilating being or human existence to a logic of universals that moves around in genera and species, and without carving up the world into a set of distinct regions of being. (This is partly what I take to be at issue in Heidegger's critique of the logic of *definitio* in SS 1924. Recall our remarks on exemplary definition in Chapter 3.)

Readers of the Introduction to *Sein und Zeit* who come to the work without the help of the early lecture courses are likely to be puzzled by Heidegger's curt refusal to speak of the universality of being as if it were a

---

[24] Heidegger's appropriation of Husserl's phenomenology is clearly indebted to Dilthey's subtle hermeneutic account of lived experience, understanding, and expression. For a discussion of Dilthey's mature theory of *Verstehen*, see my "Dilthey's Epistemology of the *Geisteswissenschaften*" in *JHP*.

highest genus.[25] Nor are they likely to be reassured when Heidegger cites, apparently with approval, the medieval designation of being as the "*transcendens* pure and simple."[26] It appears natural to begin by examining the familiar objects we encounter in the world, noting similarities and differences, and moving gradually toward a system of classification in which each object can be confidently placed. Not only does it appear natural, but the development of rigorous, specialized scientific research and the emergence of distinctive philosophical disciplines, the possibility, in short, of concrete work as opposed to mere conceptual babble about meaningless abstractions, depend upon the differentiation of material domains or regions of objects. We might note, for example, important differences between objects that must be moved from without and objects that seem capable of moving themselves. In this way inanimate nature is distinguished from the world of animals, in contrast to the confused modes of thought one finds in animism and hylozoism, and both domains become fields of independent scientific research that can be pursued without interference.[27] At a more developed stage of thought, we might draw distinctions between the real objects encountered in perception and ideal objects, between stones, and plants, and animals, on the one hand, and numbers, geometrical objects, and logical propositions, on the other.[28] We might add the apparently empty observation that everything we can possibly consider must after all *be* in order to be considered and classified at all. Being is, after all, the highest genus. Even nothing must, in the end, somehow *be* in order to be thought.

Throughout the early lecture courses, Heidegger repeatedly insists that philosophical concepts do not function in this way; that formal indications contribute nothing to our efforts to organize and classify things; and that, more paradoxically, they do not really capture something like a universal *at all*.[29] The "ordering, totalizing, typifying tendency to classify" and the subsuming of particulars under universals are anchored in the assumption

---

[25] *Sein und Zeit*, 3.   [26] *Sein und Zeit*, 2 and 38.

[27] This is how Husserl generally understands the gradual emergence of relatively independent domains of scientific research.

[28] The distinction between the real and the ideal, taken up by early Heidegger from Lotze, Husserl, and others, is in a sense the first fundamental ontological difference to be pursued in the earliest writings. After KNS 1919, the distinction is subjected to rigorous phenomenological critique and traced back, ultimately, to the temporality of Dasein. For an extended discussion of the distinction, see the *Vorbetrachtung* of WS 1925/6 (*GA* 21).

[29] In WS 1921/2, Heidegger associates the idea of a highest genus with the "logic of the Greeks," which develops out of a particular experience of the world as the field of things "made, produced, fabricated" (*GA* 61, 25).

that philosophy and its objects are "matters of fact and things." But in the self-interpreting movement of life, we find nothing like matters of fact and mere things, devoid of meaningful contexts. To see things in this way is already to occupy a theoretical standpoint divorced from the proper field of phenomenological research. If formal indications are not to be construed as concepts of an object, if they do not organize our experience and its contents in terms of *genera* and *species*, if a formally indicative concept is not a scientific concept, but is rather something like an expression of self-interpreting life, then we should ask: How are these peculiar "philosoph-ical" statements, statements ultimately about nothing less than "being," to be understood? Isn't *every* concept, even one that applies to the situations and experiences of everyday life, a general representation, something that applies uniformly to every object that falls under it? And if not, why speak of *concepts*?

*

If there is a philosophical project tied to the idea of formal indication in the early lecture courses, and if we hope to clarify Heidegger's cryptic claims on behalf of philosophical concept-formation, the *Begrifflichkeit* of philo-sophical inquiry will have to be pursued and interpreted against the backdrop of Husserl's phenomenology. Throughout the phenomeno-logical period, Heidegger takes over and modifies a number of basic Husserlian concepts.[30] Intentionality becomes a situated, caring relation to the world, explicated according to three senses of direction (*Bezugssin, Vollzugssinn, Gehaltssinn*).[31] The phenomenological reduction becomes a regress to the space of significance in which each of us dwells, before the world is placed at a distance from the contemplative subject.[32] Husserl's famous "principle of all principles" becomes the "primal intention of

---

[30] The Husserlian orientation is compatible with the recognition that Heidegger is frequently criticizing Husserl, as Carman, among many others, has argued in *Heidegger's Analytic*. But the accent on Heidegger's critical departures from Husserl often conceals deeper levels of continuity. See Dahlstrom's extended account of Husserl in *Heidegger's Concept of Truth* and Marion's *Reduction and Givenness*.

[31] In WS 1919/20, these three senses of direction (*Sinnelemente* or *Sinnführungen*) are said to belong to the *Urstruktur* of the situation of philosophical understanding (*GA* 58, 261). Heidegger adds a *Zeitigungssinn* to the list of directional senses in WS 1921/2, where they are treated as moments in the structure of *Verhalten*, and deployed in an effort to understand the nature of the philosophical life (*GA* 61, 52–3). As it turns out, the directional sense of life (pre-philosophical and philosophical) is precisely the "object" of formal indication. We shall return to this point below.

[32] "Alles   Bedeutsamkeitslose,   nicht   Verstehbare   wird   *ausgeschaltet*   oder   aufgesogen [phänomenologische Reduktion!!]" (*GA* 58, 156). Five pages earlier in the same volume, Heidegger objects to the Husserlian conception of reduction on the grounds that it is not by

truthful life as such, the absolute *life-sympathy*, that is itself identical with
living experience itself."³³ Phenomenological intuition, the self-givenness
of something *leibhaft* (in the flesh, bodily), the locus of evidence for every
genuine phenomenological claim, is transformed into the vital "hermeneutic intuition" that grounds the concept-formation of a less intrusive and
disruptive approach to life.³⁴ Most importantly for our purposes, the
Husserlian notion of formalization is developed in the direction of formal
indication.

The fullest account of formal indication begins where Husserl left off,
with the important phenomenological distinction between *formalization*
and *generalization* drawn in the *Logische Untersuchungen* and sketched out
in the first book of the *Ideen*, section 13. On Husserl's view, generalization
or conceptualization of something in terms of *genera* and *species* is an
operation that bears upon the material content of an object of thought;
in Heidegger's terms, generalization is "in its accomplishment tied to a
definite *material domain*."³⁵ Red, for instance, is an instance of color, color
a sensible quality, sensible qualities representations, and representations
are, in the end, modes of consciousness. Formalization, by contrast, is not
tethered to specific material domains. The transition from "sensible quality" or "color" to *object as such* and the transition from color to the essence
of color involve a unique (non-generalizing) operation of thought. In
formalization, the attitude or expressive intention is not bound to any
Sachhaltigkeit, but is materially free³⁶ and free, likewise, of every ordering
step: it is not necessary to run through each stage of generalization in order
to consider something (anything) as an *object as such* or to consider the
object as an instance of its essence. Formalization is an essential possibility
of consciousness at every stage of the process of generalization or specifica-
tion. I can always turn away from *this* particular content and ask: In what
way is this very thing an object? What must it be like in order to be an
object at all? In order to focus on objectivity as such, I must look away
from every *Wasgehalt* (what-content).³⁷ Although formalization involves
no material determination, it must still be motivated. And its motivation
lies in the "attitude of relation," in a certain way of being related to the
object of thought.³⁸

---

itself productive, and is ultimately bound up with transcendental, epistemological modes of
questioning (Ibid., 151).
³³ *GA* 56/7, 110.   ³⁴ See *GA* 56/7, 117.   ³⁵ *GA* 60, 58.   ³⁶ *GA* 60, 58.   ³⁷ Ibid., 58.
³⁸ "Die formale Prädikation ist sachhaltig nicht gebunden, aber sie muß doch irgendwie motiviert
sein. Wie ist sie motiviert? Sie entspringt dem *Sinn des Einstellungsbezugs* selbst" (*GA* 60, 58). The
introduction of relational and performance or actualization senses is itself an "indication" of the

This distinction between formalization and generalization has important phenomenological implications. What is at issue in the idea of formalization is nothing less than the possibility of (a certain kind of) ontology. For Husserl, the ability to consider something without taking an interest in its material content, the ability to formalize, to abstract from every regional domain of being, makes possible the development of *formal ontology*, a science of the necessary structure of the thought of an object as such, or a science of the general structure of any object insofar as it can become an object of thought. To determine something merely as an object is not to say anything about the sort of object it is, but simply to determine the way in which it *gives itself* (objectively) to me. Husserl's idea of a formal ontology is already an important step in the right (ontological) direction, even if (as we saw in Chapter 2) Heidegger is suspicious of *mathesis universalis*. Phenomenology is possible because there is a difference between *what* displays itself to me and *how* it shows itself.[39] If Heidegger is a critic of Husserl throughout the phenomenological decade, it is partly because his mentor is already on the way toward (a deficient) ontology.

As important as Husserl's ontological breakthrough is, it does not advance far enough to satisfy Heidegger's demand for a radical phenomenology of pre-theoretical life. Formalization and generalization are both species of *universalization*; and universals are concepts that grip things only insofar as they become objects about which something indifferent might be said, something that fails to capture *how* they are, what purposes they might, in certain contexts, be said to serve, and what aim they might be said to make possible. "What formalization and generalization have in common is that they stand in the sense of the 'universal,' while formal indication has nothing to do with the universal."[40] Husserl's ontology privileges only one mode of givenness, a mode of givenness that finds its measure in objectivity, as correlate of the theoretical attitude. Aristotle already recognized that *to on pollachôs legetai*. If every being is not an object, and if every attitude or comportment is not theoretical, is not trained upon something universal, then we need a concept of formalization liberated from every reference to objectivity and universality, at least as

---

method of formal indication, which deals not so much with the content of experience but with its way of appearing and being lived, and an announcement of the terrain upon which criticism of the Husserlian idea of formalization should be conducted.

[39] For a discussion of the central importance of Husserl's discovery of the essential difference between the appearing or giving of something and what appears or is given, see Marion's *Reduction and Givenness*, 31–2.

[40] Ibid., 59.

these characteristics of truthful expression come forward in the theoretical attitude, under some description.[41]

It is tempting to look for non-objective expressions in the realm of ordinary language, and to seek out non-theoretical attitudes in the various ways we speak to one another in concrete linguistic situations, in the living discourse of face-to-face encounters. The language of everyday life appears to be free of any reference to objectivity and the theoretical attitude. We speak about the world above all as something that matters to us, in contexts of concern that precede and condition the observational stance of theory. Grammarians notwithstanding, the heavy or broken hammer is not a subject of predication, but "this thing here that's getting in the way of a project." To speak about the hammer in the context of trying to work with it is not to theorize about it (to classify it, to subsume it under a universal, to examine its *eidos*, etc.), but to request another hammer or to express a sense of frustration. If I merely look at the hammer, I still typically understand it in the sense that I could take it in hand and use it if I wished to get back to work. To see it as a hammer is just to take it up as something capable of disappearing in the work to be done. Even if my gaze is trained upon a tool the use of which is unknown to me, I still see it *as* a tool, as something with which I could work if I learned how properly to use it.

Although he often begins with the linguistic richness of everyday expressions, Heidegger is no ordinary language philosopher. Despite Heidegger's early efforts to bring philosophy back to (everyday) life, everyday life is not philosophy.[42] As well-suited as everyday speech is to speak about the specific contents that concern us in the normal, uninterrupted course of everyday life, it has not developed with an eye on *how* these contents show up for us.[43] In the language of *Being and Time*, everyday life and its

---

[41] This distinction between the being of an object, as the correlate of a theoretical attitude, and the being of the non-objective, as it gives itself in self-interpreting, self-actualizing life, is the *basic* ontological "difference" in early Heidegger.

[42] This, I take it, is part of what Heidegger means by the *self-sufficiency* of life in WS 1919/20. In WS 1920/1, Heidegger observes that factical life "zeigt eine *Indifferenz* in Bezug auf die Weise des Erfahrens," and this very indifference "begründet also die *Selbstgenügsamkeit* der faktischen Lebenserfahrung" (*GA* 60, 12). Talk of "self-sufficiency" in the lecture course on the phenomenology of religious life and, a bit later, in WS 1921/2 assumes a slightly pejorative tone, as if self-sufficiency were an obstacle to the development of phenomenology.

[43] "For our language, for reasons which we shall have to consider, in following its natural bent, first addresses and expresses the entity as a world and not the entity which is speech itself, so that our stock of words and expressions is first oriented in its sense to entities which we in our case here really do not have as our theme. But even when we try to explicate the being of the entity of the world as it is there for us, even here there are enough difficulties in finding suitable formulation for the

ways of speaking out about itself are remarkably insensitive to the *being* of what there is in the world. When it does speak out about being, when it becomes philosophical, it tends to interpret beings uniformly and to work with a single (and inadequate) concept of being. If formal indications grow out of the richness of a living linguistic tradition, they are nevertheless supposed to express something frequently neglected.

Everyday life is already in some sense fragmented, its "objects" experienced as things among things, each having its own place in an order of things, even if we rarely speak about the items of our *Umwelt* in the language of *genera* and *species*. As Heidegger notes in *Sein und Zeit*, the facticity of being-in-the-world means that "Dasein is already dispersed in definite ways of being-in, perhaps even spilt up."[44] We care for flowers in the garden, human beings at a local hospital, the animals who help us cultivate the fields and provide companionship, works of art in museums, and ancient documents in the archive. And we do so in different ways, depending on the sort of object at issue in our cares and concerns. We *understand* the difference between an animal and a plant, a tool and a work of art, even if we are unable to say explicitly and precisely what we mean or understand in our concrete dealings with these things. In the discussion of science as a *Bekundungszusammenhang* in WS 1919/20, presented at length in Chapter 1, Heidegger claims that the scientific treatment of an object is an accomplishment that rests upon a certain *pregiven* foundation.[45] Every non-primordial science, even formal logic, is the development of a *Sachgebeit*, a material domain of objects that become more clearly delimited and sharply fixed as the science in question develops.

Primordial science, by contrast, has no fixed domain of objects. This means that an original science of factical life does not come into conflict with the special sciences. Phenomenology is not in competition with physics over the true conception of material reality. Its interest lies in life before it becomes the theme of physical science. Every objective domain is distinct, but none has any priority over any other. None of them motivates a return to the *Ursprung*. If phenomenology continues to speak about history, earth, sky, life, art, etc., it does not consider them primarily in terms of a specific material content, but in terms of *how* they are lived and appropriated in life itself, not in terms of some *Wasgehalt*, but rather in terms of the *Wie* of life, its *Wiegehalt*. The phenomenological return to the

---

structures of the being of the entity; for here too the propensity is first toward the entity and not toward being" (*History of the Concept of Time*, 151).

[44] *Sein und Zeit*, 56.   [45] GA 58, 66.

Urpsrung is a distinctive regress to the ways of life's self-interpreting movement in spaces of significance; and formal indication is, from this point of view, the proper way of talking about this peculiar way of experiencing the pre-theoretical world of daily life.[46]

To say, then, that phenomenology has to pursue the *Wie* of life and experience, is to say that philosophy is somehow concerned about how things are *had* in pre-theoretical life. The notion of formally indicative concepts develops in an effort to speak about the rich field of pre-scientific *Haben*. Pre-theoretical life and the life of theory are both instances of comportment (*Verhalten*), are both ways of *having* things. This recognition does not provide the phenomenologist with a place to rest, but opens up paths of further inquiry. The initially empty identification of theory and life as ways of having invites reflection on the differences between having something as an object of theoretical comportment and having something in life itself. To have something in life itself is, roughly (and repeating an argument presented earlier), to relate to the world as the horizon of meaningful content in the way of being *familiar* with things, to *understand* how to behave in complex situations of action, and to actualize or perform life in the manner of caring for my own being and taking care of those things that come within the scope of my *Umwelt* and in the world I have in common with others (*Mitwelt*). If there is a basic insight that drives Heidegger's appropriation of phenomenology in early lecture courses, it would have to be this: *Wissen* and *Wissenschaft* grow out of non-theoretical ways of having things in the world of everyday life.

Formal indications turn out to be rather *informal*. They are neutralizing with respect to *one* way of determining the sense of comportment or having, but fertilizing in relation to the further explication of the senses of being. The problem of formal indication is essentially the problem of *Zugänglichkeit*, the problem of gaining access to the domain of pre-theoretical life, finding one's way around *in* it, and saying something essential about it without theoretical interruption or intrusion. In a word, formal indications indicate the concrete ways in which life has *itself*.[47] Heidegger's earliest critique of the ideal of theory amounts roughly to the charge that theory is a deficient and inauthentic way of having those things that matter to me in the *Lebenswelt*.

---

[46] For the distinction between *Wasgehalt* and *Wiegehalt*, see section 19 of WS 1919/20 (*GA* 58).

[47] The much-maligned "jargon of authenticity" in *Being and Time* must be traced back to these early efforts to speak about the genuineness of personal life.

But what, after all, does it mean to *have* something pre-theoretically? And how does formal indication play out (concretely) in the interpretation of life? We speak of having in a variety of contexts, and often mean very different things. I do not have a headache in the same way that I have a pet or a wife. If I say, "I have a mother" I don't mean to suggest that the person who gave birth to me is in my possession like a package from the post-office. I have a mother means: *This* woman gave me birth, cared for me when I was very young, was frustrated with me when I disobeyed, was proud of my accomplishments, was supportive when I was struggling, and so on. To spell out the sense of *Haben* in this context is to say something about what concretely it means to *be* a mother and to be *related* to a mother.[48] Sometimes having does amount to being in possession of something. But even here, possession means very different things depending on the sort of thing possessed. Having a collection of rare books is not akin to having a body or a mind; and having a mind as such is not the same as having a mind to get revenge. Having a heart (an organ) is not having a heart (compassion). I have a talent differently than I have three (Biblical) talents. And each of these ways of having something cannot be compared with the way in which I have a *world* and have myself in the world.

If there is a focal or fundamental sense of "having" in early Heidegger, it is tied to the concept of self-*movement*, of worldly self-comportment in the concrete shape of history. *Haben* is not static possession, but active appropriation, not a fixed relation to something finished, but the vital struggle to be in a certain way. To have something genuinely is to *enact* or perform in relation to something, to *appropriate* an object of vital concern in the manner of a history.[49]

We can see how formal indications work in one of the more detailed instances of its employment during the first Freiburg period. In the opening part of SS 1920, devoted to the problem of the *a priori* in neo-

[48] The connection between having and being lies at the heart of Heidegger's early remarks on the Aristotelian concept of *ousia*. According to SS 1924 (section 7), the common or pre-philosophical sense of *ousia* is as much as *Vermögen, Besitzstand, Hab und Gut, Anwesen*. As a name for being, *ousia* names the *how* (*Wie*) of being, being itself in the sense of being-there (See *GA* 18, 24–5.).
[49] As we move closer to the concrete sense of formal indication, the influence of Husserl gives way to the influence of Kierkegaard. What Heidegger means by formal indication is akin to what in the *Concluding Unscientific Postscript* is called the *truth of appropriation*. The similarities are far too striking to be coincidental and far too numerous to mention in full here. Climacus insists that the way to objective (systematic, definitive, scientific) truth is a movement away from the subject, in the direction of a truth that becomes *indifferent*, and even draws the distinction between *what* is said, important from an objective point of view, and *how* what is said is said (*Postscript*, 202).

Kantianism, Heidegger distinguishes between six meanings of history, and examines each in some depth with the overarching intention of discovering the most basic way of having a relation to the historical.[50] (1) If I say "My friend studies history" I mean history and not law or natural science. To study history is not merely to read, collect, excerpt, or take up certain items of information, but to develop knowledge of the past methodically, to make the historical world accessible in scientific research. History in this sense is historical *science*. (2) When someone is grappling with a philo-sophical problem, one often advises her to get oriented in the *history* of the problem, i.e., to familiarize herself with the factual realizations of the development of the problem. In this case, the individual is in possession of a body of information without necessarily taking an interest in it *as past*. All that is relevant is the *Wasgehalt*, a content that can be taken up and explored without regard for historical context. (3) One speaks of tribes and peoples *without history*. This does not mean that they have no science of history, although this might be true, and not that they have no relation to the past, but that they possess nothing like *tradition*. Those lacking a history in this sense are a people without a sense of being indebted to a heritage, people for whom the ancestral is a matter of indifference. They live, like those in the early modern infatuation with savages, from day to day and care only about what each day brings. In this light, "history" means as much as "tradition" – a body of customs and values and points of view that stems from an ancestral past to which one feels somehow indebted. (4) We also speak of history as the great magister of life, e.g.,

---

[50] Heidegger's discussion of history in this pivotal text illustrates the concrete use of formal indication rather well, and helps pave the way for an account of the various philosophical functions of formally indicative concepts. That Heidegger chooses *history* is nothing arbitrary. History turns out to be the very being of the human being. Already in KNS 1919, Heidegger is speaking out against the "unliving" and "reifying" description of lived experience in scientific theory and its epistemological shadow. Later in the same year, in SS 1919, Heidegger is calling for a phenomenology of the "historical I" living out its life in concrete situations of engagement and concern in opposition to phenomenological reflection that represses the historical life of consciousness, that emerges by way of a certain *Entgeschichtlichung*. "Das Ich ist selbst Situations-Ich; das Ich ist histor*isch* " (*GA* 56/7, 206). In WS 1920/1, history is said to be the "core phenomenon" of the phenomenology of religious life and, indeed, of factical life itself. According to a famous remark in the same course, the primitive Christian does not just live *in* time, as if time were a neutral container in which objects and events have a fixed place, but "lives time itself." "Die faktische Lebenserfahrung ist historisch. Nachsatz: Die christliche Erfahrung lebt die Zeit selbst (*leben* als verbum transitivum verstanden)" (*GA* 60, 82). The rejection of theoretical appropriations of experience is the negative side of an effort to return to the original historicity of factical life. A hermeneutics of facticity is meant to be an ontological explication of the historical sense or structure of Dasein, an explication that becomes, as we draw closer to 1927, an ontological interpretation of the original *Zeitlichkeit* of being-there. And formal indication is the method of grasping a being that is self-interpreting in the form of a historical life.

in politics. History in this sense is not a science or the object of a science, and it is not tradition in the previous sense. The present sense of history is related in some way to my own life. History is supposed to give directions for the present, insofar as life in the present is a striving, is related to an open future. For the politician, history is accessible as something living, not as an object of theoretical contemplation, but as something that *warns* and *guides*, that shows up for me in the light of definite projects and pursuits. (5) Or one says things like "This person has a sorry history." History is meant in this instance as *my own past*, what distinguishes me from others, insofar as my life is a story to be told, a sense that captures something like my very identity. To speak of a sorry history is to narrate a series of events that collectively shape the sort of person I consider myself to be, a series of events that includes relations to parents and other influential persons, the various twists and turns of fortune that open paths and close others, and the specific things about which I cared and, in some cases, continue to care. (6) Finally, I can say: "Today I went through an unpleasant history." History here means a *happening*, something that *befalls* me, something that engages and concerns me, something that really gets to me.

History functions here as a formal indication, as an initial gesture that points toward a group of loosely affiliated experiences and the conceptual resources at our disposal for interpreting them. What each of these expressions has in common, at first, is just an obscure relation to becoming or happening in time. Generally speaking, history means something like *Werden, Entstehen, in der Zeit Verlaufen.*[51] This is why it is possible for us to speak of the histories of non-human things – the history of a species of plant, the history of the earth, even the history of the material universe. The point of the initial enumeration is not simply to juxtapose various meanings, perhaps with the intention of clarifying isolated expressions for the sake of cleaning up the language, but rather to consider each with an eye on their remoteness from or proximity to the domain of vital human experience. The aim of this consideration is not to arrive at a bloodless abstraction that would cover each sense of history uniformly, but to reach an *original sense* (an *archê*) from out of which each of these initially isolated senses can be seen to derive. In keeping with the methodological strictures of formal indication, an evaluation of expressions of history will not involve a detailed analysis of the various historical contents expressed, but will consider each only in terms of the way in which they are

---

[51] *GA* 60, 32.

experienced or possessed in life itself. The only relevant question is: To what extent do I genuinely *find myself* in each of these expressions?[52] Does the expression capture something of the genuine sense of living out a life? Or does the expression refer to a way of living that is remote from genuine (historical) life?

As ways of having the historical, assessed in SS 1920 in terms of their *Bezugssinn*, the first two senses are clearly derivative. In each case, history is an object for the contemplative subject, not something had in a distinctive way of (personal) life. The third sense is also derivative, precisely because the history of a people is tied, for early Heidegger, to the concrete, historical lives of individuals. (It bears mentioning how far removed this evaluation is from Heidegger's subsequent views on the *Volk* and the anti-individualism that comes forward in the 1930s.) The fourth sense brings us closer to the genuine sense of the historical, but it remains, after all, an episodic moment of the concrete life of the politician. That leaves only senses five and six. The last sense clearly relates to the life of the individual, but it, too, is episodic. Only the fifth sense captures an authentic experience of the life of someone for whom the past really matters, in a direct and personal way. Here, history is neither something I occasionally pursue in a theoretical attitude nor the tradition in which my personal life somehow stands nor an isolated happening that stands out against the backdrop of my life as a whole, but *my very life itself,* a life had not as an object of reflection or detached observation, but had in simply living out, actualizing or performing my own life.

*

We are now in a better position to see how formal indications function in the early lecture courses. As the example of history shows, formal indication forms the methodological core of the practice of phenomenological criticism or *Destruktion*. Philosophy throughout the early lecture courses is meant to transform our thinking, an attempt to make philosophical common sense "stand on its head," in Hegel's phrase, not in order to invert common wisdom for its own sake, but because the forms of language that shape the contemporary practice of philosophy are somehow preventing us from seeing the genuine puzzles beneath the pseudo-problems. Formal indication in this context gives expression to

---

[52] Genuine self-experience is the measure of phenomenological reflection and description in KNS 1919, where formal indication is already operating without a name.

philosophical dissatisfaction; it is a gesture of protest, a refusal to allow traditional philosophical concepts and expressions to get in the way of the "things themselves," rooted in dissatisfaction with the tradition sedimented in our current ways of speaking about the issue in question.

Its initial function as an instrument of philosophical critique is prohibitive, more like a warning than the deposit of a definite insight. At first, a formal indication tells us where the truthful account is *not* to be found, where something has come to disfiguring expression. When Heidegger announces in *Sein und Zeit* that the essence of Dasein lies in its existence, we have, at first (that is, as first-time readers), no clear conception of what precisely this means. If we have some philosophical training, we can surmise that traditional accounts of the *essentia* of a thing are somehow insufficient here, that the human being is not like any of the beings that have essences in the common philosophical sense, and that, by implication, the *Existenz* of Dasein will not be further defined in opposition to its *Wesen*. But initially the indication is empty. If it points in a positive direction, the direction itself remains vague and indeterminate and the categories or concepts that will eventually come to fill in the empty indication are clearly pre-delineated in the point of departure. The intellectual value of a formal indication at this stage is what we might call its shock value. To the extent that the expression does *not* sound strange, insofar as it can be readily assimilated to a language that is familiar, a formal indication has failed to do its work.

The critical practice of formal indication is similar in intention to the Socratic *elenchos*; its use is intended to draw attention to our ignorance, to make us less comfortable in our philosophical orientation, and to call into question the propositions we spontaneously utter and the standpoints in which we typically move.

Formal Indication and Productive Logic in Nuce

Although Heidegger repeatedly insists that phenomenological criticism is not simply the negative prelude to the construction of a philosophical system, that phenomenology somehow *is* radical criticism of the self-objectification of life in philosophical theory, it should by now be clear that formal indications open up paths that lead to positive insights. A Heidegger who did little more than criticize the epistemological standpoint of modern thought, who exposed the limitations of neo-Kantian philosophy of value, and questioned the primacy of consciousness in Husserl's phenomenology, a Heidegger, in short, who never went on to write *Sein und Zeit*, would scarcely be worthy of serious philosophical consideration, his reputation confined to those students present at the earliest lecture courses. The Heideggerian corpus would include only a handful of polemical lecture courses that gesture, vaguely enough, in the direction of *Leben an und für sich*, and make obscure references to the mysterious *Ereignis* of life and employ provocative impersonals like *es weltet*. But as we draw closer to 1927, Heidegger's appropriation of phenomenology develops into a hermeneutic ontology of factical life or Dasein, a project devoted to explicating the basic *categorial sense* of the self-interpreting movement of human life. Formal indication becomes something like a *productive logic* of human experience.[53] We begin with a formal indication in order to *detach* the consideration from a fossilized conception taken over, without criticism, from the tradition. But the work of philosophy does not come to an end in critical detachment from the philosophical tradition. To follow up a formal indication is to move toward another, more concrete conception of the matter at issue.

I have nothing more to say about this conception here, at least not in the abstract. It should be fairly obvious to anyone conversant with early Heidegger that he is doing more than merely saying "No" to certain traditional, inherited conceptions of the phenomena he treats. And there is another function assigned to formal indication, at once critical and positive, that calls for more careful consideration.

The Ethical Function of Formal Indication and the "Jargon" of Authenticity

The constructive role played by formal indication in categorial and existential analysis clearly resembles a transcendental function, as Crowell rightly insists. Heidegger continues to speak the language of method, grasp of principles, orders of founding and grounding, logic of basic experience, science of life, and so on. The earliest account of the idea of a self-grounding, primordial science, in section 2 of KNS 1919, invites comparison with Fichte's meta-philosophical reflections on the circularity of transcendental philosophy in *Über den Begriff der Wissenschaftslehre*. The first sketch of what will subsequently be called "formal indication," again in KNS 1919, takes up Kant's conception of the *Ideen* of pure reason as non-objectifying concepts of the whole, concepts that present no object,

---

[53] For a sketch of the idea of a productive logic, see section 1 *History of the Concept of Time* (SS 1925), and *Being and Time*, 10 and 399.

but *guide* further efforts to clarify and define something that can never become an object without hypostasis.[54] The very idea of an *a priori* account of the genesis of the theoretical, and the various accounts of the origins of scientific comportment in pre-scientific life, are difficult to interpret without the help of some version, however modified, of transcendental grounding. From this point of view, it is possible to construe Heidegger's account of the *Selbstwelt* as the original domain of radical phenomenology as a deepening of the transcendental problematic, where the conditions necessary for the possibility of certain things (e.g., knowing the world in scientific theory, puzzling over the meaning of a life, reflecting upon moral norms and standards) are traced back to the historical structure of situated, factical life.

But interpretation focused narrowly on the transcendental structure of Heidegger's arguments, however illuminating, often ignores questions touching upon the *motives* of philosophical research, questions pursued throughout the early lecture courses, and runs the risk of marginalizing the prominently ethical function of formal indication in early Heidegger. Throughout the early lecture courses we have been considering, reflections on method and matter are linked in subtle ways to the question of motivation. Before the *Seinsfrage* becomes Heidegger's passion, the basic question of philosophy is *Why philosophize?* And the measure of phenomenological criticism of the philosophical tradition, as proximity to or estrangement from the "origin," is not fidelity to fixed transcendental conditions of experience, but resonance with or faithfulness to the existential or ethical situation of the critic. Situations are not only conditions necessary for the possibility of transcendental reflection, but sources of motivation and living tendencies of (ethical) life. Natorp's descriptions of lived experience are rejected by the phenomenological critic, not (or at least not most importantly) because they are insufficiently grounded in a science of pre-theoretical life, but because they are descriptions of a world in which no one is able to live, descriptions of a world in which everything essential has already been decided.[55] But world "is something within which

---

[54] The idea of *Urwissenschaft* is sketched out in terms of the *Idee als bestimmte Bestimmtheit* in section 2a and the *Zirkelhaftigkeit der Idee der Urwissenschaft* in section 2b of KNS 1919. For Kant's concept of the concepts of pure reason, see the first book of the Transcendental Dialectic of the first *Critique*.

[55] See section 15 of SS 1920 (*GA* 59). Heidegger's criticism of Natorp here is essentially ethical criticism. The guiding *Vorgriff* of constitution in consciousness is the philosophical appropriation of life's tendency to take things lightly, to retire from the difficulties of living as quickly as possible, and to reassure oneself that everything is in order. The movement toward constitution is a retreat

one can live (one cannot live in an object)."[56] The point of doing philosophy is not, in the end, merely to know something (life, world, space, time) more scientifically – although Heidegger's project, from the very beginning, is clearly cast in the language of *Wissenschaft* – or to ground what we somehow already know, but to live more genuinely and more truthfully. The truth that matters is not the truth of a proposition or the truth of an argument in support of a proposition, but the truth of and in a life, the truth of a certain kind of *ethos*, an ethical truth.

Ethical truth need not be universally binding truth, as Heidegger makes clear in an important passage from *Plato's Sophist* (WS 1924/5) that deserves to be quoted in full: "If we hold fast to the meaning of truth as unconcealedness or uncoveredness, then it becomes clear that truth means the same as *Sachlichkeit*, understood as a comportment of Dasein to the world and to itself in which beings are present in conformity with the way they are. This is objectivity correctly understood. The original sense of this concept of truth does not yet include objectivity as universal validity, universal binding force. That has *nothing to do with truth*. Something can very well have universal validity and be binding universally and still not be true. Most prejudices and things taken as obvious have such universal validity and yet are characterized by the fact that they distort beings. Conversely, something can indeed be true which is not binding for everyone but only for a single individual."[57] (There are deeper questions concerning motivation and grounding that come forward in later Heidegger, and that we touch on briefly below in the Conclusion.)

We need to be cautious, however, in speaking about the ethical function of formal indication, and not only because Heidegger repudiates disciplinary distinctions in philosophy. If there is a vision of ethical life embodied in the early lecture courses, if formal indications indicate concrete (ethical) situations of understanding, they nevertheless have nothing explicit to say about the specific form of life one ought to live in order to be happy or to live earnestly. Formal indications are not prescriptions dispensed from the pulpit or offered from a superior philosophical standpoint, but ways of speaking driven by something like what Foucault called *care for the self*, motivated in an abiding concern to let the non-reified self experience itself, and speak about itself and its world. The problem of language, the problem of philosophical *Begrifflichkeit* and concept-formation, is at

---

from concrete, actual Dasein (*GA* 59, 143). The regress to the *Ursprung* of factical life reaches nothing like a stable *Grund* or fund of transcendental truths or conditions, but essentially *unsettles*.
[56] *GA* 60, 11.   [57] *Plato's Sophist*, 17.

bottom a *care-problem*, the problem, roughly, of working out non-dogmatic and non-reifying ways of talking about the caring individual, in relation to a world of concern. As instruments of phenomenological criticism, formal indications serve to clear away the conceptual debris that occludes facticity, that ignores the *unum necessarium*, "historisch vollzogene Dasein jedes Einzelnen als Einzelnen."[58] In this sense, the ethical function of formal indication and phenomenological destruction is to unmask the distortions that prevent us from confronting ourselves, to make existence insecure, to introduce a note of restlessness and genuine concern in everyday life.

But insecurity is not the last word on the authentic (human) life. There are, as we saw in Chapter 1, ways of living in the absence of security that are equally removed from genuine care and concern, ways of taking up the flux of life that are just as incoherent, ways of trying to preserve insecurity that err on the side of disintegration and easy, if sometimes anxious, relativism. As the conceptual or methodological core of a productive logic, formal indications indicate the structure of an integral life, leaving it for the individual to decide on what is significantly at stake in her own concrete way of life. As Heidegger notes in an important essay on Dilthey (1925), his theme involves "a basic problem that pervades the whole of Western philosophy: the problem of the sense of [personal, self-worldly] life."[59]

All of Heidegger's youthful phenomenological criticisms terminate in the *Selbstwelt* as an original domain of experience that is overlooked, suppressed, or otherwise distorted in the Cartesian philosophies of consciousness and subjectivity. Phenomenological destruction, as we saw in Chapter 1, is more like self-examination than detached scrutiny of isolated propositions or consideration of the coherence or internal consistency of a philosophical system. If Heidegger accuses Descartes more than once of failing to ask about the "being" of the *sum*, the question that follows, at least in 1921, is not "What sort of being *am* I?" but, simply "Am I?" A strange question to put to a being that clearly exists, unless "being" is something other than mere existence, the *Vorhandenheit* of *Sein und Zeit*, and has more to do with self-interpret*ing* life unfolding in spaces of significance, with what Heidegger in 1922 called *Existenz*.[60] Not "what

---

[58] GA 59, 169.

[59] "Wilhelm Dilthey's Research and the Current Struggle for a Historical Worldview" in *Becoming Heidegger*, 242.

[60] In the "Natorp Essay" of 1922, Heidegger employs the term *Existenz* to name the being that I can appropriate or fail to appropriate. I always somehow *am*, whether I genuinely exist or not: "The

am I?" – a question that harkens back to the philosophical search for a fixed *essentia* or *eidos* – but "Is my life significant or am I stranded in trivial pursuits, living out my life on its surface?" Am I on the way toward myself, or missing myself? What constitutes the genuine richness of an integral life, in contrast to a life that merely appears rich because it is pulled in so many colorful directions?[61] How do I know or recognize the difference between life in the depths and life on the surface, between a life that is my own and a life that is borrowed, cliché, unoriginal? It makes sense to speak of depth and originality in human life and to criticize a life in which these "properties" are absent, because life is owned in the spaces of memory and unfolds in and as the intimate, self-defining history of a personal existence. If Heidegger develops an ontology of the self in response to this fundamental (Cartesian) neglect, it is not in order to theorize about subjectivity, but in order to draw the *self*-alienated individual's attention to the challenge of living more intensely and honestly. Formal indication forms the core of a method aimed at bringing the self back to itself, of developing what, in SS 1923, Heidegger called a *wakefulness* of Dasein for itself. And, we might add (in keeping with our chapter on Heidegger's Kantianism), a wakefulness for *others*. Formal indications are meant to allow others to make of our pronouncements what *they* will.

It is a fundamental fact of life that its significance can fade. To say that life lives in a world saturated with significance is not to say that all things are significant. The familiar items of my life-world – the table, chairs, books, and other items that form the holistic context of my scholarly life – give themselves to me in the most immediate way as significant things, but the meanings in question are subordinate to the work they serve and this, in turn, depends upon the significance of my life as a whole. This significance can break down in a moment of crisis. Sometimes, as we saw, I can longer find reasons to continue my work, the items of my *Werkwelt* become colorless and indifferent, mere things that serve only as reminders of a once vital area of concern. This situation can be an occasion to reflect upon my life, to take stock of my projects, and to place my vital energies in the service of other projects that better embody a sense of what genuinely matters to me. The fading of

---

possibility of seizing upon and stirring the being of life in its worry about itself is simultaneously the possibility of failing to exist" (*Supplements*, 120).

[61] Heidegger's interest in this Augustinian question goes back at least to SS 1920, where Heidegger explores the significance of the rise of historical consciousness in the nineteenth century.

significance in this context is temporary and altogether consistent with the vigilance of a careful and conscientious life.

Philosophy as metaphysics or epistemology or determination of ultimate values or the construction of a worldview is the satisfaction of a human, all-too-human need to find a place of rest, to feel finally at home in a reliable world, one that puts an end to the questions that disturb our peace of mind. Early Heidegger often associates this tendency with the public sphere. A careful look at the early lecture courses suffices to dispel the impression that Dasein is, at its best, absorbed coping in and with a world of public concerns, as if Dasein were nothing but a socially determined way of being in a world of concerns that reflect socially determined values, norms, and priorities. Public life under a certain description is a life of evasion, for early Heidegger, a life spent in pursuit of reassurance from my peers, conforming to norms that have not been clarified and appropriated, and lived at a distance from myself. But a life that I ought to take into consideration as I choose to speak.

Formal indication is not merely a powerful weapon in the battle against philosophical theory, but an instrument in the critique of everyday life. Heidegger urges his students to return from the cold and indifferent world of theory to the richly significant life of everyday encounter, not in order to find a place of rest in the immediate certainties of animal faith, but to question what gives itself immediately, to take up the worldly way of life each of us must live in a questioning way, to live more truthfully, more critically, and, in a sense, more skeptically. The unquestioned world of everyday life is inhabited as a fixed abode, more like a set of paths mapped out in advance and directions to be assumed and taken up blindly than the site of questioning comportment. The world into which each of us is socialized is, at first, what others have said about the world: "Factical life moves at any time within a certain state of *having-been-interpreted* that has been handed down to it, and it has reworked or worked out anew."[62] And the life of everyday care is outside of itself, lost in things that give support and reassurance and "intent on maintaining this life" at all costs.[63] There is

---

[62] "Phenomenological Interpretations of Aristotle" in *Supplements*, 116. World as a social space of significance is, of course, necessary to the concrete life of Dasein, but it can also serve as a refuge that prevents the individual from thinking too deeply. Heidegger's early conception of the world as a temptation obviously has theological sources, as the lecture on "The Problem of Sin in Luther" of 1924 delivered in Bultmann's seminar on the ethics of Paul invites us to think, but the concept of world in Heidegger is not itself theological but "formal," and has implications not limited to the theological sphere.

[63] *GA* 61, 130.

more than one way to get lost in the world; the modern preoccupation
with culture, the alienation of the worker in capitalist societies, and the
fetishism of the entertainment industry are only more recent manifest-
ations of the tendency to "fall," to take the easy way out, inherent in
factical life.

As we saw in Chapter 1, the movement running counter to falling is
nothing like "escapist flight from the world."[64] Everyday life is inescapable,
its demands unavoidable, its claims worthy of our attention. Every attempt
to escape its demands or to avoid its claims is either self-deception or
insanity. The world may be a holistic network of (socially and historically
determined) paths for the actualization of care, but some of those paths,
well-worn though they might be, must inevitably be traveled. Still, there
are paths that deserve to be scrutinized, paths that ought to be avoided,
paths, for example, that lead to racism and intolerance or religious fanati-
cism, and there are paths the criticism or avoidance of which betrays a
failure to appreciate the distinction between what matters and what is
unworthy of my (critical) concern. Authenticity is, among other things,
the capacity to discern the difference. It would be absurd to refuse to ride
on the subway, to shop at the local grocery store, to mail letters, to go to
concerts and museums, or to listen to the radio on the grounds that
complicity with the banalities of the world of everyday life would somehow
spoil an otherwise authentic life, as if everydayness were identical with
inauthenticity. The point is not to flee it, but to live it in the right way.
"Our everyday life," according to Novalis, "consists of nothing but life-
sustaining tasks which recur again and again."[65] It is a necessary means to
earthly life. But only philistines "live only an everyday life." What needs
considering is "the how of the movement of one's life."[66]

Heidegger's phenomenology is not merely a critique of everyday life,
without positive conceptual ambitions. If formal indication were not also
categorial research trained upon the structure of an integral life, then the
vision of life embodied in the early lecture courses would collapse into an
intolerable skepticism, and the way of life at stake would fall victim to the
sorts of errors Kierkegaard described in his portrait of the aesthetic sphere
of existence in the first volume of *Either/Or*. In WS 1920/1, a course in
which the skeptical nature of the philosophical life is, as we saw, especially

---

[64] "Phenomenological Interpretations of Aristotle" in *Supplements*, 120.
[65] *Miscellaneous Observations* (published in a slightly different version in 1798 as *Pollen*), fragment 76
(in *Philosophical Writings*, 37). I discuss these and related claims in *Novalis's Philosophical Fictions:
Magical Idealism in Context* (Northwestern University Press, forthcoming).
[66] "Phenomenological Interpretations of Aristotle" in *Supplements*, 120.

prominent, Heidegger concludes a dense account of *Ruinanz* with a terse sketch of the questioning life as a counter-movement to the tendency to lapse that places skepticism in its proper light: "maintaining oneself in genuine questioning does not consist in reacting mechanically, as it were, according to an empty maxim that requires nothing but questioning at all times, on every possible occasion, and in any way whatsoever. On the contrary, genuine questioning arises from motives that have been clarified in the ... factical situation and that receive *direction* from factical life. Likewise, genuine questioning consists in *living in the answer* itself in a searching way, such that the answering maintains a constant relation to the questioning, i.e., such that the latter remains alive, or, in other words, such that the basic experiences retain a factically historical vitality in factical life and in its ontological sense."[67] The critical function of formal indication disquiets an otherwise peaceful and complacent life; the disclosive and directing function of formal indication points the way toward a life beyond disintegration, restlessness, and despair. Just as formal indication functions philosophically as both an instrument of criticism and a productive logic, it also throws into relief the general structure of a life well lived, a life that includes questioning as a basic experience. Formal indications of the structures of factical life, while not tied to any *specific* "ontic" ideal of human existence, nonetheless articulate something like a paradigm of genuine life, capturing something like a *logic* of meaningful and earnest individuation.

Philosophy as a Truthful Way of Life

At the risk of treating Heidegger's conception of philosophy as an object to be pinned down and discussed, and distinguished from other, less adequate conceptions of the nature of philosophy, a risk that every discussion of Heidegger inevitably takes upon itself, it is now time to consider how the method of formal indication and its philosophical and ethical functions, discussed separately and perhaps one-sidedly, converge in early Heidegger's conception of the philosophical life, a conception I will risk calling *minimal transcendentalism*.[68] Although it often appears in the guise of transcendental reflection, perhaps even *must* appear in this

---

[67] *Phenomenological Interpretations of Aristotle*, 114.

[68] I have in mind a conception of transcendental philosophy as a general project of elucidating *grounds* or *conditions*, taking the *Grund* of something in a broad (formally indicative) sense, one that might even shed light on later Heidegger's reflections on metaphysics and post-metaphysical thinking as the attempt to elucidate the neglected soil of metaphysical concepts.

way, philosophy is above all a *Verhalten*, an illuminating, cognitive comportment, perhaps, but still chiefly a style of behavior and a *Wie des Lebens*. Heidegger repeatedly insists that philosophy "is intended as something that we appropriate originally, the basic relation we want to gain in which it is authentically there."[69] Philosophical method is not a *technê* that can be developed and taught to everyone, like the procedure of geometrical thought in Euclid's *Elements*. Philosophical work can be clarified only in philosophizing itself, in being willing to take upon oneself the risks a life of radical questioning.[70] Formal indications serve throughout the early period to draw attention to the performance of a philosophical way of life, and *for others* as well as for the philosopher herself. If transcendental philosophy is an attempt to overcome skepticism once and for all in a definitive account of the essence of human cognition; if the transcendental philosopher takes certain facts for granted and attempts merely to ground or explain them; if transcendental thinking is retrospective, ruminating rather than anticipatory; if transcendental reflection leaves life itself unchanged; and if transcendental philosophy aims at the construction of a static system of concepts,[71] then Heidegger's hermeneutics of facticity is *nothing transcendental*, and formally indicative concepts have nothing in common with transcendental concepts except the name.

A minimal transcendentalism, by contrast, remains committed generally to the project of grounding, but is directed toward the future, and in a way that invites others to carry the philosophical indications forward in their own way. It traffics in concepts that do not leave the inquirer indifferent, but (if genuinely appropriated) participate in the transformation of a way of life. Grounding means something like leading the derived back to a more genuine and original mode of life, and inviting (but not compelling) others to follow suit.

When Heidegger employs transcendental arguments in the early lecture courses, they are almost always critical, not system-building, but dismantling, arguments (or phenomenological descriptions) intended to convince us that certain ways of posing questions and traditional ways of expressing experience are *unecht*, derived from and forgetful of a domain of experience

---

[69] *GA* 61, 41.   [70] *GA*60, 8.

[71] Again, one might protest in the name of Fichte, a transcendental philosopher who introduced the idea of a dialectical movement of philosophical concepts and never tired of beginning the work of developing a *Wissenschaftslehre* anew. But there persists in Fichte (and in Kant, Schelling, and Hegel) the ideal of an adequate system of reason that we are always striving to approximate, a system the intimation of which provides the standard or measure for evaluating every particular approximation of it.

in such a way that the questions and their solutions no longer make sense, or make sense only because our experience of the world has been shaped by inauthentic traditions. The regressive method of reflection leads, e.g., from the idea of a subject of constitution and the ideal of totalizing self-knowledge to concrete, actual, self-worldly life or from the idea of truth as correspondence between concept and thing to the original experience of truth as unconcealment. Once we reach the original domain, we are not given a system of ordering concepts, but the indication of an experience that cannot be fully objectified. What is considered a relevant point of access to the domain of origin depends upon a relatively unique situation of access that will differ with each Dasein.

Early Heidegger never tires of reminding us that philosophy is always situated. It grows out of and embodies concerns tied to a unique historical situation, and, if it acknowledges its own unavoidable involvement in a situation, reflects upon the situation in which it is embedded. As situated, philosophy speaks for its own time, without regard for the concerns of the previous or the next generation, but always with other (prospective) readers still clearly in view. The situation of factical life, and the situation of philosophy as a movement *of* factical life, is not simply something to be considered in transcendental reflection, but the "stand taken by life in which it has made itself transparent to itself in its falling and has, in worrying about itself in a concrete manner at the particular time, *seized upon itself and stirred itself* in its possibility of a motion running counter to the falling of its care."[72] This is just another way of saying that philosophy is *intrinsically* historical, that philosophical problems are not timeless but tied to a unique set of historical concerns and exposed to further questioning in the light of future historical situations of concern.

As we saw in Chapter 2, a situation is not an object, but a context in which we find ourselves meaningfully but uncertainly placed. It is not spread out before the philosopher's timeless gaze, but permeates and predelineates the paths of our concrete relations to the world, to ourselves, and to others. Its unity is not the unity of a multiplicity of properties in a substance, but a unity of motivation, tendency, and above all *sense*.[73] Appropriation of a unique situation is an affair of the understanding in

---

[72] "Phenomenological Interpretations of Aristotle," *Supplements*, 118.

[73] For the concept of situation in an early lecture course, see the Becker *Nachschrift* of SS 1919 in *GA* 56/7 (205–14). The basic "scientific" contrast in SS 1919, or at least in Becker's transcript of the course, is between an understanding that preserves the unity of the situation and various forms of explanation that essentially destroy the unity of the situation and reify its isolated elements. Phenomenology falls naturally under the "understanding sciences." (See *GA* 56/7, 208).

pursuit of holistic contexts of sense; and because situation cannot be
clarified fully in a system of propositions or concepts or captured in a
narrative account of the experience of being in a specific situation, it makes
some sense to claim that philosophical understanding is itself *phronetic*:
philosophical reflection involves moments of insight or vision trained upon
the salient features of a unique and unrepeatable philosophical situation.
In the words of SS 1923, philosophical possibilities "concretely come into
being and are there not by having a cleverly thought-out philosophical
system ... laid before them as a plan of operation, but rather only through
the fact that at a certain time [*jewels*] in 'this' discipline the right man at
the right place and at the right time steps in and takes hold of it in a
decisive manner."⁷⁴ Philosophical decisions and the insights they antici-
pate are rooted in the time of an occasion, a *kairos*.⁷⁵ And *kairoi* are always
at least potentially shared, or reflect a common situation.

Why, for instance, take up Natorp or Dilthey in 1920? Why stress the
concept of the historical as the *Kernphänomen* of the phenomenology of
religious life in 1920/1? Why is epistemology a target of criticism? Why
single out the university as the ontic site of ontological research in WS
1921/2? Why a treatise with the title *Sein und Zeit*? Why (for those who
pursue transcendental philosophy as an end in itself) ask questions concerning conditions of possibility and not, rather, questions concerning
how I ought to live?

Answers to these questions reflect fundamental philosophical decisions
that can be neither predicted in advance nor fully justified in retrospect,
decisions that develop in engagement with one's own philosophical situ-
ation.⁷⁶ They show up in the heat of what one used to call *inspiration*
(Heidegger calls it the *passion* of questioning). Such questions do not
exclude subsequent development along quasi-transcendental lines (and

⁷⁴ *Ontology – The Hermeneutics of Facticity*, 45. Compare with Aristotle's discussion of ethical *aretê* or
   excellence of character as determined by the *phronimos* in *Nicomachean Ethics* II.6. Aristotle's
   remark on feeling at the right time, for the right things and the right people, for the right end,
   and in the right way at *EN* 1106b closely resembles Heidegger's gloss on taking up philosophy.
⁷⁵ The "kairological" determination of Dasein's temporality is discussed briefly in WS 1921/2 and
   again in SS 1923, but oddly enough makes no appearance in *Sein und Zeit*, although it seems to
   capture what is meant by the *Augenblick* in Heidegger's major work. A useful study of the
   Augenblick and the limits of the theory and Heidegger's appropriation of Aristotle is McNeill's
   The Glance of an Eye.
⁷⁶ See the *Vorbemerkung* in WS 1923/4 for a revealing "phronetic" indication of scientific research,
   anticipating the "existential concept of science" in *Sein und Zeit*, as "eine Möglichkeit des Daseins
   und seiner Auseinandersetzung mit sich selbst" (GA 17, 3). For further remarks on the existential
   concept of science, see *Plato's Sophist*, 7, *Being and Time*, 11 and 357, and *Phenomenological
   Interpretations of Kant's Critique of Pure Reason*, section 3.

on the reading I'm proposing, they ought to be), but the transcendental explication is parasitic on the phronetic disclosure, on an initially indeterminate sense or conviction that *this here* matters, that *this* particular path of thought might lead to something worthy of my concern, in light of what others have said about "the same." To press transcendental clarification too far – as though the experiences that need grounding are fixed once and for all – is to come close to reifying an insight that ought to remain questionable. Phenomenology, like the life itself in which it is rooted and for which the philosopher is supposed to speak, is always *on the move*, not only retrospective, but equally and importantly prospective.

Both functions of formal indication discussed earlier cohere in the idea of a critical and skeptical but truthful way of life. Skeptical: we are never at rest, always searching and seeking, always on the way toward ourselves and a life of one's own. Philosophy and the life it strives to express are essentially *homesickness*.[77] We philosophize, not because there is a truth *an sich* waiting to be discovered, but because we are uneasily at home in the world, because, in the pregnant words of Levinas, the true life is absent, but we are in the world.

Truthful: there is something that it is like to live a meaningful life, cares that better express myself in relation to the *Umwelt* and *Mitwelt*, concerns that speak more directly to *our* unique situation of concern. As a philosophical tool, formal indication liberates the phenomenologist from an ossified intellectual tradition and opens up domains of experience that come distortedly into focus in the philosophical and scientific traditions. As an ethical instrument, formal indication brings the individual back to herself, reminding her to pay closer attention to the truths that define her own unique situation in a shared world of human concern. But these two functions are really two faces of a single critical function, as long as philosophy is not just detached discourse *about* life, but a way of getting around in it. If transcendental philosophy is the self-fixation of life in a system of categories, then philosophy must always endeavor to overcome its own transcendental pretensions. It might occasionally employ the language of transcendental reflection and grounding, but its interests will flow in another direction, beyond any concern for systematic order and completeness. The categories of facticity (later *existentialia*) are not ordering concepts intended to fix factical life or Dasein, but elucidations

---

[77] Heidegger takes over and "ontologizes" Novalis's famous definition of philosophy as homesickness, "the desire or drive to be at home everywhere," in WS 1929/30, *The Basic Concepts of Metaphysics* (*GA* 29/30).

of the motility of life in the directions of falling away from and returning to itself. And the categories interpret the self-interpreting movement of life only if they are appropriated in concrete *concern*.[78] As we saw, they are not structures that hold for each and every instance of human life in the same way, but concepts that give probing expression to a paradigmatic configuration of life. The paradigm itself is neither a specific life-style (Christian or political or artistic) involving certain facts or truths to be believed and tasks to be performed, nor a static model that has only to be imitated in order to be realized, however imperfectly, in a particular life, but a set of structures that places certain constraints upon the self-interpreting movement of an individual life in general. There is no *particular* ideal of human life at the heart of Heidegger's fundamental ontology.

There is, to be sure, an "ontic ideal" placed squarely at the basis of the phenomenology of temporality in the second division of *Being and Time*, an ideal of *Eigentlichkeit* or earnestness, one that includes explicit attitudes toward death, history, time, the situation of human action, and the anonymous dictatorship of *das Man*, but it remains no less formal than Kant's categorical imperative. If we approach the early lecture courses and *Being and Time* hoping to find out what we must do in order to become virtuous or happy or wise, we are likely to be disappointed, beyond the apparently formal demand to own up to the condition of being human. *Being and Time* is nothing like a philosophical self-help book, precisely because Heidegger's essential structures of human existence are meant to allow others to decide for themselves how their lives are supposed to be. Fundamental ontology is neither a *Tugendlehre* nor a theory of *eudaimonia*, is nothing like a moral psychology that teaches us how better to love, in the manner of psychoanalytic theorists like Erich Fromm, and contains no positive insight, grounded in philosophical anthropology, into the concrete sort of life that is best for a human being to live.

If the path to *Being and Time* was influenced by Kierkegaard and the theological tradition – Heidegger proclaimed himself a "Christian theo*logian*" in a famous letter to Löwith – the texts themselves, with two important exceptions,[79] have very little to say about religious issues, at least not directly, and none of them contains anything comparable to a Christian apologetics. Although fundamental ontology refuses to speak specifically about ethical or religious life as objects of distinct philosophical

---

[78] "*Kategorie ist interpretierend* und ist nur interpretierend, und zwar das faktische Leben, angeeignet in existentieller Bekümmerung" (*GA* 61, 86).

[79] I refer, of course, to the two courses on religion published in GA 60.

disciplines, it does indicate *formally* certain directions or paths that might be pursued in our efforts to live a more truthful and careful life, a life that (to take just a few famous examples or "formal indications" from *Being and Time*) does not suppress the fact of human mortality; that acknowledges the importance of the *pathê* as disclosures of significance; that takes the temporality of human experience seriously; that does not repress uncertainty in the face of the future; that recognizes the importance of heroic figures in opposition to contemporary tendencies to deny every perception of greatness; that does not seek an escape route from the difficulty of life in detached theoretical activity, in idle contemplation of the past, or in utopian visions of a way of life regulated and tranquilized by scientific authorities.

Heidegger, as we saw in the opening chapter, rejects the idea of philosophy as a worldview, not because worldview philosophy fails to live up to the rigors of scientific discourse, but because it shares with scientific philosophy certain assumptions about knowledge and life, because the pursuit of a worldview is an attempt to imprison life in a system of highest values, an attempt ultimately to still the stream of philosophical and everyday life. Heidegger's own development toward (and beyond) *Sein und Zeit* embodies these youthful insights into the nature of the life of a philosopher content to remain a perpetual *beginner*.

Conclusion

> If the name 'ethics,' in keeping with the basic meaning of the word *êthos*, should now say that ethics ponders the abode of the human being, then that thinking which thinks the truth of being as the primordial element of the human being, as the one who eksists, is in itself original ethics. However, this thinking is not ethics in the first instance because it is ontology.
>
> Heidegger, *Letter on Humanism*

In lieu of a more conventional conclusion, intended to summarize the argument presented above, a few final words are in order about where I think the line of thought traced in the foregoing chapters leaves us and, just as importantly, what might come next. There are good reasons to be suspicious of conclusions, in the same way that Hegel was skeptical of prefaces. There is no definitive stance on work of this sort, and more work that needs doing. Not so much a conclusion, then, but an opening and a transition.

Heidegger's master question, as he never tires of reminding his readers, is the *Seinsfrage*, the question concerning the meaning or the sense of being. If the argument developed in the preceding pages is sound, it is no longer possible to view Heidegger's distinctive, early way of responding to the question as a merely theoretical or metaphysical affair; not because, at this stage, Heidegger is a critic of metaphysics as such, but because his ontology is at some level an ethical affair, an exercise in *moral* ontology. Heidegger's early analyses of being-in-the-world, his critique of such thinkers as Descartes, Husserl, and the neo-Kantians, his account of authenticity as a necessary condition of the philosophic life, his attempt to ground intentionality in a more original mode of understanding, his views on authentic and original truth, and so on can fruitfully be viewed as elucidations of the normativity of human existence and the good life, under some description. The experiences that stand at the center of Heidegger's analysis of concernful being-in-the-world are ethical, in a

broad sense articulated in the Introduction. At times the accent falls on an
Aristotelian ideal of practical wisdom (*phronêsis*), in other contexts Kant's
distinction between things and persons and the life of freedom come more
sharply into focus. In the first Freiburg period, under the influence of
Dilthey, the accent falls upon the demands of something more nebulous,
call it "life." But there is a persistent ethical agenda running throughout
early Heidegger's engagement with the tradition, under the official aegis of
ontology, between 1919 and 1927. If *that* much remains in question still,
the preceding chapters should be judged a collective failure.

But as we know, Heidegger himself saw his youthful phenomenology,
culminating in *Sein und Zeit*, as marking only the *beginning* of a course of
philosophical reflection that continued for nearly five more decades. *Sein
und Zeit* ends on a remarkably inconclusive note, in the form of a series of
questions, including the following: "Is there a way leading primordial *time*
to the meaning of *being*? Does *time* itself reveal itself as the horizon of
being?"[1] The canny reader is likely to be surprised. Had Heidegger not
opened the work by stating, if only as a working hypothesis, that time just
is the horizon within which the meaning of being is necessarily determined? Why is Heidegger's unquestioned starting point now suddenly in
question? In any event, the promised third division never appeared; the
work remained an "astonishing torso." And Heidegger continued to
rethink the very meaning of the *Seinsfrage*, in increasingly historical and
poetic terms. From his own point of view, to remain fixated on the path
that led to *Sein und Zeit*, as the definitive statement on human existence
and the meaning of being as such, would be comparable to preferring
classical physics over more recent developments in relativity theory and
quantum mechanics and the ambition to find the common root of both.
The early period is to be seen as one of re-awakening a sense of the
fundamental importance of the elusive meaning of being and not as a
definitive answer to the *Seinsfrage*. (There is some reason to believe that
Heidegger came to think that the very greatness and dignity of the
question is tied to its insolubility. Only technical questions are able to
be really answered.)

The question we are left with, in terms of the scope and intention of the
present study, is this: What, if anything, becomes of the ethical *after* 1927,
in light of Heidegger's famous *Kehre*? The question is not only a pressing
one because the moral ontology I have been interpreting and partially
defending here was developed by a philosopher who lent his thought to the

---

[1] *SZ*, 437.

cause of National Socialism, although it is pressing for that reason, too. Its urgency is also tethered to the possibility that the move toward "being-historical thinking" does not ground ethical and moral life more deeply, but simply leaves the moral fabric of human existence behind, in favor of a poetic disclosure of being, say, or in an attempt to replace ethical life with a more fatalistic variety of religious existence, or to prepare the way for an unchosen return of the divine: "Only a god can save us." If the later work can be said plausibly to ground what comes forward in the earlier work, and Heidegger certainly thinks that it does, then we cannot afford to ignore the post-phenomenological period, despite what I said in the Introduction about the dubiousness of allowing the later work to over-shadow the earlier, or to provide its proper interpretation and foundation. That may still be a valid hermeneutical principle – "Be open to the possibility that a writer has gone astray" – but we should not assume, *a priori*, that later Heidegger sheds no compelling light on his earlier coun-terpart. I do not mean to say that the later work is a necessary development from the earlier, but there are motives and intentions embedded in and underwriting the early work that find an outlet and a response in what comes next. Heidegger's turn to the work of art and, more specifically, to certain privileged poets can seem like the natural outgrowth of lines of thought on language and disclosure developed in Chapter 6.

It is not as though Heidegger merely changes the subject. Several phenomena continue to play an important part in Heidegger's subsequent philosophical labor, but in a decidedly different key. If Heidegger con-tinues to speak, for instance, of "decision" after 1927, the term seems to have an altered significance: No longer is decision a practical or a moral affair – the sort of thing responsible agents reach, after careful deliber-ation – but something that *happens*, something like a novel way of having world that comes over us and alters our way of interpreting things. It would be closer to the (Heideggerian) truth to say, not that we (or I) decide, but that we are *decided* (by something mysterious, call it *Seyn*). And decision in this sense is supposed to ground and condition decision in the earlier sense. Our being able to decide is conditioned by our *being* decided, in advance of every merely "ontic" decision and choice.

One can discern in *Sein und Zeit* and the early lecture courses some anticipations of later Heidegger's views on history and being, centered on *Geschichtlichkeit* and *Geworfenheit*, and tied to the task of destroying the history of ontology, all in keeping with early Heidegger's insistence upon the essential *finitude* of Dasein. I don't take this as sufficient reason to think that early Heidegger's views on the historicity of human existence are inherently fascist, but some degree of continuity is clearly in evidence. Already in early Heidegger our capacity for deliberation and choice is hedged in by certain structures of human existence, enabled by unchosen facts about us, and made possible by the historical matrix into which we find ourselves cast. There may be timelessly valid structures of human life, as I tried to show in Chapter 5, but the specific alternatives we face are always particular embodiments of the various ways in which historical individuals understand themselves, their possibilities, and the horizon within which self-understanding is condemned to move. Philosophical research into past Daseins can play some liberating role, but we are never without an unchosen way of taking up with the things and persons of this world. There is, it seems, no timelessly valid norm, rule, or law that places necessary constraints on the uses and abuses of human freedom. And freedom itself becomes synonymous with something like original truth: to be free is to stand within a clearing (*Lichtung*) opened up by being itself.

The real worry here, and it is one I take seriously, is that ontological deepening will reveal the ethical or the moral to be, if not quite inauthentic, at least superficial, unoriginal, and removed from the dark soil out of which our commitments and attitudes somehow grow. Again, something like this move is apparent in early Heidegger, in the analysis of conscience in the vulgar sense. But the account of conscience from an ontological perspective in *Sein und Zeit* is still tied to certain experiences of a moral variety, of which the account is supposed to provide the necessary "conditions of possibility." It isn't at all clear, however, that Heidegger's later views are meant to elucidate anything like our moral experiences. The worry, in short, is that the moral life is in danger of being left behind altogether, that Heidegger's subsequent ontology is no longer a *moral* ontology.

We might take ourselves to be free to ignore what happens next in the story. There's Heidegger I and Heidegger II, and let's just stick with the former.[2] That is, I think, a respectable option. And there are good students of Heidegger (John Haugeland, for example) who refuse to consider Heidegger's subsequent work on principle. But that won't suffice in my own case. I find some of later Heidegger's musings on the disclosive power of the work of art compelling; so, too, his powerful interpretation of modern technology and human bondage to the technological apparatus, his views on dwelling (poetically), his worries about encroaching

---

[2] We owe the terms of the distinction between Heidegger I and II to Richardson's *Heidegger: Through Phenomenology to Thought.*

nihilism – that uncanniest of all guests – and his terse but suggestive remarks in the "Letter on Humanism" on what he calls "original ethics."

This last topic suggests that ethical concerns, very broadly construed, don't disappear from Heidegger's radar but continue to shape his sense of what it means to ask about the very meaning of being. Heidegger's problems remain centered on the difficulties of finding meaning in our various pursuits in the modern age, or flourishing as mortals in an age dominated by a technological understanding of being, and so remain "ethical" in at least one broad sense of the term. But it remains an open question: the ethical under what description? The absence of Kant in the Letter, combined with the remark that the tragedies of Sophocles are more ethically relevant and primordial "than Aristotle's lectures on 'ethics,'" don't exactly bode well for the Aristotelian and Kantian perspectives that inform our work on Heidegger's early moral ontology.[3] Heidegger's explicit claim that authenticity and inauthenticity "do not imply a moral-existentiell . . . distinction" at all is hard to square with my efforts to show that the distinction is itself a moral one, or tailored to abiding moral concerns.[4]

There is one problem in particular that needs addressing in the sequel, a problem at stake in both Heidegger I and Heidegger II. It came forward in one form in Chapters 4 and 6 under the auspices of the problem of *motivation*, my response to which is likely to frustrate both the Heidegger scholar in search of a more definitive answer the question "Why be authentic?" and the Kantian, who thinks that the problem of motivation is fairly clear, because being an agent of a certain sort just is being responsive to moral reasons. (If there is any topic of ethical salience neglected in the present study, it is surely the topic of mood, attunement (*Stimmung*), and *Befindlichkeit*, which plays, for Heidegger, a fundamental role in orienting human beings in the space of reason, argument, and debate.) But it is also implicit in our previous discussion of Heidegger's recovery of ethical truth in the sixth book of the *Nicomachean Ethics*, where nothing was said, at least not directly, about why we ought to care about being virtuous in the specifically Aristotelian sense, or how, on what basis, Aristotle defends the specific set of virtues at issue throughout the bulk of the *Ethics*. Aristotle's own list of virtues or excellences is likely to strike some as parochial, anchored less in his definition of the human being as such and more in certain contingent facts about life in the ancient Greek

---

[3] *Pathmarks*, 269.   [4] *Pathmarks*, 253.

polis. And his curt analysis of the distinctive work or function (*ergon*) of human life in *EN* 1.7 has its critics.

In the broadest sense we could call it the problem of *ground*. In the shape of a question: What *grounds* our sense that some things matter and others don't, that the life of moral excellence and virtue (a life of courage on the field of battle or temperance or friendship) is preferable to a life of vice, or that treating others as ends and not merely as means is more admirable (or, in the Kantian account, *absolutely* required) than reducing others to instruments in our own selfish pursuits? It doesn't seem arbitrary that some things are judged to be worthwhile. Nor that we are encouraged to take an interest in the lives of others. But what grounds our various commitments remains a pressing question, especially in theories that, like Heidegger's, see the life of reason in historical terms, according to which what counts as a reason to do x or to pursue y cannot be divorced from apparently contingent facts about when and where we happen to find ourselves placed, but the apparent contingency of our reasons is not taken to be arbitrary. *That* we are necessarily norm-bound creatures, concerned to live well and to do right, seems beyond dispute, a descriptive fact about us, but the ultimate "sources of normativity," in Korsgaard's suggestive phrase, remain obscure throughout the early period. And this leaves the question concerning why we should care about the ideal of life defended in various guises between 1919 and 1927 troublingly open.

Blank appeals to mood, comparable to what we had to say in Chapter 4, run the risk of asserting that, as a matter of fact, we, or at least some of us, just *do* care. Appeals to motives in play in everyday life, or in life but against the proverbial "grey everyday," are comparable to appeals to brute fact. We need something like a more compelling account of why some moods are better than others, or at least more fundamental (but, as we've seen, their being "fundamental" is insufficiently motivating). The accounts of anxiety in *Sein und Zeit* and boredom in WS 1929/30 try to do just that, but they are exceptional experiences of human life that leave us uncertain about how and why to get reoriented in the space of practical reason and concern in a certain way. In *Angst* and *Langweile* I am suspended in an ether without proper ground or sufficient reason *to be*. Being unsettled (*unheimlich*) is not an end in itself, although it may be our most basic condition, but an invitation to find the proper grounds of a more adequate way of life and reasons to press ahead.

Heidegger's interest in the problem of grounds and grounding intensifies in the later period, in part because his sense of the historical conditions of meaning and intelligibility is exacerbated, and in a way that troubles the more universalizing aspects and scientific (*wissenschaftlich*) ambitions of his early thought. The move toward more thoroughgoing historical ways of thinking is a consequence of Heidegger's suspicions, shared, for instance, by Karen Horney in her critique of Freudian psychoanalysis, that the reduction of questions concerning motive and intention, thought, belief, and desire (and their various pathological distortions) to matters of individual psychology is insensitive to the historical conditions that help give the soul its distinctive shape. What we (secularized North Americans or good Europeans) might find neurotic – an obsessive concern about preserving the nuclear family at all costs, for instance – would be perfectly normal and healthy in another sort of community. The historical shape and conditions of our ethical concerns now seem inescapable facts about us, although we still often argue with the passionate intensity of the essentialist, committed to certain truths about human dignity, for reasons spelled out, if inconclusively, in Chapter 5.

But that recognition gives rise to another question or two: Are the historical shapes of the human soul arbitrary? And if not, what grounds historically inflected interpretations and embodiments of what human beings are, do, and aspire to be? Heidegger consistently refuses to think that human history is just "one damned thing after another." But whether his account of the necessary shapes of historical life over time is convincing or not remains to be decided, especially in light of Hegel's thesis that history can best be read as a progressive unfolding of human freedom and reason, even if human history is a "slaughter-bench" that sacrifices the life of the individual for its own, more progressive or self-enlightening purposes, combined with Nietzsche's view that such "meta-narratives" are merely delusional bulwarks against encroaching nihilism, if not themselves nihilistic. At the end of the day, our deepest grounds may prove groundless (cf. Lee Braver's study of groundless grounds in Wittgenstein and Heidegger), in the sense that nothing like Cartesian certainty or Aristotelian confidence regarding first principles in *intuitus* or *nous* is available to us. (We can always ask *why* the quest for certainty is itself plausible, or what grounds our commitment to the pursuit. Descartes supplies an answer of sorts in the *Discourse on the Method*, but it is hardly a rigorous, deductive argument that leads to Cartesian metaphysics as its rational conclusion. I'll risk calling Descartes's attempt to motivate the interest in the quest for certainty *existential*.) But this position on "groundless grounds" calls for argument of some kind. In any case, Heidegger's persistent attention to the problem of locating the deepest grounds of our cares and concerns, and the world in which they might find a place, is one more reason, perhaps the weightiest, to take into consideration what happens after 1927.

All of which is to say that there is more work to be done, both *with* Heidegger and, in light of the political commitments of the 1930s and the disturbing revelations in the *Black Notebooks*, also *against* Heidegger, but in a spirit of open, non-partisan inquiry into the the *Sache selbst* and what Heidegger has to say about the grounds of our efforts to find meaning and sources of moral normativity in the modern – or, if you prefer, our post-modern – age. Whether I will be the one to do some humble portion of it remains an open question.

Bibliography

Adorno, Theodore, and Max Horkheimer. *Dialectic of Enlightenment.* Translated by John Cumming. New York, NY: Seabury Press, 1972.

Appiah, Kwame Anthony. *The Ethics of Identity.* Princeton, NJ: Princeton University Press, 2005.

Arendt, Hannah. *The Human Condition.* Chicago, IL: University of Chicago Press, 1958.

Aristotle. *Metaphysics, Books I-IX.* Translated by Hugh Tredennick. Rev. ed. Cambridge, MA: Harvard University Press, 1996.

Metaphysics, Books X-XIV. Translated by Hugh Tredennick. Cambridge, MA: Harvard University Press, 1990.

Nicomachean Ethics. Translated by H. Rackham. Cambridge, MA: Harvard University Press, 1982.

Bambach, Charles R. *Heidegger, Dilthey, and the Crisis of Historicism.* Ithaca, NY: Cornell University Press, 1995.

Heidegger's Roots: Nietzsche, National Socialism, and the Greeks. Ithaca, NY: Cornell University Press, 2003.

Becker, Ernest. *The Denial of Death.* New York, NY: Free Press, 1973.

Beiser, Frederick. *The Fate of Reason: German Philosophy Between Kant and Fichte.* Cambridge, MA: Harvard University Press, 1987.

Berlin, Isaiah. *The Roots of Romanticism.* Princeton, NJ: Princeton University Press, 2001.

Three Critics of Enlightenment: Vico, Hamann, Herder. Princeton, NJ: Princeton University Press, 2000.

Bernet, Rudolf, Iso Kern, and Eduard Marbach. *An Introduction to Husserlian Phenomenology.* Evanston, IL: Northwestern University Press, 1993.

Blackburn, Simon. *Being Good: A Short Introduction to Ethics.* Oxford: Oxford University Press, 2014.

Essays in Quasi-realism. Oxford: Oxford University Press, 1993.

Ruling Passions: A Theory of Practical Reasoning. Oxford: Clarendon Press, 2009.

Blanchot, Maurice. *The Space of Literature.* Translated by Ann Smock. Lincoln, NE: University of Nebraska Press, 1982.

Blattner, William D. *Heidegger's Temporal Idealism.* Cambridge: Cambridge University Press, 2005.

Bloom, Harold. *The American Religion: The Emergence of the Post-Christian Nation.* New York, NY: Simon & Schuster, 1992.

Shakespeare: The Invention of the Human. New York, NY: Riverhead Books, 1998.

Blumenberg, Hans. *The Legitimacy of the Modern Age.* Translated by Robert M. Wallace. Cambridge, MA: MIT Press, 1993.

Work on Myth. Translated by Robert M. Wallace. Cambridge, MA: MIT Press, 1990.

Booth, Wayne. *The Company We Keep: An Ethics of Fiction.* Berkeley, CA: University of California Press, 1988.

Brandom, Robert B. *Tales of the Mighty Dead: Historical Essays in the Metaphysics of Intentionality.* Cambridge, MA: Harvard University Press, 2002.

Campbell, Scott M. *The Early Heidegger's Philosophy of Life: Facticity, Being, and Language.* New York, NY: Fordham University Press, 2012.

Camus, Albert. *The Myth of Sisyphus and Other Essays.* Translated by Justin O'Brien. New York, NY: Vintage Books, 1983.

Caputo, John. *Radical Hermeneutics: Repetition, Deconstruction, and the Hermeneutic Project.* Bloomington, IN: Indiana University Press, 1987.

Carlyle, Thomas. *Sartor Resartus.* Edited by Kerry McSweeney and Peter Sabor. Oxford: Oxford University Press, 1987.

Carman, Taylor. *Heidegger's Analytic: Interpretation, Discourse, and Authenticity in "Being and Time".* Cambridge: Cambridge University Press, 2003.

Carr, David. *Phenomenology and the Problem of History: A Study of Husserl's Transcendental Philosophy.* Evanston, IN: Northwestern University Press, 1974.

Cavell, Stanley. *Cities of Words: Pedagogical Letters on a Register of the Moral Life.* Cambridge, MA: Belknap Press of Harvard University Press, 2005.

The Claim of Reason: Wittgenstein, Skepticism, Morality, and Tragedy. Oxford: Oxford University Press, 1999.

Coyne, Ryan. *Heidegger's Confessions: The Remains of Saint Augustine in 'Being and Time' and Beyond.* Chicago, IL: University of Chicago Press, 2015.

Craig, Candace R. *Education and Identity in Faulkner's Light in August: "This is not my life."* New York, NY: Amazon Publishing, 2014. Digital file.

Crowe, Benjamin D. *Heidegger's Religious Origins: Destruction and Authenticity.* Bloomington, IN: Indiana University Press, 2006.

Crowell, Stephen Galt. *Husserl, Heidegger, and the Space of Meaning: Paths toward Transcendental Phenomenology.* Evanston, IL: Northwestern University Press, 2001.

Normativity and Phenomenology in Husserl and Heidegger. New York, NY: Cambridge University Press, 2013.

"Sorge or Selbstbewußtein? Heidegger and Korsgaard on the Sources of Normativity." *European Journal of Philosophy* 15 (2007): 315–33.

Crowell, Steven Galt, and Jeff Malpas, eds. *Transcendental Heidegger.* Stanford, CA: Stanford University Press, 2007.

Dahlstrom, Daniel. *Heidegger's Concept of Truth*. Cambridge: Cambridge University Press, 2000.

Davidson, Hugh MacCullough. *The Origins of Certainty: Means and Meanings in Pascal's 'Pensées.'* Chicago, IL: University of Chicago Press, 1979.

De Beauvoir, Simone. *The Ethics of Ambiguity*. Translated by Bernard Frechtman. Secaucus, NJ: Citadel Press, 1997.

De Muralt, André. *The Idea of Phenomenology: Husserlian Exemplarism*. Translated by Garry L. Breckon. Evanston, IL: Northwestern University Press, 1974.

Descartes, Rene. *The Philosophical Writings of Descartes*. Translated by John Cottingham, Robert Stoothoff, and Dugald Murdoch. Cambridge: Cambridge University Press, 1984.

Dewey, John. *The Quest for Certainty*. Edited by Jo Ann Boydston. Vol. 4 of *The Later Works, 1925–1953*. Carbondale, IL: Southern Illinois University Press, 1988.

Dickinson, Emily. *The Complete Poems of Emily Dickinson*. Edited by Thomas H. Johnson. Boston, MA: Little, Brown and Company, 1961.

Dilthey, Wilhelm. *Gesammelte Schriften*. Edited by H. Johach and F. Rodi. Vol. 19. Gottingen: Vandenhoeck & Ruprecht, 1982.

Dreyfus, Hubert L. *Being-in-the-World: A Commentary on Heidegger's "Being and Time," Division I*. Cambridge, MA: MIT Press, 1991.

Dreyfus, Hubert, and Harrison Hall. *Heidegger: A Critical Reader*. Oxford: Blackwell, 1993.

Eliade, Mircea. *The Sacred and the Profane: The Nature of Religion*. Translated by Willard R. Trask. New York, NY: Harcourt, Brace & Company, 1987.

Engelland, Chad. *Heidegger's Shadow: Kant, Husserl, and the Transcendental Turn*. New York, NY: Routledge, 2017.

Faulkner, William. *The Sound and the Fury*. New York, NY: Vintage, 1984.

Faye, Emmanuel. *Heidegger, the Introduction of Nazism into Philosophy in Light of the Unpublished Seminars of 1933–1935*. Translated by Michael B. Smith. New Haven, CT: Yale University Press, 2009.

Fichte, Johann Gottlieb. *Early Philosophical Writings*. Edited and translated by Daniel Breazeale. Ithaca, NY: Cornell University Press, 1993.

Foundations of Transcendental Philosophy (Wissenschaftslehre) Nova Methodo (1796/99). Edited and translated by Daniel Breazeale. Ithaca, NY: Cornell University Press, 1992.

Introductions to the Wissenschaftslehre and Other Writings. Edited and translated by Daniel Breazeale. Indianapolis, IN: Hackett Publishing Company, 1994.

Forster, Michael N. *Hegel and Skepticism*. Cambridge, MA: Harvard University Press, 1989.

Hegel's Idea of a Phenomenology of Spirit. Chicago, IL: Chicago University Press, 1998.

Foucault, Michel. *Michel Foucault: Ethics: Subjectivity and Truth*. Edited by Paul Rabinow. Translated by Robert Hurley. New York, NY: New Press, 1997.

Frankfurt, Harry G. *The Importance of What We Care About: Philosophical Essays*. Cambridge: Cambridge University Press, 2005.

The Reasons of Love. Princeton, NJ: Princeton University Press, 2004.

Freud, Sigmund. *General Psychological Theory: Papers on Metapsychology*. Edited by Philip Rieff. New York, NY: Simon & Schuster, 1997.

Frye, Northrop. *Fearful Symmetry: A Study of William Blake*. Princeton, NJ: Princeton University Press, 1990.

Furtak, Rick Anthony. *Knowing Emotions: Truthfulness and Recognition in Affective Experience*. Oxford: Oxford University Press, 2018.

Wisdom in Love: Kierkegaard and the Ancient Quest for Emotional Integrity. Notre Dame, IN: University of Notre Dame Press, 2005.

Furtak, Rick Anthony, Jonathan Ellsworth and James D. Reid, eds. *Thoreau's Importance for Philosophy*. New York, NY: Fordham University Press, 2012.

Gadamer, Hans-Georg. *Heidegger's Ways*. Translated by John W. Stanley. Albany, NY: State University of New York Press, 1994.

Truth and Method, Translated by J. Weinsheimer and D. G. Marshall. New York, NY: Continuum, 1997.

Garber, Daniel. *Descartes' Metaphysical Physics*. Chicago, IL: University of Chicago Press, 1992.

Goethe, Johann Wolfgang von. *The Collected Works: Essays on Art and Literature*. Edited by John Gearey. Vol. 3. Princeton, NJ: Princeton University Press, 1986.

Elective Affinities. Translated by R.J. Hollingdale. London: Penguin Books, 1971.

Golob, Sacha. *Heidegger on Concepts, Freedom and Normativity*. Cambridge: Cambridge University Press, 2014.

Guignon, Charles. *The Cambridge Companion to Heidegger*. Cambridge: Cambridge University Press, 1993.

Guthrie, W. K. C. *A History of Greek Philosophy*, Vol. VI. Cambridge: Cambridge University Press, 1993.

Habermas, Jürgen. *Moral Consciousness and Communicative Action*. Translated by Christian Lenhardt and Shierry Weber Nicholsen. Cambridge, MA: MIT Press, 1990.

The Philosophical Discourse of Modernity. Translated by Frederick Lawrence. Cambridge: Polity Press, 1987.

The Theory of Communicative Action, Volume One. Translated by Thomas McCarthy. Boston, MA: Beacon Press, 1984.

The Theory of Communicative Action, Volume Two. Translated by Thomas McCarthy. Boston, MA: Beacon Press, 1989.

Hadot, Pierre. *Philosophy as a Way of Life*. Translated by Michael Chase. Oxford: Blackwell, 1995.

Haugeland, John. *Dasein Disclosed: John Haugeland's Heidegger*. Edited by Joseph Rouse. Cambridge, MA: Harvard University Press, 2013.

Hegel, George Wilhelm Friedrich. *Elements of the Philosophy of Right*. Edited by Allen Wood and translated by H. B. Nisbet. Cambridge: Cambridge University Press, 1991.

Phenomenology of Spirit. Translated by A. V. Miller. Oxford: Oxford University Press, 1977.

Heidegger, Martin. *The Basic Problems of Phenomenology*. Translated by Albert Hofstadter. Bloomington, IN: Indiana University Press, 1988.

Becoming Heidegger: On the Trail of his Early Occasional Writing, 1910–1927. Edited by Theodore Kisiel and Thomas Sheehan. 2nd, revised and expanded edition ed. Seattle, WA: Noesis Press, 2009.

Being and Time. Translated by Joan Stambaugh. Albany, NY: State University of New York Press, 1996.

The Concept of Time. Translated by William McNeill. Oxford: Blackwell, 1992.

The Essence of Truth: On Plato's Cave Allegory and 'Theaetetus'. Translated by Ted Sadler. New York, NY: Continuum, 2002.

The Fundamental Concepts of Metaphysics: World, Finitude, Solitude. Translated by William McNeill and Nicholas Walker. Bloomington, IN: Indiana University Press, 1995.

Gesamtausgabe. Klostermann, 1975.

Band 17: *Einführung in die phänomenologische Forschung*. Edited by Friedrich-Wilhelm von Hermann, 1994.

Band 18: *Grundbegriffe der aristotelischen Philosophie*. Edited by Mark Michalski, 2002.

Band 19: *Platon: Sophistes*. Edited by Ingeborg Schüßler, 1992.

Band 20: *Prolegomena zur Geschichte des Zeitbegriffs*. Edited by Petra Jaeger, 1994.

Band 21: *Logik. Die Frage nach der Wahrheit*. Edited by Walter Biemel, 1995.

Band 56/7: *Zur Bestimmung der Philosophie*. Edited by Bernd Heimbüchel, 1999.

Band 58: *Grundprobleme der Phänomenologie*. Edited by Hans-Helmuth Gander, 1992.

Band 59: *Phänomenologie der Anschauung und des Ausdrucks*. Edited by Claudius Strube, 1993.

Band 60: *Phänomenologie des religiösen Lebens*. Edited by Matthias Jung and Thomas Regehly, 1995.

Band 61: *Phänomenologische Interpretationen zu Aristoteles*. Edited by Walter Bröcker and Käte Bröcker-Oltmanns, 1994.

Band 63: *Ontologie. Hermeneutik der Faktizität*. Edited by Käte Bröcker-Oltmanns, 1995.

History of the Concept of Time: Prolegomena. Edited and translated by Theodore Kisiel. Bloomington, IN: Indiana University Press, 1985.

Hölderlin's Hymn 'The Ister'. Translated by W. McNeill and J. Davis. Bloomington, IN: Indiana University Press, 1996.

Introduction to Metaphysics. Translated by G. Fried and R. Polt. New Haven, CT: Yale University Press, 2000.

Introduction to Phenomenological Research. Translated by Daniel Dahlstrom. Bloomington, IN: Indiana University Press, 2005.

Logic: The Question of Truth. Translated by Thomas Sheehan. Bloomington, IN: Indiana University Press, 2010.

The Metaphysical Foundations of Logic. Translated by M. Heim. Bloomington, IN: Indiana University Press, 1984.

Nietzsche, Volumes One and Two. Edited by D. F. Krell. New York, NY: Harper & Row, 1991.

Off the Beaten Track. Translated by Julian Young and Kenneth Haynes. Cambridge: Cambridge University Press, 2002.

Ontology – The Hermeneutics of Facticity. Translated by John van Buren. Bloomington, IN: Indiana University Press, 1999.

Pathmarks. Edited by William McNeill. Cambridge: Cambridge University Press, 1998.

Phenomenological Interpretations of Aristotle. Translated by Richard Rojcewicz. Bloomington, IN: Indiana University Press, 2001.

Phenomenological Interpretations of Kant's 'Critique of Pure Reason'. Translated by Parvis Emad and Kenneth Maly. Bloomington, IN: Indiana University Press, 1997.

The Phenomenology of Religious Life. Translated by Matthias Fritsch and Jennifer Anna Gosetti-Ferencei. Bloomington, IN: Indiana University Press, 2004.

Poetry, Language, Thought. Edited and translated by Albert Hofstadter. New York, NY: Harper & Row, 1971.

Ponderings II-VI: Black Notebooks 1931–1938. Translated by Richard Rojcewicz. Bloomington, IN: Indiana University Press, 2016.

Ponderings VII-XI: Black Notebooks 1938–1939. Translated by Richard Rojcewicz. Bloomington, IN: Indiana University Press, 2017.

Ponderings XII-XV: Black Notebooks 1939–1941. Translated by Richard Rojcewicz. Bloomington, IN: Indiana University Press, 2017.

The Principle of Reason. Translated by Reginald Lilly. Bloomington, IN: Indiana University Press, 1996.

Plato's 'Sophist'. Translated by Richard Rojcewicz and André Schuwer. Bloomington, IN: Indiana University Press, 1997.

The Question Concerning Technology and Other Essays. Translated by William Lovitt. New York, NY: Harper & Row, 1977.

The Question Concerning the Thing: On Kant's Doctrine of the Transcendental Principles. Translated by James D. Reid and Benjamin D. Crowe. London: Roman & Littlefield, 2018.

Sein und Zeit. Tübingen: Max Niemeyer Verlag, 1993.

Supplements: From the Earliest Essays to 'Being and Time' and Beyond. Edited by John van Buren. Albany, NY: State University of New York Press, 2002.

Heller, Erich. *The Disinherited Mind: Essays in Modern German Literature and Thought.* Expanded ed. San Diego, CA: Harcourt Brace Jovanovich, 1975.

Herman, Barbara. *The Practice of Moral Judgment.* Cambridge, MA: Harvard University Press, 1993.

Hodge, Joanna. *Heidegger and Ethics.* London: Routledge, 1995.

Husserl, Edmund. *Analyses Concerning Passive and Active Synthesis: Lectures on Transcendental Logic.* Translated by Anthony J. Steinbock. Dordrecht: Kluwer Academic Publishers, 2001.

Cartesian Meditations: An Introduction to Phenomenology. Translated by Dorion Cairns. Dordrecht: Martinus Nijhoff Publishers, 1960.

The Crisis of European Sciences and Transcendental Phenomenology. Translated by David Carr. Evanston, IL: Northwestern University Press, 1970.

Experience and Judgment: Investigations in a Genealogy of Logic. Edited Ludwig Landgrebe and translated by James S. Churchill and Karl Ameriks. Evanston, IL: Northwestern University Press, 1973.

Formal and Transcendental Logic. Translated by Dorion Cairns. The Hague: Martinus Nijhoff Publisher, 1978.

Ideas Pertaining to a Pure Phenomenology and to a Phenomenological Philosophy, First Book. Translated by F. Kersten. Dordrecht: Kluwer Academic Publishers, 1982.

Ideas Pertaining to a Pure Phenomenology and to a Phenomenological Philosophy, Second Book. Translated by R. Rojcewicz and A. Schuwer. Dordrecht: Kluwer Academic Publishers, 1989.

Logical Investigations. Translated by J. N. Findlay. Atlantic Highlands, NJ: Humanities Press Inc., 1970.

On the Phenomenology of the Consciousness of Internal Time (1893–1917). Translated by John Barnett Brough. Dordrecht: Kluwer Academic Publishers, 1991.

Irwin, Terence. *Aristotle's First Principles.* Oxford: Clarendon Press, 1995.

James, William. *Pragmatism and the Meaning of Truth.* Cambridge, MA: Harvard University Press, 1998.

The Varieties of Religious Experience: A Study in Human Nature. Edited by Martin E. Marty. London: Penguin Books, 1985.

The Will to Believe and Other Essays in Popular Philosophy/Human Immortality: Two Supposed Objections to the Doctrine. New York, NY: Dover Publications, 1956.

Jaran, François, and Christophe Perrin. *The Heidegger Concordance.* London: Bloomsbury Academic, 2013.

Jonas, Hans. *The Phenomenon of Life: Towards a Philosophical Biology.* New York, NY: Delta Publishing, 1966.

Kant, Immanuel. *Critique of Judgment.* Translated by Werner S. Pluhar. Indianapolis, IN: Hacket Publishing Company, 1987.

Critique of Pure Reason. Translated by Norman Kemp Smith. New York, NY: St. Martin's Press, 1965.

Groundwork of the Metaphysics of Morals. Edited and translated by Mary J. Gregor. Cambridge: Cambridge University Press, 1998.

The Metaphysics of Morals. Translated by Mary J. Gregor. Cambridge: Cambridge University Press, 1993.

Practical Philosophy. Translated by Mary J. Gregor. Cambridge: Cambridge University Press, 2006.

Religion within the Limits of Reason Alone. Translated by Theodore M. Greene and Hoyt H. Hudsom. New York, NY: Harper & Row, 1960.

Kermode, Frank. *The Sense of an Ending: Studies in the Theory of Fiction*. Oxford: Oxford University Press, 1967.

Kierkegaard Søren. *The Concept of Irony*. Edited and translated by Howard V. Hong and Edna H. Hong. Princeton, NJ: Princeton University Press, 1989.

Concluding Unscientific Postscript. Edited and translated by Howard V. Hong and Edna H. Hong. Princeton, NJ: Princeton University Press, 1992.

Either/Or: Part I. Edited and translated by Howard V. Hong and Edna H. Hong. Princeton, NJ: Princeton University Press, 1987.

Either/Or: Part II. Edited and translated by Howard V. Hong and Edna H. Hong. Princeton, NJ: Princeton University Press, 1987.

Fear and Trembling. Translated by Alastair Hannay. New York, NY: Penguin, 1985.

The Sickness Unto Death: A Christian Psychological Exposition for Upbuilding and Awakening. Edited and translated by Howard V. Hong and Edna H. Hong. Princeton, NJ: Princeton University Press, 1983.

Kisiel, Theodore. *The Genesis of Heidegger's 'Being and Time'*. Berkeley, CA: University of California Press, 1993.

Kisiel, Theodore, and van Buren, John, eds. *Reading Heidegger from the Start*. Albany, NY: State University of New York Press, 1994.

Kraut, Richard. *Aristotle on the Human Good*. Princeton, NJ: Princeton University Press, 1989.

Krell, David Farrell. *Ecstasy, Catastrophe: Heidegger from Being and Time to the Black Notebooks*. Albany, NY: SUNY Press, 2015.

Lafont, Cristina. *Heidegger, Language, and World-Disclosure*. Translated by Graham Harman. Cambridge: Cambridge University Press, 2000.

The Linguistic Turn in Hermeneutic Philosophy. Translated by José Medina. Cambridge, MA: MIT Press, 1999.

Larmore, Charles. *The Morals of Modernity*. Cambridge: Cambridge University Press, 1996.

The Romantic Legacy. New York, NY: Columbia University Press, 1996.

Lear, Jonathan. *Happiness, Death, and the Remainder of Life*. Cambridge, MA: Harvard University Press, 2001.

Love and Its Place in Nature: A Philosophical Interpretation of Freudian Psycho-analysis. New York, NY: Farrar, Straus & Giroux, 1990.

Levinas, Emmanuel. *Totality and Infinity: An Essay on Exteriority*. Translated by Alphonso Lingis. Pittsburgh, PA: Duquesne University Press, 1961.

Lewis, C. S. *A Grief Observed*. New York, NY: Harper Collins, 2001.

Lilla, Mark. *The Reckless Mind: Intellectuals in Politics*. New York, NY: New York Review Books, 2001.

Locke, John. *Some Thoughts Concerning Education and Of the Conduct of the Understanding*. Edited by Ruth W. Grant and Nathan Tarcov. Indianapolis, IN: Hackett Publishing Company, 1996.

Löwith, Karl. *Martin Heidegger and European Nihilism*. Edited by Richard Wolin. New York, NY: Columbia University Press, 1995.

My Life in Germany before and after 1933: A Report. Translated by Elizabeth King. Urbana, IL: University of Illinois Press, 1994.

MacIntyre, Alasdair. *After Virtue.* Notre Dame, IN: University of Notre Dame Press, 1991.

Mackie, J. L. *Ethics: Inventing Right and Wrong.* New York, NY: Penguin, 1990.

Marion, Jean Luc. *Being Given: Toward a Phenomenology of Givenness.* Translated by Jeffrey L. Kosky. Stanford, CA: Stanford University Press, 2002.

Cartesian Questions: Method and Metaphysics. Chicago, IL: University of Chicago Press, 1999.

Prolegomena to Charity. Translated by Stephen Lewis. New York, NY: Fordham University Press, 2002.

Reduction and Givenness: Investigations of Husserl, Heidegger, and Phenomenology. Translated by Thomas Carlson. Evanston, IL: Northwestern University Press, 1998.

Sur L'ontologie Grise De Descartes: Science Cartésienne Et Savoir Aristotélicien Dans Les Regulae. Paris: J. Vrin, 1981.

Marshall, John. *Descartes's Moral Theory.* Ithaca, NY: Cornell University Press, 1998.

McManus, Denis. *Heidegger and the Measure of Truth: Themes from His Early Philosophy.* Oxford: Oxford University Press, 2012.

ed. Heidegger, *Authenticity and the Self: Themes from Division Two of 'Being and Time'.* London: Routledge, 2015.

McMullin, Irene. *Time and the Shared World: Heidegger on Social Relations.* Evanston, IL: Northwestern University Press, 2013.

McNeill, William. *The Glance of an Eye: Heidegger, Aristotle, and the Ends of Theory.* Albany, NY: State University of New York Press, 1999.

Mensch, James Richard. *Intersubjectivity and Transcendental Idealism.* Albany, NY: State University of New York Press, 1988.

Merleau-Ponty, Maurice. *Phenomenology of Perception.* Translated by Colin Smith. New York, NY: Routledge, 1962.

The Primacy of Perception. Edited by James M. Edie. Evanston, IL: Northwestern University Press, 1989.

The Prose of the World. Translated by John O'Neill. Evanston, IL: Northwestern University Press, 1973.

Mill, John Stuart. *The Basic Writings of John Stuart Mill: On Liberty, The Subjection of Women & Utilitarianism.* New York, NY: Random House, 2002.

Miller, J. Hillis. *The Disappearance of God: Five Nineteenth-Century Writers.* Urbana, IL: University of Illinois Press, 2000.

Poets of Reality: Six Twentieth-Century Writers. Cambridge, MA: Harvard University Press, 1966.

Murdoch, Iris. *Existentialists and Mystics: Writings on Philosophy and Literature.* Edited by Peter Conradi. New York, NY: Penguin, 1997.

Metaphysics as a Guide for Morals. London: Penguin, 1993.

Musil, Robert. *The Confusions of Young Törless.* Translated by Shaun Whiteside. New York, NY: Penguin, 2001.

The Man without Qualities. Translated by Sophie Wilkins. New York, NY: Vintage Books, 1996.

Nagel, Thomas. *Mortal Questions*. Cambridge: Cambridge University Press, 2000.
The View from Nowhere. Oxford: Oxford University Press, 1986.

Nehamas, Alexander. *The Art of Living: Socratic Reflections from Plato to Foucault*. Berkeley, CA: University of California Press, 2000.

Nietzsche, Friedrich. *The Gay Science: With a Prelude in Rhymes and an Appendix of Songs*. Translated by Walter Kaufmann. New York, NY: Vintage Books, 1974.
Philosophy in the Tragic Age of the Greeks. Translated by Marianne Cowan. Washington, DC: Regnery Gateway, 1987.
Thus Spoke Zarathustra. Translated by Walter Kaufmann. New York, NY: Penguin, 1978.
Untimely Meditations. Edited by Daniel Breazeale and translated by R. J. Hollingdale. Cambridge: Cambridge University Press, 1997.
The Will to Power. Translated by Walter Kaufmann and R.J. Hollingdale. New York, NY: Random House, 1968.

Novalis. *Hymns to the Night*. Translated by Dick Higgins. New York, NY: McPherson & Company, 1988.
Philosophical Writings. Translated by Margaret Mahony Stoljar. Albany, NY: State University of New York Press, 1997.

Nussbaum, Martha. *Cultivating Humanity: A Classical Defense of Reform in Liberal Education*. Cambridge, MA: Harvard University Press, 1998.
The Fragility of Goodness: Luck and Ethics in Greek Tragedy and Philosophy. Cambridge: Cambridge University Press, 1986.
Love's Knowledge: Essays on Philosophy and Literature. Oxford: Oxford University Press, 1990.
The Therapy of Desire: Theory and Practice in Hellenistic Ethics. Princeton, NJ: Princeton University Press, 1994.
Upheavals of Thought: The Intelligence of Emotions. Cambridge: Cambridge University Press, 2001.

Okrent, Mark. *Heidegger's Pragmatism: Understanding, Being, and the Critique of Metaphysics*. Ithaca, NY: Cornell University Press, 1988.

Olafson, Frederick A. *Heidegger and the Ground of Ethics: A Study of "Mitsein."* Cambridge: Cambridge University Press, 1999.

Ott, Hugo. *Martin Heidegger: A Political Life*. Translated by Allan Blunden. London: HarperCollins, 1993.

Pater, Walter. *Essays on Art and Literature*. Edited by Jennifer Uglow. London: Everyman's, 1990.
Marius the Epicurean. Edited by Michael Levey. New York, NY: Penguin, 1985.
The Renaissance. Edited by Adam Phillips. Oxford: Oxford University Press, 1998.

Philipse, Herman. *Heidegger's Philosophy of Being*. Princeton, NJ: Princeton University Press, 1998.

Pippin, Robert. *Henry James and the Modern Moral Life*. Cambridge: Cambridge University Press, 2001.
Idealism as Modernism: Hegelian Variations. Cambridge: Cambridge University Press, 1997.
Modernism as a Philosophical Problem. Oxford: Blackwell, 1991.

Plato. *The Collected Dialogues of Plato.* Edited by Edith Hamilton and Huntington Cairns. Princeton, NJ: Princeton University Press, 1961.

    Euthyphro, Apology, Crito, Phaedo, Phaedrus. Translated by Harold North Fowler. Cambridge, MA: Harvard University Press, 1995.

    The Republic of Plato. Translated by Allan Bloom. New York, NY: Basic Books, 1968.

Putnam, Hilary. *Ethics without Ontology.* Cambridge, MA: Harvard University Press, 2004.

Quine, W. V. O. *Pursuit of Truth.* Cambridge, MA: Harvard University Press, 1992.

Ratcliffe, Matthew. *Feelings of Being: Phenomenology, Psychiatry and the Sense of Reality.* Oxford: Oxford University Press, 2008.

Reid, James D. *Being Here Is Glorious: On Rilke, Poetry, and Philosophy, with a New Translation of the Duino Elegies.* Evanston, IL: Northwestern University Press, 2015.

    "Dilthey's Epistemology of the Geisteswissenschaften: Between Lebensphilosophie and Wissenschaftstheorie." *The Journal of the History of Philosophy* 39, no. 3 (July 2001): 407–36.

    "Morality and Sensibility in Kant: Toward a Theory of Virtue." *Kantian Review* 8 (2004): 89–114.

    Novalis's Philosophical Fictions: Magical Idealism in Context. Evanston, IL: Northwestern University Press, forthcoming.

    "On the Unity of Theoretical Subjectivity in Kant and Fichte." *Review of Metaphysics* 57, no. 2 (December 2003): 243–77.

Richardson, William J. *Heidegger: Through Phenomenology to Thought.* 4th ed. New York, NY: Fordham University Press, 2003.

Rilke, Rainer Maria. *Letters to a Young Poet.* Translated by M. D. Herter Norton. New York, NY: Norton, 1993.

    New Poems [1907]. Translated by Edward Snow. New York, NY: Farrar, Straus and Giroux, 1995.

    The Selected Poetry of Rainer Maria Rilke. Edited and translated by Stephen Mitchell. New York, NY: Vintage, 1989.

Risser, James, ed. *Heidegger toward the Turn: Essays on the Work of the 1930s.* Albany, NY: State University of New York Press, 1999.

Rockmore, Tom. *On Heidegger's Nazism and Philosophy.* Berkeley, CA: University of California Press, 1992.

Rorty, Amélie. *Essays on Aristotle's Ethics.* Berkeley, CA: University of California Press, 1980.

Rorty, Richard. *Contingency, Irony, and Solidarity.* Cambridge: Cambridge University Press, 1989.

    Essays on Heidegger and Others: Philosophical Papers Volume 2. Cambridge: Cambridge University Press, 1995.

    Philosophy and the Mirror of Nature. Princeton, NJ: Princeton University Press, 1980.

Rousseau, Jean-Jacques. *Emile: Or, On Education*. Translated by Allan Bloom. New York, NY: Basic Books: 1979.

Russell, Bertrand. *The Conquest of Happiness*. New York, NY: Liveright, 1996.

Rust, Joshua. *John Searle and the Construction of Social Reality*. London: Continuum, 2006.

Safranski, Rudiger. *Martin Heidegger: Between Good and Evil*. Translated by Ewald Osers. Cambridge, MA: Harvard University Press, 1999.

Sartre, Jean Paul. *Being and Nothingness*. Translated by Hazel Barnes. New York, NY: Philosophical Library, 1956.

   Critique of Dialectical Reason, Vol. 1. Translated by Alan Sheridan-Smith. New York, NY: Verso, 1982.

   Existentialism and Humanism. Translated by Philip Mairet. Brooklyn, NY: Haskell House Publishers, 1948.

   Nausea. Translated by Lloyd Alexander. New York, NY: New Directions Books, 1964.

   Notebooks for an Ethics. Translated by David Pellauer. Chicago, IL: University of Chicago Press, 1992.

   Truth and Existence. Translated by Adrian van den Hoven. Chicago, IL: Chicago University Press, 1992.

Schalow, Frank. *The Renewal of the Heidegger-Kant Dialogue: Action, Thought, and Responsibility*. Albany, NY: SUNY Press, 1992.

Schelling, F. W. J. *System of Transcendental Idealism (1800)*. Translated by Peter Heath. Charlottesville, VA: University Press of Virginia, 1993.

Schlegel, Friedrich. *Friedrich Schlegel's 'Lucinde' and the Fragments*. Translated by Peter Firchow. Minneapolis, MN: University of Minnesota Press, 1971.

Schutz, Alfred, and Luckmann, Thomas. *The Structures of the Life-World*, Volume 1. Translated by Richard M. Zaner and H. Tristram Engelhardt, Jr. Evanston, IL: Northwestern University Press, 1973.

   The Structures of the Life-World, Vol. 2. Translated by Richard M. Zaner and David J. Parent. Evanston, IL: Northwestern University Press, 1989.

Searle, John R. *The Construction of Social Reality*. New York, NY: Free Press, 2007.

   Mind, Language, and Society: Philosophy in the Real World. New York, NY: Basic Books, 1999.

Sherman, Nancy. *Making a Necessity of Virtue: Aristotle and Kant on Virtue*. Cambridge: Cambridge University Press, 1997.

Sherover, Charles. "Founding an Existentialist Ethic." *Human Studies* 4 (1981): 223–36.

   Heidegger, Kant and Time. Bloomington, IN: Indiana University Press, 1972.

Shockey, Matthew. "Heidegger's Descartes and Heidegger's Cartesianism." *European Journal of Philosophy* 20, no. 2 (June 2012): 285–311.

Sikka, Sonia. "Kantian Ethics in *Being and Time*." *Journal of Philosophical Research* 31 (2006): 309–34.

Stevens, Wallace. *The Palm at the End of the Mind: Selected Poems and a Play.* Edited by Holly Stevens. New York, NY: Vintage, 1990.

Ströker, Elisabeth. *Husserl's Transcendental Phenomenology.* Translated by Lee Hardy. Stanford, CA: Stanford University Press, 1993.

Investigations in Philosophy of Space. Translated by Algis Mickunas. Athens, OH: Ohio University Press, 1987.

Taminiaux, Jacques. *Heidegger and the Project of Fundamental Ontology.* Translated by Michael Gendre. Albany, NY: State University of New York Press, 1991.

The Thracian Maid and the Professional Thinker: Arendt and Heidegger. Translated by Michael Gendre. Albany, NY: State University of New York Press, 1997.

Taylor, Charles. *The Ethics of Authenticity.* Cambridge, MA: Harvard University Press, 1992.

Philosophical Arguments. Cambridge, MA: Harvard University Press, 1997.

Sources of the Self. Cambridge, MA: Harvard University Press, 1989.

Thiele, Leslie Paul. *Timely Meditations: Martin Heidegger and Postmodern Politics.* Princeton, NJ: Princeton University Press, 1995.

Thomson, Iain D. *Heidegger on Ontotheology: Technology and the Politics of Education.* Cambridge: Cambridge University Press, 2005.

"Heidegger's Perfectionist Philosophy of Education in *Being and Time*." *Continental Philosophy Review* 37 (2004): 439–67.

Thoreau, Henry David. *Walden and Resistance to Civil Government.* Edited by William Rossi. New York, NY: Norton, 1992.

Trawny, Peter. *Heidegger and the Myth of a Jewish World Conspiracy.* Translated by Andrew J. Mitchell. Chicago, IL: University of Chicago Press, 2015.

Trilling, Lionel. *Sincerity and Authenticity.* Cambridge, MA: Harvard University Press, 1972.

Van Buren, John. *The Young Heidegger: Rumor of the Hidden King.* Bloomington, IN: Indiana University Press, 1994.

Vlastos, Gregory. *Socratic Studies.* Edited by Myles Burnyeat. Cambridge: Cambridge University Press, 1994.

Vogel, Lawrence. *The Fragile "We": Ethical Implications of Heidegger's "Being and Time."* Evanston, IL: Northwestern University Press, 1994.

Wachterhauser, Brice, ed. *Phenomenology and Skepticism: Essays in Honor of James M. Edie.* Evanston, IL: Northwestern University Press, 1996.

Williams, Bernard. *Ethics and the Limits of Philosophy.* Cambridge, MA: Harvard University Press, 1985.

Withy, Katherine. *Heidegger on Being Uncanny.* Cambridge, MA: Harvard University Press, 2015.

Wittgenstein, Ludwig. *On Certainty.* Edited by G. E. M Anscombe and G. H. von Wright. New York, NY: Harper Torchbooks, 1972.

Wolin, Richard. *Heidegger's Children: Hannah Arendt, Karl Löwith, Hans Jonas, and Herbert Marcuse.* Princeton, NJ: Princeton University Press, 2001.

The Politics of Being: The Political Thought of Martin Heidegger. New York, NY: Columbia University Press, 1980.

Wordsworth, William. *The Prelude: The Four Texts (1798, 1799, 1805, 1850)*. Edited by Jonathan Wordsworth. New York, NY: Penguin Books, 1995.

Wrathall, Mark A. *Heidegger and Unconcealment: Truth, Language, and History*. Cambridge: Cambridge University Press, 2011.

Zimmerman, Michael. *Heidegger's Confrontation with Modernity: Technology, Politics and Art*. Bloomington, IN: Indiana University Press, 1990.

Index

absorption, 43, 57, 170

Ackrill, J. L., 95

action, 3, 17, 40, 44, 56, 61, 81, 89, 93, 108, 135, 151–6, 158–60, 168, 175, 182, 192

agency, 5, 9, 91, 117, 122, 126, 130–1, 133, 139, 172

alienation
self-alienation, 53, 202
of the worker, 204

ambiguity, 58, 73, 127

antimodernism, 22, 27, 63

anxiety (*Angst*), 44, 103, 105, 122, 125–6, 147–8, 169, 217, *See* death

archê (first principle), 8, 85–6, 195, 218

Arendt, Hannah, 173

Aristotle, 3, 17–18, 20, 25, 40, 51–3, 65–6, 70, 73, 82–3, 93, 95–6, 99, 101, 103, 107–10, 114, 137, 144, 155–6, 161, 175, 189, 208, 216–17

Aron, Raymond, 164

art, 36, 191

attunement (*Stimmung*), 93, 136, 149, 216, *See* mood, disposition

Augustine, 99, 112

authenticity, owning up (*Eigentlichkeit*), 3, 6, 10, 99, 104–9, 120, 125, 133, 139, 144–5, 204, 210, 212, 216
jargon of, 6, 192

autonomy, 4, 63, 127, 134, 137

bad faith, 47, 155

Bambach, Charles R., 21, 63

Bäumler, Alfred, 22

beata vita (the happy life), 99

beautiful soul, the, 106

being, 2, 4–5, 18, 20, 35, 52, 57, 61–2, 68, 72, 76, 86, 97–8, 100, 102, 106–7, 112–13, 117, 129–30, 133, 139, 182, 185–7, 189, 191–2, 201, 212–16
being-historical thinking, 14, 214

being-there, 53, 108, 194

being-with (*Mitsein*), 128, 131
of care, 67
of Dasein, 3, 5, 89, 105–6
poetic disclosure of, 214
political, 116
Sein, 53, 79
Seinsfrage, 14, 26, 62, 111, 199, 212–13
ways of, 125

Being and Time, 2–5, 7, 9, 14, 21–2, 24–8, 30, 35, 40, 52, 54, 57, 63, 82, 92, 97–109, 111–28, 130–1, 133, 145–7, 149–51, 157, 159–63, 178–9, 185, 191–2, 198, 210–11, 213–15, 217

being unsettled (*Unheimlichkeit*), 126, 217

being-in-the-world, 14, 16, 34, 101, 103, 105, 109–10, 118, 129, 191, 212

Blackburn, Simon, 14–15

Blattner, William, 112, 119–21, 128

Blumenberg, Hans, 157

Bohr, Niels, 14

boredom, 217

Brandom, Robert, 4

Braver, Lee, 218

breakdown, 121–2, 124

Brogan, Walter, 82

Bultmann, Rudolph, 203

Campbell, Scott M., 1

care (*Sorge*), 3, 6–10, 15–16, 22, 33, 35, 43, 54–60, 67–8, 79, 86, 97–8, 102, 106–7, 112, 123, 126, 128, 130–1, 133, 136, 144, 150–2, 160, 163, 169, 171–3, 176, 183–4, 191–2, 200–1, 207, 216–18
care-structure, 8, 25, 113, 131
life of everyday care, 203–4
shared care (*Mitsorge*), 131
Sorgen, 7, 9, 58, 112, 139, 157
Sorgenwelt, 9, 34, 59

Carman, Taylor, 112, 117–18, 128, 187

234